Origins and Growth of the Global Economy

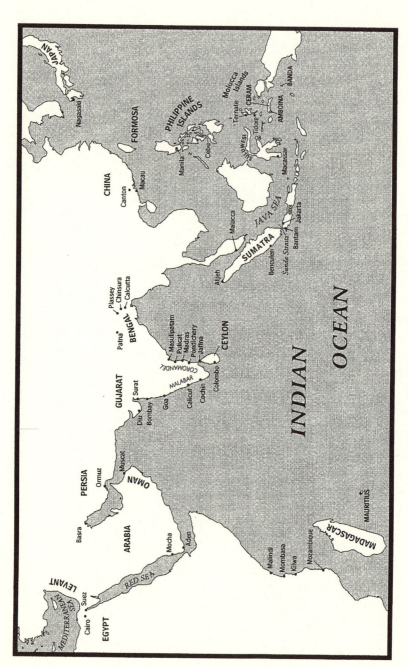

IMPERIAL COMMERCE IN THE SIXTEENTH AND SEVENTEENTH CENTURIES

Origins and Growth of the Global Economy

From the Fifteenth Century Onward

_____ Ronald E. Seavoy _____

Westport, Connecticut
London

Library of Congress Cataloging-in-Publication Data

Seavoy, Ronald E.
    Origins and growth of the global economy : from the fifteenth century onward / Ronald
E. Seavoy.
     p. cm.
    Includes bibliographical references and index.
    ISBN 0–275–97912–1 (alk. paper)
    1. Commerce—History.   2. Economic history.   3. Globalization.   I. Title.
HF352.S357 2003
382′.09—dc21   2002029898

British Library Cataloguing in Publication Data is available.

Library of Congress Catalog Card Number: 2002029898
ISBN: 0–275–97912–1

First published in 2003

Greenwood Press, 88 Post Road West, Westport, CT 06881
An imprint of Greenwood Publishing Group, Inc.
www.praeger.com

Printed in the United States of America

The paper used in this book complies with the
Permanent Paper Standard issued by the National
Information Standards Organization (Z39.48–1984).

10 9 8 7 6 5 4 3 2 1

CONTENTS

INTRODUCTION

There are two purposes for writing this book. The first is to show that the global economy in the twenty-first century is built on the foundation of European commercial imperialism. The second is to show that the global economy as it is currently evolving is capable of producing consumer cultures in all nations that adopt policies to increase exports. Consumer cultures are especially visible in the industrial nations of western Europe, North America, and Japan; and it is becoming increasingly visible in the few post-colonial nations that have actively expanded commercial sectors inherited from imperial governance (South Korea, Taiwan, Singapore).

This book is not about aggression, atrocities, brutality, greed, racism, slavery, and other unsavory imperial practices that many investigators have described. Many of these studies, while accurate, have the purpose to convince readers that European commercial imperialism was exploitation. This is not a fair picture. When observed and analyzed in a long perspective, European commercial imperialism was a strongly positive event because it is the foundation for the globalization of commerce and industry. Put another way, European commercial imperialism was the propellant for creating the global economy of the twenty-first century that can produce consumer cultures in all nations that actively participate.

The rules for participation in the global market have been defined by industrial nations for their benefit, but the rules are open ended. All nations are invited to participate in the World Trade Organization (WTO), International Monetary Fund (IMF), World Bank, Organization of Economic Cooperation and Development (OECD), or to organize regional trade associations like the European Union (EU) and North American Free Trade Association (NAFTA). Beneficial participation in any of these organizations, however, depends on central governments actively promoting the production of products for export.

In practice, active participation in the global economy means that nations must be receptive to investments by global and multinational corporations. As the global market has evolved since the end of WWII (1945), global and multinational corporations have been one of the principal agents for creating and enlarging consumer cultures in industrial nations because of their ability to transfer technologies and management skills across national boundaries. They can perform the same function for nations with small commercial sectors if governing elites adopt and enforce the requisite policies of political economy. The material abundance that is possible by actively commercializing culture is an opportunity waiting to be grasped by the governing elites of post-colonial nations because they are no longer constrained by dependent imperial relationships.

BEGINNINGS OF
EUROPEAN COMMERCIAL EXPANSION

In the fifteenth century the central governments (dynastic monarchies) of European nations encouraged and protected commerce because it increased tax revenues. Most of their commerce was among themselves. This was also true from the sixteenth through the twentieth centuries, and is equally true in the twenty-first century. Portugal was the first European nation to begin broadening European maritime commerce away from the Mediterranean and Baltic. They began in the fifteenth century with a series of exploration voyages down the west coast of Africa that were capped by the voyages of Vasco da Gama to India and Christopher Columbus to America. Voyages of commerce immediately followed voyages of discovery.

The imperialism that followed these discoveries was commercial imperialism. From its beginning in the fifteenth century to the collapse of the Soviet Union at the end of the twentieth, the primary motive for encouraging long distance commerce was to increase the power of central governments. In western Europe, Russia, and Japan, these were dynastic monarchies. Dynastic monarchies in the sixteenth and seventeenth centuries actively encouraged and protected merchant adventurers because it was mutually profitable. Wealth earned by merchant adventurers could be taxed and increased tax revenue was the foundation of increased political and military power. Long distance merchants benefited because contract law guaranteed possession of the commercial wealth they accumulated. Promotion and protection of long distance commerce was a bargain in which both central governments and merchant adventurers profited.

Merchant adventurers used superior marine and armament technology reinforced by superior navigational, financial, and military skills to intrude imperial commerce into the social fabric of subsistence cultures. Intrusion often required armed intervention by European soldiers who used superior armaments and discipline to compensate for their small numbers. Superior military, governing, transportation, and commercial skills usually sustained the continued presence of imperial merchants.

There were three types of European commercial imperialism. The first was settling its citizens on vacant land, depopulated land, or sparsely populated land; the second was settling citizens on land where indigenous populations remained the majority but Europeans became the governing elite. The third was where European merchants traded with long established feudal kingdoms. In these places imperial merchants were visitors in an alien culture rather than an integral part of the governing elite.

The first type of imperialism was practiced in North America, a large part of South America, Australia, New Zealand, Hawaii, parts of the Republic of South Africa, and Siberia. The second type of European imperialism incorporated indigenous inhabitants within the social, political, and economic fabric established by European settlers because imperial nations did not have the population or resources to displace resident populations. This type of imperialism occurred most prominently in Mexico, Peru, Bolivia, Equador, Paraguay, parts of the Republic of South Africa, and parts of Russia. The third type of imperialism operated in territories governed by feudal emperors, kings, rajahs, or sultans where population densities were high. These principalities may or may not have been conquered. In any case the imperial merchants operating in these territories were visitors in alien cultures. This imperialism operated in north Africa, the Levant, India, Indonesian archipelago (Indies), China, and Japan.

The purpose of commercial imperialism in all of its diversity was to mobilize the labor of resident populations (usually peasants) to produce larger amounts of exchange commodities than they would normally produce so that the surplus could be exported and sold on anonymous markets anywhere in the world. All three types of European commercial imperialism became permanent because European nations had sufficient military and naval power to maintain a permanent presence and because the managers of European commercial imperialism coopted a receptive minority of indigenous merchants to participate in the revolutionary changes necessary to make large scale, long distance commerce profitable.

The foundation for sustaining imperial commerce was enforcing internal peace. Wherever possible, European commercial empires suppressed internecine warfare because peace was necessary to maximize the production of export commodities. Alternatively, the governments of the principalities where imperial merchants traded were strong enough to maintain domestic peace. On the other hand, the European nations that maximized imperial commerce were continuously at war with each other in order to engross profits at the expense of their rivals. Imperial commerce was an extension of European power politics.

The export commodities produced by peasants were purchased with precious metal coins or exchanged for manufactured items that peasants desired. The favorable terms of trade for precious metals and manufactured items induced peasants to increase the production of export commodities. Alternatively, imperial merchants managed the exchange of products produced in one peasant society with products produced in another peasant society. In this exchange, imperial merchants acquired a surplus of products that could be shipped to Europe. The sale of commodities that peasants produced for export to Europe was the measure of profitability of imperial commerce in the sixteenth, seventeenth, and eighteenth centuries. For the most part, the production of export commodities was voluntary because it was a bargain that benefited both peasants and imperial merchants.

In the nineteenth and twentieth centuries the industrial revolution dictated a revolutionary change in the structure of global commerce. The volume of trade vastly increased. Most of the increased volume and value of trade was between the principal industrial nations, and it was in manufactured products and related services. There was, however, a residuum of the older imperial commerce. It was between industrial nations and post-colonial peasant nations with small commercial sectors.

In the twenty-first century, peasant societies in post-colonial nations continue to produce export commodities as they have been doing for 400 years, and the terms of trade for these communities operate in exactly the same way.

Soon after monetization, most peasant societies become dependent on trade for a limited number of items that are easier to purchase than to make by handicraft methods. In order to acquire these items, the peasantry expends enough additional labor to produce commodities that can be sold for money in order to purchase them. These products are called exchange commodities. . . . Peasants compute the superiority of manufactured items over handicraft items by comparing the amount of labor it takes to make a handicraft item with the amount of labor required to produce an exchange commodity that can be sold in order to purchase a manufactured item of superior utility. Part of the comparison formula is how long the manufactured item will last, measured against how frequently a handicraft item needs replacement. [1]

Contemporary peasants produce sheet rubber, kopra, coffee beans, cocoa beans, tea leaves, peanuts, or the fruit of oil palms as exchange commodities. These commodities are assembled by village storekeepers who are the agents of merchants engaged in export trade. Peasants exchange these commodities for machine made textiles that replace hand woven textiles, or for steel or aluminum cooking pots that replace ceramic pots, for steel hoes and machetes that replace iron tools made by village blacksmiths, for plastic buckets that replace gourds, or for food in poor crop years. The ability of village storekeepers to obtain manufactured items of superior utility and food during seasons of hunger, to exchange for export commodities, makes peasants participants in global commerce.

MEDITERRANEAN COMMERCE

At its inception, European imperialism was guided by the commercial and governing skills that were developed in the twelfth and thirteenth centuries when Genoa and Venice established seaport colonies along the southern and eastern rims of the Mediterranean sea and in the port cities of the Black sea. Commerce from these colonies made Genoa and Venice rich compared to the other principalities of Italy and especially compared to the dynastic monarchies of western and northern Europe.

The prosperity of Genoa and Venice was based on promoting and protecting commerce and taxing commercial wealth. This was the development model for the dynastic monarchies of western and northern Europe that were in the process of centralizing political power at the expense of feudal aristocracies. It was clear to these monarchs and their principal advisors that commerce could be a more reliable source of revenue than the indefinite dues owed by feudal aristocrats; and that taxing commerce posed a lesser threat to dynastic claims to govern than the pretensions of feudal aristocrats. Put another way, money taxation was a safer and more reliable source of revenue than dues from feudal aristocrats. It was, therefore, strongly in the interests of dynastic monarchs to encourage, protect, and tax internal and external commerce. It was equally in the interests of dynastic monarchs to convert poorly defined (often ambiguous) feudal dues into monetized taxation.

When and how did European imperialism begin? After the loss of most their colonies in the Levant in the thirteenth century, Venice and Genoa turned west and employed their commercial skills in the service of the monarchies of Portugal and Spain. During the fourteenth and fifteenth centuries, Portuguese and Spanish merchants steadily expanded their trade with northern Europe by adapting Mediterranean commercial and navigational skills to new opportunities to earn profits. The developments that made northern commerce profitable were: 1) larger ships of sturdy construction; 2) that could sail in the rough waters of the Atlantic; 3) navigational skills that allowed captains to know their locations at great distances from land; 4) heavy caliber naval artillery to defend against piracy or to control the maritime commerce of competitors. These were the same innovations that insured continuous armed intrusion of European imperial commerce into subsistence cultures worldwide.

During the fourteenth and fifteenth centuries, in the course of expanding trade, five hidden ingredients assumed increasing importance: 1) "a technological attitude to knowledge;" 2) "an extreme readiness to apply science in immediately practical ways;"[2]   3) monarchies that encouraged merchants to earn commercial profits; 4) a willingness to use armed force to protect merchants because predictable taxation of commercial wealth made monarchies more powerful than their neighbors; 5) a social attitude that money earned from commerce was beneficial to both central governments and private citizens.

Large scale north-south trade began with the Champagne fairs in the thirteenth century. Most commodities carried north of the Alps had a high value, like spices and sugar that could bear the high cost of overland transportation from the distant places where they were produced. Genoese and Venetian bankers financed this commerce with capital accumulated in Mediterranean trade. The Champagne fairs declined in direct ratio to the growth of the coastal cities of the Rhine delta. The decline was accelerated as ships were built of new design with larger carrying capacity in order to carry bulk commodities. Marine transportation made it possible to carry many bulk commodities with low unit values for long distances and find profitable markets.

In 1277 the first ships from Genoa arrived at Bruges. This trade was a northern extension of Genoese and Venetian trade with Spain and Portugal in commodities procured in the Levant and the hinterlands of the Ottoman empire. Coincident with these voyages was the transfer of the credit skills of Genoese and Venetian bankers to northern bankers and the transfer of the oceanic navigational skills devised by Portuguese and Spanish navigators to northern navigators. Bruges, Antwerp, and other cities clustered around the delta of the Rhine rapidly grew in population and wealth because diverse commodities were assembled there by: 1) Hanseatic merchants who traded with cities on the shores of the Baltic sea; 2) merchants who traded into the interior of Europe using the Rhine river; 3) English merchants from London and elsewhere.

The principal high value commodities produced in northern Europe that had strong Mediterranean and Iberian markets were wool and linen textiles and hemp sailcloth. Much of the raw wool came from England and Spain and hemp fiber from the Baltic. Weaving and dying were done in the city of Bruges and surrounding villages. The principal high value Mediterranean commodities imported into northern Europe were spices acquired from Arab merchants in the Levant, sugar produced in Sicily and elsewhere, and Spanish and Portuguese wines. The bulk commodities imported from the south were salt and vinegar. The salt and vinegar were used to preserve meat and fish; and profits earned by southern merchants were used to purchase food grains and dried, salted, and pickled fish.

The profitability of northern commerce accumulated enough capital and trained enough entrepreneurial merchants and ship captains for merchants from Portugal and Spain to invest in voyages of discovery in the fifteenth century. Bankers from Genoa, Venice, and other Italian city states helped finance these speculative voyages. The earliest of these voyages were undertaken to find new markets on the west coast of Africa; and were then extended to find a direct maritime route to the spices of India and the Indies.

VOYAGES OF DISCOVERY

John H. Parry in *The Age of Reconnaissance*, summarizes the commercial motivation for European imperialism.

The great discoverers of the fifteenth and sixteenth centuries were not primarily interested in discovery for its own sake. Their main interest, the main task entrusted to them by the rulers and investors who sent them out, was to link Europe, or particular European countries, with other areas known or believed to be of economic importance. The discovery of distant, unknown islands and continents, like much scientific discovery, was incidental, often fortuitous. [3]

Most voyages of discovery were partnerships between merchants, bankers, and monarchs. The partners were looking for markets beyond the Mediterranean and northern Europe. They sought to find kingdoms that could be induced to produce commodities for export to Europe or concentrations of populations where indigenous rulers could mobilize labor to produce commodities for sale in Europe. These voyages usually had a veneer of proselytizing Christianity and nearly as frequently, commercial relations began with an interlude of looting the ships of indigenous merchants.

The Portuguese were the earliest explorationists seeking a direct maritime route to India because the resources of Spain were focused on conquering Grenada (1492) in order to expel the last Muslim influence from Iberia, as Portugal had done in 1253. Direct maritime trade with India would eliminate Arab, Levantine, and Venetian middlemen and the profits of the spice trade would accrue to long voyage merchants operating out of Lisbon and other port cities of Portugal.

Prince Henry the Navigator (1394-1460) used the fiscal resources of the Portuguese crown to finance voyages of discovery down the west coast of Africa. The ultimate objective of these voyages was finding a direct sea route to the pepper and spice producing regions of India and the Indies. The commodities exchanged on the African voyages were European weapons, metal implements, and textiles for which they received gold, ivory, and negro slaves. These ventures were supported by Henry's father, king Joao I, until his death in 1433, and then by his brother, king Duarte (1433-1438), and another brother, prince regent Pedro (1438-1448). Henry's nephew, king Afonso V, also contributed financial support from 1448 until Henry's death in 1460. Henry was also a conduit of crown resources for lending to merchants who undertook to settle people on three groups of Atlantic islands that were imperfectly known or newly discovered during his lifetime (Azores, Madeira, Cape Verde).

The Madeira islands began to be settled about 1420, the Azores about 1427, and the Cape Verde islands about 1466. Spain did the same for the Canary islands that had been discovered about 1341 but colonization did not begin until about 1410. By 1460, the Madeira islands had become prosperous outposts of long distance commerce by producing exportable quantities of wheat, sugar, and wine. Their prosperity made them advance supply bases for further exploration along the west coast of Africa by Portuguese navigators. The Cape Verde, Madeira, and Azores islands performed the same function for fleets going to India after 1498, and for navigators exploring Brazil after 1500. Likewise, Spanish explorers and merchants used settlements on the Canary islands as advance supply bases for voyages of exploration to the Americas.

Who were the navigators who undertook the voyages of discovery to India and the Americas? Among the earliest were Bartolomeu Dias, Christopher Columbus, Vasco da Gama, Pedro Alverez Cabral, and Ferdinand Magellan. Dias, da Gama, and Cabral were in the service of the Portuguese crown and Columbus and Magellan in the service of the Spanish crown. Dias rounded the Cape of Good Hope at the southern tip of Africa in 1487 and returned in 1488. His voyage opened the way for direct maritime commerce with the Indies. Columbus was in Lisbon when he returned.

Columbus convinced the Spanish crown that there was a shorter route to the Indies by sailing west and the Spanish crown financed his voyage of exploration in 1492-1493. Because of affairs of state, the Portuguese crown did not follow Dias's discovery until 1497 when a flotilla of four ships commanded by da Gama was sent to find India and establish trade. Da Gama arrived at Calicut in 1498, acquired a small cargo of pepper and other spices, and returned in 1499. Cabral commanded the second fleet of 13 ships that sailed to the Indies in 1500. He was to establish trade by force if necessary. After leaving the Cape Verde islands, the fastest route to the Cape of Good Hope was using southwesterly winds to cross the equator. In the process, Cabral discovered the northeast coast of Brazil.

The merchant adventurers who followed the voyages of discovery were extremely vulnerable because of their tenuous contact with bases of power that could protect them. Their survival and prosperity usually depended on cooperation with indigenous feudal rulers; however, the commercial social values that motivated imperial merchants inevitably came into conflict with indigenous feudal elites. The principal cause of conflict was unpredictable rules governing commerce and taxation. By necessity, the commercial enclaves established by Portugal in Africa, India, and the Indies were usually fortified warehouses (factories) on near shore islands or walled settlements on the mainland. They were frequently under siege. Most had precarious existences but they survived. Their survival was directly related to the technical superiority of European ships, guns, and navigation skills that evolved during the fifteenth and sixteenth centuries. In the hinterlands of these factories the rulers of feudal principalities often directed the labor of indigenous inhabitants or slaves to produce export commodities.

The risks of imperial commerce were high but the rewards for merchant adventurers were equally high. The rewards were equally high for European monarchies; therefore, when indigenous rulers failed to adequately protect the commerce of merchant adventurers, they reluctantly used expensive warfare to protect it. At the same time they were defending their presence in enclaves, they also had to protect their long distance commerce from encroachment. If political conditions warranted, they fought to expand their imperial commerce at the expense of European rivals because there were no rules of commerce at remote locations. When armed merchant ships of European rivals met on the ocean or in the unfortified harbors of weak indigenous governments, armed conflicts were frequent. In the sixteenth and in most of the seventeenth centuries, discovery, commerce, and war were interchangeable terms. In order to protect the profits of long voyage merchants the central governments of European nations increased the size of their navies because tax revenues from this commerce outweighed the costs of defense.

The remainder of this chapter will describe and analyze the fifteenth and sixteenth century voyages of discovery made by Portuguese, Spanish, Dutch, and English navigators. The long voyage merchants who followed voyages of discovery established a source of supply for a small number of high value commodities. These commodities were assembled in enclaves established by European merchant adventurers on all continents except Australia. By the end of the eighteenth century these enclaves were permanent presences in the subsistence cultures where they were located, and there was a steady increase in the variety, volume, and value of commodities that were produced for sale in Europe and in other markets where European merchants had entry. In the 500 years after da Gama sailed east and Columbus sailed west, European commerce impinged on, intruded into, and overwhelmed all subsistence cultures.

PORTUGUESE COMMERCIAL EMPIRE

In 1505, Francisco de Almeida sailed for India in command of a fleet of 22 merchant ships financed by Genoese and Florentine bankers. Almeida had participated in the siege of Grenada in 1492 that expelled the remaining Muslims from Spain, and was a veteran of earlier wars against the Muslims in north Africa. He was an experienced empire builder. After his arrival he accurately assessed the situation. In 1508 he wrote King Manuel, "In so far as you are powerful on the sea, all India will be as yours, but if you do not possess this kind of power on the sea, fortresses ashore will do you precious little good." [4]

It was clear from the beginning that Portuguese merchant ships had to have naval protection. The first protection was sailing from Europe in annual convoys. The second protection was requiring all merchant ships engaged in long distance trade to be capable of waging naval warfare. Portuguese control of maritime commerce in India and the Indies was secured by establishing fortified warehouses (factories) with resident Portuguese merchants. After a sufficient number of ports in India and the Indies were under Portuguese control, the coastal trade of indigenous merchants was controlled by a system of licensing (taxation). Unlicensed ships and cargoes were confiscated. Controlling the trade of indigenous merchants guaranteed that their cargoes of desirable products were first offered to Portuguese merchants for purchase. After they were acquired they were consigned to Portuguese ships and carried to Europe or other places where Portuguese merchants traded.

This strategy required a secure base of operations. A secure base meant a fortified enclave around a capacious harbor where there was always a garrison of European soldiers and a flotilla of armed ships. Garrisons defended the land frontier and the flotilla inspected the ships of indigenous merchants. Garrisons of professional soldiers and ships to move them, gave commanders of enclaves the power to negotiate from strength or, alternatively, to intimidate local rulers to establish warehouses so that commerce would be on a continuing basis. Finally, the activities of all factors and fortified enclaves had to be centrally coordinated so that there was only one policy of trade and war. All enclaves, from undefended warehouses in small ports to the most strongly fortified harbors, had a precarious existence but Portuguese control of the sea in the sixteenth and early seventeenth centuries ensured their survival if attacked by indigenous rulers—but not if attacked by European commercial rivals.

The Portuguese crown managed long distance trade by licensing Portuguese merchants who traded into specific geographic areas. This commerce made the Portuguese crown into a giant mercantile corporation that operated on shares. The revenue acquired by licensing Portuguese merchants helped sustain the crown's claim to govern Portugal with minimal interference from feudal aristocrats. Likewise, the licensing and taxing of indigenous merchants engaged in trade along the west coast of India (Malabar coast) and the east coast of Africa helped defray the costs of governing and defending the empire. After Portuguese ships arrived at enclaves, shipboard merchants had full access to the warehouses of resident Portuguese merchants who assembled export commodities, food, and the naval stores necessary for completing the voyage. These supplies were procured from indigenous merchants who traded into the interior.

In the 30 years after their arrival in India, the Portuguese acquired a series of trading enclaves on the rim of the Indian Ocean by forcibly displacing Arab and Gujarati merchants. Arab and Gujarati commerce was easy prey to Portuguese sea power because: 1) Arab ships were small and flimsy; 2) they could be smashed and sunk by naval artillery without boarding; 3) sultans along the west coast of India paid little attention to maritime commerce because there were no organized maritime enemies (but there were pirates); 4) the political and military focus of these sultanates was always their land frontiers; 5) sultans, therefore, had no navies to protect merchants while they were at sea; 6) nor did sultans promote trade because Arab and Gujarati merchants came to them and voluntarily paid taxes levied on them.

The advantages of the Portuguese were: 1) vastly superior ships; 2) vastly superior naval artillery; 3) veteran commanders and soldiers who had crusaded against Muslims in north Africa and were eager to do the same in India; 4) a centralized command of their naval and military forces. Even though they were at the far end of communication with Lisbon, Portuguese naval power could displace Arab and Gujarati merchants because marine mobility allowed them to concentrate their limited but highly motivated manpower at one place. In most situations, this tactic gave them the advantage of surprise that was often enhanced because they were opposed by poorly organized and poorly led indigenous levies.

It was, therefore, relatively easy for the Portuguese to forcibly appropriate the long distance trade of Arab and Gujarati merchants along the Malabar coast and tax the coastal trade that remained. It was relatively easy because the political structure of the Malabar coast was fragmented. Finally, and most important, the Portuguese knew exactly why they came to India and what they wanted.

Between 1500 and 1535 the Portuguese established a commercial empire in the Indian ocean by capturing the principal coastal cities that were the home ports of Arab, Gujarati, and Malay merchants. These cities were Diu in Gujarat, Ormuz in Persia, Muscat in Oman, Colombo in Ceylon, and Malacca in Malaysia. After capture they installed sufficiently strong garrisons (in forts they built) to defend the enclaves from inland attack.

The first attack to displace Arab and Gujarati merchants from long distance trade in the Indian ocean was at Diu in 1509. It was the home port of most Gujarati merchants. The assault failed but Portuguese naval artillery destroyed the combined fleets of the sultans of Egypt and Gujarat. After the failure to capture Diu in 1509, the Portuguese, under the leadership of Afonso de Albuquerque, captured Goa in 1510. Goa had a large harbor that was protected by an inshore island that could be easily fortified and defended by a small number of professional soldiers. The capture of Goa gave the Portuguese a strong base for a permanent fleet in the Indian ocean that was essential for enforcing their control of maritime commerce in the western half of the Indian ocean. In due time, many smaller ports on the east coast of Africa and Malabar coast of India were captured and fortified warehouses established.

Next, Albuquerque concentrated his power against Ormuz, at the mouth of the Persian Gulf in order to gain control of the spice trade to

Persia and the Levant. He assembled a fleet of 27 ships and 3,000 soldiers in 1515 and arrived without warning. He anchored outside the harbor and by a show of force, diplomacy, and murder, induced the sultan to allow the Portuguese to build a fort that would control all commerce entering and leaving the harbor.

Finally, in 1518, a fort was established at Colombo on the island of Ceylon that gave the Portuguese control of a large part of the cinnamon trade. At a later date the Portuguese forced the sultan of Oman to allow the Portuguese to build a fort in the harbor of Muscat, which gave them control of both ends of the trade conducted by the Arab merchants along the east coast of Africa. Control of Indian ocean commerce, however, was not complete until 1535 when the Portuguese established a fortified enclave at Diu. The capture of Goa, Malacca, Ormuz, Diu, and Colombo allowed the Portuguese to appropriate most of the long distance commerce of Arab and Gujarati merchants in both the eastern and western halves of the Indian ocean.

Portuguese control of trade to Arabia and Egypt would not be complete until they controlled Aden at the mouth of the Red Sea. Albuquerque assaulted Aden in 1513 with a fleet of 20 ships and 2,500 soldiers. He was repulsed and Aden was never captured, but it was more or less isolated by having no subsidiary trading enclaves along the east coast of Africa (Malindi, Mombasa, Kilwa, Mozambique) or along the Malabar coast of India because they were either captured or controlled by the Portuguese. The east African enclaves were important to the Portuguese because they were sources of ivory and slaves. They also supplied ships with fresh water and food on their voyages to Goa and when returning to Portugal.

The capture of Goa (1509) was immediately followed by the capture of Malacca in 1511. Immediately after the capture of Malacca, three armed ships were sent into the Java sea to search for the Banda islands where nutmeg and mace were produced, and the islands of Ternate and Tidore where cloves were produced. After these islands were located, Portuguese merchants visited them in 1516, 1517, 1518, and 1519 and returned with highly profitable cargoes of spices. In 1522 the Portuguese sent an expedition to Ternate to depose the sultan and build a fortified warehouse in order to control the clove trade.

Control of trade from Malacca displaced Arab, Gujarati, and Malay merchants from long distance commerce in spices. In 1513, Muslim merchants from Atjeh, at the northern tip of Sumatra, organized a counter-attack. Naval artillery destroyed their fleet. Thereafter, on the land side, Malay sultans besieged Malacca in 1517, 1525, 1550, 1567, and 1571. All of these assaults were unsuccessful, but they stretched Portuguese resources.

Shortly after Portuguese merchants arrived at Ternate and Tidore, the Spanish arrived. Ferdinand Magellan's surviving ships stopped there during his voyage of circum-navigation (1519-1522) and traded for a cargo of cloves. Magellan was Portuguese and, like Columbus he was serving the Spanish crown; and like Columbus, he sailed west to find the spice islands (Molucca islands). He began his voyage with five ships and 240 men. His first major stop in the orient was the Philippine islands where he was killed while trying to mediate a tribal dispute. From there a pilot guided the two surviving ships to Tidore in the Molucca islands where they loaded cargoes of cloves and other spices. One ship was immediately captured by the Portuguese but the other, with 15 crewmen, returned to Spain in 1522. The spices repaid the cost of the voyage plus a large profit.

In 1525 the Spanish sent an expedition to Tidore to establish permanent trade. The Portuguese strongly objected. Potential armed rivalry was ended in 1529 by the Portuguese king paying a large sum of money to Spain for their peaceable withdrawal. The Portuguese commercial empire that began in the Indian ocean when da Gama arrived at Calicut in 1498 as an armed visitor was more or less complete in 1535 when the Portuguese captured Diu and gained control of most of the maritime trade of Arab and Gujarat sultans, and built fortified warehouses in the spice islands. Thereafter, until the arrival of the Dutch in 1599, Portuguese merchants controlled the spice trade. Control, however, was tenuous because Portugal did not have sufficient military or naval power to enforce domination.

Malacca was the key city for conducting the spice trade. Spices produced in the sultanates of Banda, Ternate, and Tidore were assembled there and Portuguese merchants carried them across the Indian ocean to India or north to China and Japan. When Molucca and

Banda spices reached Goa, pepper from Calicut and Cochin was added and the cargoes were carried to Europe or to the warehouses of Portuguese merchants in Persia and Arabia. Arab and Gujarati merchants then carried the spices to Egypt and the Levant by sailing the length of the Red sea to the Egyptian port of Suez, or sailing to Basra at the head of the Persian gulf. From Suez and Basra they were carried overland to the shore of the Mediterranean where Venetian merchants acquired them for distribution in Europe. Malacca was also the place where locally produced tin and Chinese silk and porcelain were assembled for sale around the rim of the Indian ocean and in Europe.

In 1514, using information supplied by Chinese merchants in Malacca, Portuguese merchants sailed to China (Canton) where they found a highly profitable market for spices, ivory, and sandalwood (a dyewood). In 1515 the Portuguese king financed a flotilla of seven ships to China that included a personal emissary. The ships arrived at Canton in 1517 with a cargo of spices and acquired a highly profitable cargo of silk textiles and porcelain ware. A second trading fleet arrived in 1519 and its admiral forcibly mobilized local labor to build a fortified warehouse on an offshore island. Chinese authorities ordered the Portuguese to leave. A battle ensued in which two Portuguese ships were sunk and Canton was closed to Portuguese commerce.

The trade, however, was too profitable for the Chinese governors to ignore. In 1557 Portuguese merchants secured a permanent enclave on a small peninsula that became Macau, and agreed to pay all custom duties and not fortify themselves. Macau was a new form of Portuguese commerce. It was wholly controlled by merchants and its continued existence depended on good relations with Chinese authorities, not by controlling Chinese maritime commerce with superior ships and gunnery.

From their enclave in Macau, in 1543 Portuguese merchants discovered Japan or, more accurately, some islands off of the south coast of Kyushu. The trade that ensued was highly profitable and next year several Portuguese ships arrived. The Chinese merchants who controlled Japanese maritime trade attacked the Portuguese intruders. These merchants had not previously encountered Portuguese ships and had no experience with naval artillery. Many junks were sunk. Japanese feudal barons (daimyo) were impressed.

Within a few years a very complex trade developed. Portuguese ships at Goa were loaded with cargoes of Indian cotton textiles, pepper, cinnamon, ivory, wine, glassware, and Flemish clocks. These ships sailed to Malacca where part of the cargo was traded for hides (from Thailand), sandalwood, cloves, nutmeg, and mace. Upon arrival at Macau the cargoes were traded for Chinese silk and porcelain ware, then sailed to Japan to complete the voyage. The items going to Japan included ivory, pepper, cinnamon, spices, and some Flemish clocks. In Japan these items were traded for silver, some gold, bars of copper, Japanese lacquer ware, steel swords, and other distinctive Japanese products.

After returning to Macau, Japanese silver was converted to gold because the Chinese valued silver at a ratio of 5.5 ounces of silver for 1.0 ounce of gold. When this gold was carried to Europe it was exchanged for silver at the rate of about 12.0 ounces of silver for 1.0 ounce of gold. Much of the copper acquired in Japan went to Goa where it was alloyed with tin purchased from Malay merchants who purchased it from placer miners on the Malay peninsula (Perak, Kedah). At Goa copper and tin were alloyed and cast into bronze cannons. Some of the cannons, Chinese silk textiles, porcelain ware, and spices were shipped to Europe.

Trade with Japan, like trade at Macau, was dependent on good relations with Japanese rulers, not superior ships and naval artillery. In 1571, the port of call for Portuguese merchants was fixed at Nagasaki on the south coast of Kyushu. Portuguese merchants, and the Spanish and Dutch merchants who followed them, were confined to an unfortified near shore island where they built warehouses and residences. It was not a close confinement because Japan was experiencing a many sided civil war among feudal barons (daimyo), a conflict that did not end until 1598 when the military victories of Ieyasu Tokugawa imposed peace. Tokugawa then assumed the title of shogun, which made him the actual ruler of Japan with the power to control all international commerce.

Accompanying Portuguese merchants from Macau and Spanish

merchants from Manila (after 1586) were Roman Catholic missionaries who immediately began proselytizing the daimyo of southern Kyushu. They were favorably received and were permitted to preach a message of millennial expectations to peasants. Conversions accelerated. Ieyasu Tokugawa distrusted the influx of Roman Catholic missionaries because their preaching could ignite discontent among daimyo who were reluctant to accept the Tokugawa pacification of 1598. Tokugawa feared that millennial preaching would encourage a rebellion by daimyo who were waiting for an opportunity to contest his title of shogun. Such a rebellion would destabilize the Tokugawa peace and Japan would revert to the anarchy of warring daimyo that had disturbed Japanese society during the previous 100 years. In 1614 Spanish and Portuguese missionaries were expelled and new ones forbidden to enter.

The revolt occurred in 1615 and several rebellious daimyo fought under Christian banners, and when Osaka castle was captured at least seven Spanish missionaries were among the dead. In spite of the interference of Spanish missionaries in the internal affairs of Japan, the Manila trade continued because Tokugawa shoguns wanted access to European learning, particularly European armaments and how to make them. After 1624, Spanish ships were denied entry to Japan but Portuguese merchants retained access and continued to smuggle missionaries into Japan.

The worst fears of Tokugawa shoguns were confirmed in 1637-1638. Christian daimyo along the south coast of Kyushu led a peasant rebellion that was suppressed with great difficulty. Following its suppression, an edict excluded Portuguese ships from Japanese trade and a campaign was begun to purge Japan of Christianity. In 1640, the shogun sealed Japan to outside commerce except for Chinese and Dutch merchants in order to conserve the peace of the Togugawa social order. Dutch merchants had arrived in 1609. Their ships carried no missionary passengers and the merchants themselves had minimal interest in religion. They came to earn money and were more than happy to sell European armaments to the Japanese for a price. Thereafter, until the mid-nineteenth century, Dutch merchants were Japan's principal contact with Europe.

Like the Portuguese at Goa, the Spanish government wanted an enclave in the orient in order to trade with China, Japan, and the spice islands. In 1564 the Spanish sent a flotilla of five ships from Navidad, Mexico to the Philippine islands to establish an enclave. The Spanish used the trans-Pacific route to the Philippines in order to avoid the danger of capture by Portuguese, Dutch, or English warships if they used the route around the Cape of Good Hope. The trans-Pacific route also concealed Spanish expansion into the orient.

The flotilla was commanded by Miguel Lopez de Legaspi and arrived at the island of Cebu in 1565 where he established an enclave. In 1567 Legaspi sent a ship to Mexico with a cargo of cinnamon and a little gold. The trans-Pacific trade initiated by Legaspi in 1567 created the global market. Thereafter, the trans-Pacific link in global commerce was sustained by an annual Manila galleon and other merchant ships that often accompanied it. During the ten years that followed the establishment of a Spanish commercial enclave on Cebu island, Spanish soldiers and merchants negotiated protectorates over almost all coastal chieftains, and it was done with a minimum of warfare.

The peasants on the central islands of the Philippines did not produce sufficient amounts of commodities that could be sold on distant markets, and in 1571 the seat of government was moved to the capacious and defensible harbor at Manila. Thereafter, Manila became the entrepot for the trans-Pacific trade of Spanish merchants in the orient. Portuguese merchants in Macau supplied spices, silk textiles, and porcelain ware that were usually carried to Manila in Chinese junks. These items were purchased with silver from Mexico and Peru that arrived in the annual galleon from Acapulco, Mexico. On its return voyage the galleon carried Chinese luxury items and spices that had an instant sale to the governing elite of Mexico, or they were carried across Mexico and shipped across the Atlantic ocean to Spain.

The Spanish never developed Manila's potential for being a major entrepot of the orient because Spanish governors in the seventeenth and eighteenth centuries made little effort to establish the cultivation of pepper, cloves, or other spices on any of the islands. It was further handicapped by the expulsion of Spanish merchants from Japan (1624), and because the Spanish crown preserved Portuguese control of Macau when the monarchies of Spain and Portugal were united (1580-1640). Developing a commercial empire in the orient was always a tertiary concern of the Spanish monarchy. Increasingly, the Philippines became a missionary province to convert the peasantry to Christianity rather than a province whose commercial potential could be developed.

The sailors, soldiers, and merchants who created the Portuguese commercial empire in the orient in the late fifteenth and sixteenth centuries had a dual vision of their labors. Merchants would become rich, and the trade they conducted would be the entering wedge for evangelizing the non-Christian cultures they encountered. Merchants were a combination of speculators (seeking new sources of wealth) and adventurers (like the sailors and soldiers who accompanied and protected them). They were acutely conscious of the vulnerability of their fortified enclaves and warehouses to attacks by indigenous rulers. They were equally conscious of the tenuous nature of the empire they were helping to create because they were at the end of highly vulnerable trade routes that touched China (Macau), Japan (Nagasaki), and the Molucca islands. Holden Furber summarizes how European merchants viewed their status in India and the Indies. "The few thousands of Europeans who built these empires thought of themselves primarily as merchants rather than as rulers." [5]

SPANISH COMMERCIAL EMPIRE

The discoveries of Christopher Columbus were quickly followed by Spanish settlements on Cuba, Hispaniola, and the other large islands in the Caribbean. These islands became offshore bases for exploring the mainland, just as the Canary islands were an offshore base for crossing the Atlantic. The results of mainland exploration were spectacular. The conquest of the Aztecs in 1518-1521 and the Incas in 1533-1536 procured huge amounts of precious metals for the Spanish treasury; and active prospecting during the sixteenth and seventeenth centuries procured a continuing supply from placers and newly discovered mines.

In the immediate years following Columbus's discoveries, the crown tried to monopolize American commerce but, in the aftermath of the conquest of Granada in 1492, the crown did not have the resources. Instead, the crown centralized control of American trade by establishing the Casa de Contratacion (house of trade) in Seville in 1503. The Casa licensed only Spanish merchants or foreign merchants who were long residents in Spain and who lived in Seville. Merchants without licenses were prohibited from trading to the Americas.

Like the Spanish monarchy, Seville merchants lacked sufficient capital to finance American commerce. Genoese bankers, however, were eager to supply it as long as precious metals continued to arrive from the Americas. To cement their relationship with the Spanish monarchy and Seville merchants, Genoese bankers were made the paymasters for Spanish soldiers fighting throughout Europe. The dual function of supplying credit to merchants trading into America and to the monarchy insured that their loans would be repaid on time with money minted from American precious metals.

The Casa's licensing policy created a monopoly that could be closely regulated for the benefit of the monarchy's dynastic ambitions.

As all trade with the New World was to pass through the Casa, the control of this commerce was from the outset restricted to a single port for the whole of Spain. And for two centuries, in spite of the claims of other cities, in spite of protests from the colonies . . . the vested interests of the merchants whose prosperity depended upon the preservation of this monopoly were sufficient to bear down all opposition; and for the Crown it was much easier to maintain in a single port that rigid supervision of every detail of trade and navigation which was the Spaniard's ideal. [6]

Seville is a very awkward location for managing long distance commerce because it is not a seaport. It is 75 kilometers inland on the Guadalquivir river. Not until 1535 could Cadiz, located on the Atlantic coast, participate in American commerce. In all commerce to the Americas, Cadiz remained a satellite of Seville. After commerce was regularized, annual convoys of merchant ships could load cargoes at Cadiz, provided they followed all of the procedures required by the Casa. Return convoys, however were required to return to Seville or the small port of San Lucar at the mouth of the Guadalquivir river because San Lucar was the shortest distance from the coast to Seville. At San Lucar, all bullion listed on the ships papers was unloaded and transported to Seville where it paid taxes. This arrangement persisted until 1717 when, in a moment of reality, the king transferred the Casa to Cadiz. Cadiz and Seville reversed positions but the monopoly of the Casa was preserved.

There were three reasons why the Spanish crown favored monopoly control of American commerce by Seville merchants. 1) The overwhelming concern of the monarchy was to control bullion imports in order to control the use the gold and silver coins minted from it. The best way to control bullion imports was having only one port of entry and one convoy per year that carried bullion. 2) The monopoly of American commerce by the merchants of Seville made it possible for the monarchy to force them to pay benevolences whenever it needed money. Benevolent loans were seldom repaid. 3) Military and merchant adventurers who returned to Spain with hoards of bullion, in order to coin into money, could have their bullion seized (for reasons of state)—even after they declared the bullion and paid taxes on it. In return, they were issued bonds bearing 3.5 to 6.0 percent interest. The merchants of Seville supported the crown because the monopoly made them rich; and the crown supported monopoly merchants because of their ability to concentrate imports of bullion.

American bullion made it possible for Spanish monarchs to finance dynastic ambitions because the most efficient money for waging war was gold and silver coins. Spanish monarchs preferentially used money minted from American bullion to pay for European wars rather than for improving interior transportation, promoting artisan manufacturing, or encouraging Spanish merchants to conduct more of the nation's European trade. Spanish monarchs were oblivious to the volume and variety of manufactured products that could be produced and exported to the colonies from the hinterlands of many port cities if merchants from these cities could trade directly to America.

In the sixteenth and seventeenth centuries local merchants with more energy and imagination, but less capital than the monopoly merchants of Seville, could have supplied the American colonies with an adequate supply of products manufactured from iron because Spain had an abundance of iron ores. Nor did Mexican viceroys encourage Mexican peasants to weave cotton textiles for export to Europe, as the English were to do when they established themselves in India. In the process of establishing imperial governance, Mexican viceroys could have generated long-term tax revenues for the crown because profit opportunities in the Americas were practically limitless. Instead, the monarchy sanctioned the choking of American commerce by the monopoly merchants of Seville because of their fixation on bullion imports and dynastic concerns unrelated to commerce.

Most historians have described Spanish colonial policies in the Americas as being governed by a search for loot rather than increasing the taxable commercial wealth of Spanish and colonial merchants. This is accurate. Freer trade and self-sufficiency in artisan manufactured products were secondary concerns of Spanish monarchs. Not until the 1750s did the Spanish government begin to encourage domestic weavers to produce enough woolen cloth to make Spain self-sufficient. The lateness of the attempt at self-sufficiency in textiles was glaringly apparent because Spain was a major exporter of raw wool. Not until 1778 did the Spanish government allow free trade with the American colonies, and then from only 13 ports.

During the sixteenth century, when Spain was importing maximum amounts of precious metals, Dutch merchants were maximizing their participation in European maritime commerce. By about 1540, Dutch merchants were rapidly replacing Spanish and Portuguese merchants in commerce between northern Europe and Iberia. They were also replacing Hanseatic merchants who had long dominated the trade between the Baltic sea and the cities of the Rhine delta. The inability of Spanish artisans to produce sufficient manufactured products to satisfy the needs of American colonists meant that these products had to be purchased. Dutch, English, German, and Genoese artisans supplied them. Beginning in the second half of the sixteenth century and extending through the eighteenth, Spain was the intermediary rather than the source of supply for a high percentage of the manufactured items consumed in her American colonies.

Paralleling the inability of Spanish artisans to manufacture enough items to satisfy American needs was the inability of Spanish cultivators to grow enough food grains to feed Spanish cities. After 1560, in most crop years, imported food grain was necessary to feed Spanish cities, and dependency on imported food grains continued until the end of the eighteenth century.

Food deficits in Spain were chronic because the Spanish monarchy did not encourage feudal landholders to convert the subsistence tenures of peasants cultivating their land into leasehold tenure. Yields of food grains were among the lowest in Europe and they remained low because feudal landholders did not apply the continual coercion that was necessary to commercialize agriculture. Coercion (threat of eviction) administered by resident landowners or resident managers of their estates was essential for inducing peasants to increase per capita production of food grains for market sale. Instead, feudal landholders allowed peasants to control land use and thereby practice subsistence labor norms. In normal crop years the cities would have experienced hunger without food imports and in poor crop years food imports were required to avert famine conditions.

The lack of interest by the monarchy and feudal landholders in commercializing agriculture was mirrored in the primitive state of internal transportation. A high percentage of overland transportation was by pack mules and clumsy carts, with big solid wooden wheels, that usually moved in trains of 10 to 30. They were pulled by ox teams, were slow, and had limited carrying capacity. The roads were so primitive that it was impossible to use wagons and most roads were impassible during the winter. A further restraint on transportation was the refusal of peasants to grow forage crops to adequately feed draft animals. Oxen pulling carts had to stop early in the afternoon so they could graze in pastures reserved for their use along the route. The pastures were usually overgrazed and contained grasses of low nutrition. Only cavalry horses were adequately fed with forage crops.

Both Spain and Portugal could have been self-sufficient in food grain production if feudal landholders had been motivated to commercialize agriculture on their estates and invest in improved overland transportation, as was done by English landowners in the seventeenth and eighteenth centuries. Aristocratic landholders, however, disdained active management of their estates because it was beneath their dignity. Many were absent for prolonged periods. They consciously opted to live in symbiosis with the peasantry, a symbiosis that peasants enforced with numerous rebellions (communaros) in the sixteenth and seventeenth centuries.

Aristocratic landholders had other interests. They governed Spain, pursued careers as military commanders, colonial governors, or high offices in civil government and the church hierarchy. The purpose of their lives was to expel Muslims from Europe, stop Muslim expansion elsewhere in the world, expand the Spanish empire in order to expand the boundaries of Christendom, and reestablish the true Catholic faith as the religion of western Europe. Achievement of these goals would measure a worthy life for aristocrats and for the soldiers who served in the regiments.

If Spanish imperial expansion was to be sustained, the food grains that were not grown in Iberia had to be imported. A high percentage of the grain (wheat, barley, rye) came from the Baltic and it arrived in the same Dutch ships that supplied Amsterdam with food grains. In exchange for food grains Dutch merchants acquired salt, olive oil, wine, vinegar (to pickle herring), and wool. Exports of these products were never sufficient to pay for the food grains and manufactured items that Spain needed for domestic consumption and to supply American colonists. Precious metal money from the Americas paid for a high percentage of these imports.

In the process of engrossing much of Spain and Portugal's European commerce, the Dutch created new wealth out of proportion to their numbers. Some of the new Dutch wealth was invested in intellectual pursuits (medicine, optics, mathematics); others in improving skills in banking, insurance, navigation, shipbuilding, and engineering needed to drain land. These developments were a consequence of the social structures of Dutch society as it evolved following the reformation. The intellectual authority of the medieval church was extinguished and persons of intellect and talent could ask new questions and apply new technologies with far fewer institutional restraints on the consequences. There were no ecclesiastical trials of Galileo's disciples in the Netherlands (or in England). By the middle of the seventeenth century Dutch commerce (and learning) had eclipsed Spanish, Portuguese, Genoese, and Venetian commerce and learning, and during the eighteenth century English commerce and learning surpassed the Dutch.

Paralleling and contributing to the commercial and intellectual decline of Spain was the monarchy's extreme concern that only Catholic subjects should immigrate to the American colonies. Great efforts were made to prevent the emigration of conversos (forcibly converted Jews and Muslims), even though a high percentage of these persons were city residents who had commercial skills. Instead of going to America they emigrated to Amsterdam, Istanbul, and ports rimming the Mediterranean and took their capital and skills with them. These were people that the American colonies desperately needed to mobilize the labor of Spanish settlers and indigenous inhabitants to produce commercial wealth from newly acquired lands.

Spanish military power in Europe depended on imports of large amounts of precious metals from the Americas. When the supply declined, Spanish military and political power declined. The decline became visible by about 1570; and in 1575 the central government repudiated all contracts that supplied Spanish troops in Flanders. The central government was bankrupt. Unpaid Spanish troops mutinied and looted Antwerp in 1576. Genoese bankers helped restore the government's finances in 1577 but Antwerp was now a war zone and large numbers of merchants from Antwerp migrated to Amsterdam, Hamburg, and Cologne. The bankruptcy of 1575 did not change the European policies of the Spanish king. Reversing the reformation remained the monarchy's primary objective, which could not be done without conquering the Netherlands and England. Both attempts failed, especially the catastrophe of the Armada against England in 1588. After 1588 Spanish power in Europe steadily declined, a decline that accelerated after 1650.

After the defeat of the Armada, Spanish supremacy in the Americas and Portuguese hegemony in the Indian ocean began to be challenged by the better armed ships of Dutch, English, and French long voyage merchants. These merchants had the full support of their central governments. The chartering of the English and Dutch East India Companies (1600 and 1602) roughly corresponds with the beginning of systematic armed competition to control the long distance commerce established by Portuguese merchants in the Indian ocean and Indies and Spanish merchants in the Caribbean and the adjacent coast. Competition was relatively easy because the Portuguese and Spanish monarchies failed to use sufficient resources to protect their commerce.

The second generation of empire builders from the Netherlands, England, and France followed exactly in the footsteps of the Portuguese and Spanish empire builders who preceded them. The crucial difference was that the Dutch, English, and French governments delegated management of long distance commerce, and the armed force necessary to protect it, to monopoly corporations that exercised vice-regal powers to establish new sources of commerce and defend their interests. Compared to Portuguese and Spanish practices, the Dutch and English companies conducted their long distance trade with a minimum of government interference and a maximum of individual initiative. French practices were somewhere in between.

DUTCH COMMERCIAL EMPIRE

The roots of the Dutch commercial empire were in the mid-1500s when Dutch merchants became the principal carriers of bulk commodities from the Baltic sea (food grains, ship timbers, bar iron, naval stores) to Amsterdam and from Amsterdam to Spain and Portugal. The Dutch silently appropriated a large part of the Flemish trade with Spain while Spanish monarchs devoted much of the bullion acquired in the Americas to trying to reverse the reformation. At the same time, the smaller resources of Portugal were stretched to their limit trying to protect its overextended empire in the Indian ocean and establish sugar cultivation in Brazil.

In 1500 over 40 percent of the population of the provinces of Holland (with Amsterdam at the center) and Flanders (with Bruges at its center) were urban. Imported food grains were required to feed city residents. The principal source was the hinterlands of Baltic seaports. Food grains had to be imported because Dutch/Flemish cultivators concentrated on producing high value foods: milk, butter, cheese, and vegetables to feed city residents, plus growing flax to make linen cloth, hemp to make sailcloth, and woad to make dye. By about 1560 Dutch/ Flemish agriculture was commercialized. Dutch/Flemish cultivators were the first coherent group in western Europe to practice commercial agriculture.

At the same time the Spanish were building their commercial empire in America and the Portuguese in India, they were engaged in crusades in northern Europe and north Africa. The Portuguese sought to expand into Morocco and the Spanish into Tunisia. Spain also spent huge amounts of precious metal money to conduct a war in Flanders that: 1) captured Protestant Antwerp in 1585; 2) funded an invasion of England in 1588 (the armada); 3) funded a 30 year crusade (Thirty Years War from 1618 to 1648) in order to impose the true Catholic religion on the principalities of northern Europe.

The expenditure of resources for non-commercial purposes by Portuguese and Spanish monarchies created an opportunity for Dutch merchants to displace Spanish, Portuguese, and Flemish merchants (and the Genoese bankers who provided credit) in the carrying trade between northern and southern Europe. The profits earned by Dutch merchants and the credit skills they learned from Genoese and Florentine bankers helped them accumulate the capital that made it possible for Dutch merchants to challenge Iberian control of the long distance commerce to America and the Indies. The governing elite of the Netherlands clearly understood that there were substantial opportunities to earn high profits by contesting Iberian hegemony in long distance commerce.

The Dutch had minimal interest in propagating religious doctrines. Their interest was encouraging all varieties of artisan manufactures and maritime commerce in order to displace Portuguese merchants in their rickety Indian ocean empire and contest Spanish commercial supremacy in the Americas. The Dutch were helped in their ambitions by the unification of the Spanish and Portuguese crowns in 1580. After unification, Dutch warships did not have to make a distinction between Portuguese and Spanish ships engaged in long distance commerce; nor did the English. As long as the crowns were unified (1580 to 1640), the Dutch and English could attack the ships of both nations without distinction, and they did. The Dutch were especially motivated to attack Spanish and Portuguese ships because they had revolted against Spanish rule in 1568. The necessity of repelling attacks by Spanish troops that were occupying Flanders forced the seven northern provinces to unite in 1579, and declare independence in 1581.

After the Spanish captured Antwerp in 1585, Flemish merchants were allowed four years to leave the city with their wealth, if they wished. During a prolonged blockade of Antwerp by Dutch ships many took their wealth and skills to Amsterdam. After their migration, Antwerp ceased being the commercial rival of Amsterdam. It became a hostage of Spanish interests and a relative commercial backwater. In spite of continuing hostilities in Flanders (Spanish troops attempting to invade the Netherlands), Dutch merchants continued to supply Spanish cities food grains from the Baltic because the Spanish had no other source.

During the first half of the seventeenth century Amsterdam became the entrepot for northern Europe because Dutch merchants expanded their preeminence in Iberian commerce to preeminence in Baltic and North sea commerce. Although its Iberian trade continued to flourish, Amsterdam's commercial future was the Atlantic ocean and beyond. The rest of this section describes and analyzes the expansion of Dutch commerce into the Indian ocean, the Indies, and Japan.

The defeat of the Spanish armada removed a major constraint on Dutch and English merchants undertaking an armed intrusion into the commercial empires that Portuguese and Spanish merchants had stitched together during the previous 50 years. The basis for the Dutch global outreach was the experience of Jan Huyghan van Linschoten. He went to India in the service of the Portuguese in 1582, lived in Goa from 1583 to 1589, and returned to the Netherlands in 1592. In 1595 he published an account of his travels and accurately assessed the weakness of the Portuguese commercial empire, as well as writing clear sailing directions to India and the Indies.

At the time of Linschoten's return Dutch merchants wanted confirmation of Portuguese weakness in India and the spice islands. Cornelis de Houtman, a navigator disguised as a merchant, sailed to India on a Portuguese ship to confirm Linschoten's assessment of Portuguese weakness. He was discovered, imprisoned, and ransomed. After the Spanish king closed the port of Lisbon to Dutch shipping in 1594, nine Amsterdam merchants financed a trading voyage to the Indies. It left in 1595 with Cornelis de Houtman in command of a flotilla of four ships. He arrived at Bantam in west Java in 1596. His objective was to establish a spice trade. He traded for a small amount and returned in 1597. The cargo earned a small profit but only 89 crew members survived out of the 249 who began the voyage. He did, however, accurately assess the fragmented condition of indigenous rule on Java and the absence of Portuguese penetration.

On the basis of Houtman's information, Admiral Jacob Corneliszoon van Neck sailed to the Java sea, traded for a cargo of spices and, on his return in June 1599, sold it for a 400 percent profit. The race was on. Between 1599 and the end of 1601, eight syndicates of Dutch merchants sent out 14 fleets composed of at least 65 ships. They left factors ashore at Bantam and five other ports on Java and other islands in the Java sea; and at two ports on the Malay peninsula. In 1602 the States-General of the United Provinces forced all Dutch merchants trading into the Indies to consolidate their capital by becoming shareholders in the United Netherlands East India Company. In return for pooling their capital, participating merchants were granted a monopoly for 21 years to "trade east of the Cape of Good Hope and west of the Straits of Magellan, with authority to wage defensive war, negotiate treaties of peace and alliance, and build fortresses." [7]

The charter of incorporation of the Dutch East India Company was a copy of the charter of the English East India Company. London merchants had requested a charter to trade into the Indies in 1600 and queen Elizabeth complied. The merchant adventurers of both the Dutch and English East India companies immediately began to contest Portuguese control of commerce to the Indies. Armed merchant adventurers from England and the Netherlands also contested Spanish control of American commerce.

The stockholders of both companies were almost exclusively merchants. Both companies were monopolies that exercised similar vice-regal powers to govern and make war if necessary. The powers they received clearly indicated very close ties with their respective central governments. This relationship was necessary because the competition to earn profits in long distance commerce was also a contest for political power in Europe. Power would accrue to the European nations with the largest revenues available to fight wars for commercial advantage. The only way to protect revenues from long distance commerce was with adequate expenditures in naval construction, building fortifications at remote localities, and having garrisons of soldiers to defend them.

There were two quick results of Dutch merchant adventurers entering the Indies. One ship was wrecked on the shore of Kyushu, Japan in 1601. The captain was repatriated in 1605, but while a resident in Japan he secured a license from the shogun for Dutch ships to establish a warehouse to sustain permanent trade. The warehouse was established in 1610 and it ended the Spanish/Portuguese monopoly of trading Chinese silk textiles and spices for Japanese copper and silver.

The second result was that English merchant adventurers, like Dutch merchant adventurers, saw an opportunity to enter the Indies and compete with Portuguese and Spanish merchants. English (and Dutch) competition for the commerce of India, the Indies, and Japan would reduce the revenues of the dual monarchy of Spain and Portugal and reduce Spanish power in Europe. Particularly, it would reduce the ability of the Spanish monarchy to finance military operations that sought to impose the true Catholic religion on the Netherlands and England.

The India bound ships of both the Dutch and English East India companies were heavily armed because, in remote places, competition for trade was often armed competition. Naval battles were the usual results of Dutch and English ships encountering each or encountering Portuguese and Spanish ships in the harbors of weak rulers. Only the governments of China and Japan were strong enough to impose peaceful trade on armed European ships. Not until spheres of commercial hegemony were more clearly defined at the end of the seventeenth century did long distance commerce have some degree of order and predictability.

The fourth fleet sent out by the Dutch East India Company in 1604 followed Portuguese precedent. It anchored at Calicut, as da Gama had done in 1498, in order to establish a warehouse with a resident merchant (factor). Other unfortified warehouses were established at Aden, Surat, and Masulipatam on the east coast of India (Coromandel coast). The purposes of these warehouses was the same as the Portuguese—to acquire cotton textiles (piece goods) because textiles were the principal item desired by the peasants who grew and processed spices in the Molucca islands. Dutch factors also acquired pepper grown along the Malabar coast for sale in Europe and elsewhere. At Banda, the Dutch built a fortified warehouse in order to monopolize nutmeg and mace production and thereby control production and prices. While building the fort at Banda they came into conflict with an English East India Company ship but the Dutch retained possession.

After the Dutch gained knowledge of the spice trade, their greatest need, if they were to monopolize production and distribution, was a strongly fortified enclave with a territorial hinterland, like the Portuguese had at Goa. Portuguese ships had bypassed Java on their way to the spice islands. The Dutch found that the kingdoms of central and east Java were too strong for them to intrude a fortified enclave; however, several weak sultans governed west Java where the limited resources of the Dutch could force an entry. It was clear to the Dutch that Java was an island waiting to be incorporated into their commercial empire whenever they mobilized the ships and manpower necessary to sustain their presence.

The Dutch recognized four great assets of Java. 1) A fortified enclave on the north coast could control the entry of ships into the Java and Banda seas through the Sunda straits (between Java and Sumatra). 2) Warships based in the Jakarta enclave could choke Portuguese trade between the Molucca islands and Malacca. 3) The indigenous merchants who conducted the coastal trade of Java and elsewhere in the archipelago could be controlled by superior Dutch ships and naval artillery. 4) Java's large population could be mobilized to grow export crops. The Dutch were resolved to control the trade of indigenous merchants in the same way the Portuguese controlled the trade of indigenous merchants along the west coast of India. They would use their fortified enclave to direct the trade of export commodities through the warehouses of Dutch merchants at Jakarta.

In 1609 the directors of the company appointed a president-general who would reside in the Indies and exercise vice-regal powers. He arrived at Bantam in 1610 and in 1611 moved his headquarters to the small fishing village of Jakarta. The local sultan gave permission to build the fort because he had no choice. During his tenure the president-general made a tour of the company's fortified and unfortified warehouses. He was accompanied by Jan Pieterszoon Coen who wrote a comprehensive report on the condition of trade and he recommended policies that would increase profits. Subsequently, he was appointed resident director-general of commerce and, in 1619 he was appointed president-general and directed to increase profits by implementing the strategy he had previously recommended.

The strategy was: 1) expand regional trade (country trade) between India, the islands of Indonesia, the Malay peninsula, Thailand, Ceylon, China, and Japan; 2) use as much force as necessary to establish a monopoly in the production of three spices (cloves, mace, nutmeg). This meant preventing the planting and harvesting of spice bearing plants except on islands under firm Dutch control, and destroying plantations on islands that were not firmly controlled; 3) immigration of Dutch settlers to perform vital technical services. Coen knew that a monopoly of the spice trade could only be maintained by conquering the strongly fortified Portuguese warehouses at Ternate and Tidore and, thereafter, using warships to exclude the ships of competing nations. Coen's policies committed the company to protracted warfare to establish and maintain a production and marketing monopoly for these spices.

In both India and the Indies, the English East India Company competed with the Dutch; and both the Dutch and English were determined to evict or neutralize Portuguese commerce in India and the Indies in order to preempt their pepper and spice trade. In India, the Dutch company had to overcome two obstacles: the established Portuguese commercial network and English competition.

A regional trade (country trade) based in India was essential to both the English and Dutch companies because Indian cotton textiles and rice were necessary to trade for spices. A Dutch factor in India wrote his superiors in 1612, "The Coromandel Coast is the left arm of the Moluccas, because we have noticed that without the textiles of Coromandel, commerce is dead in the Moluccas." [8] Not all spices went to Europe. A substantial amount of spices acquired in the Moluccas were sold in India where they were prized ingredients in curries. Profits from supplying India with spices and other products helped defray the costs of protecting imperial commerce. They were equally essential for maintaining numerous warehouses in smaller harbors where diverse commodities were acquired before being assembled at an entrepot for shipment to Europe.

Silver coins from Europe, Japan (1640-1700), and America were the principal means of purchasing cotton textiles and rice in India for sale in the Moluccas, and for purchasing commodities in India and the Indies that were destined for Europe. Silver coins were supplemented by many varieties of metal implements manufactured in Europe. Among them were armaments, fittings for ships that were built in India, and bars of lead. Spices acquired by purchase with silver coins or in exchange for cotton textiles were then marketed in Europe, India, with smaller amounts going to Japan and China. Other commodities going to Europe were sugar, pepper, indigo, and saltpeter; and after 1680 Europe consumed increasing amounts of cotton textiles. Simultaneously, Japan became a regular purchaser of sugar produced on Java. The measure of corporate profitability, however, was the value of commodities that were shipped to Europe, with a high percentage of them being assembled by merchants engaged in regional trade.

Like the Portuguese before them and like their Dutch competitors, the English East India Company had to have warehouses with resident merchants (factors) at various ports in India and the Indies. Also, like the Portuguese, the English and Dutch companies had to send periodic embassies bearing gifts to rulers too strong to be intimidated to allow construction of fortified warehouses in their port cities. In

1612 the English established a warehouse at Surat in the Mughal empire, and in 1616 the Dutch did the same, but it was the English who secured the greater advantage. In 1615, they used their superior ships and naval artillery to repulse a Portuguese fleet sent from Goa to expel them. At the same time, the English company was establishing warehouses in India it was establishing them in the spice islands at places distant from Ternate and Tidore.

The Dutch, however, were one step ahead of the English in the Indies. By 1618 a fort was completed at Jakarta and the Dutch quickly expanded it into a defensible enclave that was directly governed like the Portuguese governed their fortified enclave at Goa. Like Goa, Jakarta was an entrepot where European and Indian items were distributed to the warehouses of resident merchants in the outer islands and where the commodities acquired by factors in the Indies, China, and Japan were assembled for shipment to India and Europe.

The Dutch presence in the Indies was enhanced in 1616 by sailing directly across the Indian ocean and entering the Java sea through the Sunda straits, instead of hugging the east coast of Africa and frequently stopping at fortified warehouses, which was the practice of Portuguese navigators. A second innovation was smaller crews. Smaller crews allowed greater space for cargoes and also reduced mortalities among crew members and passengers because they were better fed. A third innovation was the ability of most Dutch merchants to be naval officers when situations required it. Dutch merchants also had the advantage of superior financing from Amsterdam banks that helped them assemble cargoes for outward voyages, purchase better designed ships for the Indies trade than were used by the Spanish and Portuguese, and equip them with the latest artillery and other weaponry.

Part of the continuing success of the Dutch East India Company in the seventeenth century was the settlement in 1652 of a colony at Cape Town, at the southern tip of Africa. The region was vacant and settlers met no resistance from scattered bands of hunter-gatherers. It also had a temperate climate that was highly suitable for growing European crops. The principal purpose of the colony was to supply Dutch ships with fresh water, fresh meat, fresh vegetables, fresh fruit, and kegs of wine. At the same time it was a rest stop where crews and passengers could go ashore and recover from sicknesses. A layover reduced moralities among passengers and crews. Because there were no organized societies in the colony's hinterland whose labor could be mobilized, settlers produced only small quantities of bulk products for export: wool, hides, and wheat that returning ships from India and the Indies marketed in Amsterdam.

In 1619 the directors of the Dutch and English East India companies negotiated an agreement to reduce tensions in India and the Indies. This was necessary because a Dutch/English maritime truce with Spain/Portugal in Europe was about to expire and a maritime war in Europe would probably result. As part of the agreement the Dutch established additional warehouses in India and two in Persia. The Persian trade was highly profitable because spices were exchanged for Persian silk textiles that were highly valued in Europe. The 1619 agreement ended English competition for the clove trade in the Molucca islands, but the English company retained a small warehouse on one of the Banda islands. A Portuguese presence continued in the Molucca islands because the Dutch were not yet strong enough to expel them. The English also retained their warehouse at Benkulen on the west coast of Sumatra as a source of pepper. The Dutch could not monopolize the production and marketing of pepper because it was too widely grown.

In order to control the cultivation, processing, and marketing of nutmeg and mace the Dutch conquered all of the Banda islands, except the one where the English company had a factor, and emigrated slaves to cultivate, harvest, and process them. In order to control the cultivation and processing of cloves on Ceram and Amboina, Coen ordered the chieftains of coastal villages to assemble where they would be informed of Dutch commercial policies. These polices were to: 1) limit production to sustain prices; 2) enforce purchasing certain products only from the Dutch at their prices; 3) enforce trade with only Dutch ships or ships licensed by the Dutch. The chiefs of the coastal tribes of Ceram failed to attend and an expeditionary force was sent to harry them into submission. This was done with considerable bloodshed and resulting famine when Dutch soldiers and indigenous levies destroyed the food crops of villages ruled by non-cooperating chiefs.

From their fortified enclave at Jakarta, the Dutch searched for new markets. Hopefully, they would be markets they could monopolize. On their own initiative Dutch merchants established an unfortified warehouse in Japan in 1610 and another one on the sparsely populated island of Taiwan in 1624. The warehouse on Taiwan competed with the Portuguese at Macau. It attracted the trade of Chinese merchants originating in the other coastal cities along the south China coast. This strategy could have been hugely successful but Dutch merchants tried to force entry into Chinese port cities, as they were doing in the Indies. They were expelled and forbidden to establish warehouses in coastal cities. The Chinese captured the weakened fort on Taiwan in 1662. Direct Dutch trade with China came to an end. Cantonese trade with Europe continued to be controlled by the Portuguese; however, the Dutch continued to acquire Chinese items from Chinese merchants who traded at Nagasaki and Jakarta.

While building their sphere of influence centered at Jakarta, the Dutch blockaded the straits of Malacca from 1636 to 1641. In 1641 they conquered the city and expelled the Portuguese. After its capture, the Dutch hoped to engross the tin trade of Malaysia and prevent entry of Portuguese merchants into the spice islands. Tin minerals were found in alluvial gravels inland from the coast and were easily recovered by the same technology used to recover placer gold. Tin minerals are easily smelted into metal. Tin was in steady demand in China, Japan, and Europe for alloying with copper to form bronze.

The Dutch failed to gain full control of the tin trade because Gujarati merchants controlled transportation from the interior to the coast and had a long relationship with local sultans to whom they sold cotton textiles on credit. Late in the seventeenth century and during the first half of the eighteenth century, English regional traders increasingly acquired Malay tin at the expense of Dutch and Gujarati merchants because they had a more reliable supply of cotton textiles. The Dutch, however, still acquired some Malaysian tin but after 1710 a much more reliable supply came from the discovery of alluvial tin on the islands of Bangka and Billiton (in the Java sea) where the Dutch could exercise full control over production and marketing.

After the capture of Malacca the Dutch made repeated attempts, between 1610 and 1648, to expel the Spanish from the Philippines as a means of excluding them from the spice trade. They failed, but in 1662 they forced the sultans of Ternate and Tidore to become vassals and, in 1668 they forced the sultan of Macassar to accept a resident advisor. He was forced to exclude English, Portuguese, and non-licensed indigenous merchants who attempted to circumvent Dutch control of the spice trade. The Java and Banda seas became the center of Dutch imperial commerce in the orient and control of the spice trade became a near monopoly.

In India the Dutch used their superior naval and military power to conquer Colombo in 1656 and Jaffna in 1658. These conquests gave them control of most of the trade of Ceylon. Where they could, the Dutch levied commodity taxes (tributes) on local rajahs in Ceylon. The two principal commodities desired by the Dutch were cinnamon and rice. Cinnamon was second only to Moluccan spices in value and rice was needed to feed Dutch garrisons and the peasants in the Banda and Molucca islands who minimized the cultivation of food crops because of the favorable terms of trade between spices and rice. The Dutch liked this arrangement because the dependency of peasants on imported rice guaranteed that adequate amounts of spices would be produced.

Thereafter, from their base at Colombo, the Dutch conquered numerous small Portuguese warehouses along the Coromandel coast in order to increase their supply of cotton textiles; and in 1663 they forced the sultan of Cochin (Malabar coast) to accept a Dutch factor that gave them access to a supply of superior quality pepper.

During the first half of the seventeenth century, superior Dutch naval power, with the cooperation of the English, displaced the Portuguese from a large part of their Indian commercial empire. Dutch merchants also established themselves in Bengal where there were no Portuguese merchants. They built a fortified warehouse at Chinsura (near Calcutta) and initiated a highly profitable trade in cotton textiles, rice, saltpeter, and sugar. Sugar produced in Bengal was traded for Persian silk textiles; and after 1680 cotton textiles (calicoes, chintzes) from the Coromandel coast and Bengal found a rapidly increasing market in Europe.

Coffee first entered Europe early in the 1650s. It came from the Levant where it was the preferred beverage of Arab merchants and Turkish rulers. The coffee came from Mocha in Yemen where peasants cultivated it as their exchange commodity. Prior to 1690, most of it was exported to Egypt, Turkey, the Levant, and other feudal dependencies in the Ottoman empire. It arrived at Suez in Arab ships that carried it the length of the Red Sea. It then went overland to Egypt and the Levant where Venetian merchants carried it to Europe. London had a coffeehouse in 1652.

The first direct shipments of Mocha coffee arrived in Europe in the 1660s in Dutch and English ships, but not until the 1690s was it a regular item of commerce in Dutch ships, and then only in small amounts. The slow introduction of coffee into Europe is surprising because, almost from the beginning of Dutch commerce in India Dutch factors drank coffee, and it was an item in their country trade to all Muslim sultanates where it was the preferred nonalcoholic drink. Not until 1696 did they establish a warehouse at Mocha. The factor at Mocha had difficulty purchasing sufficient quantities of coffee at profitable prices. There were a number of reasons for low profitability. Chief among them were competition from English, French, and Turkish merchants, fluctuating demand in Europe because of variable supplies, and extortionate taxation by feudal rulers when coffee beans were transported to the coast from the highlands where coffee bushes were grown.

Dutch merchants wanted a reliable supply and it was not forthcoming from Arab cultivators. It would come from Java. The success of commodity tributes on local rajahs on Ceylon was repeated on Java. In 1696 resident advisors to local sultans ordered them to induce their peasant subjects to pay their feudal tax obligation in coffee beans instead of rice. Peasants were coerced to plant sufficient coffee bushes to satisfy their tax obligations. Half of the annual harvest went to sultans for their use and half went to the Dutch as tribute. Sultans sold their share to the Dutch in order to indulge in ostentatious living; and both shares became an export commodity. The demand in Europe, however, was greater than the supply.

In 1707 the managers of the Dutch East India Company acted with a purpose. Large scale planting of coffee was initiated on Java. Coercion was not required to induce peasants to increase their planting because they recognized its value as an exchange commodity. They were attracted to its cultivation because children could do most of the harvest labor. After peasants satisfied their tax obligations, additional coffee was sold and the money acquired was used to purchase Indian cotton textiles and iron implements made in Europe. In 1720, 90 percent of the coffee sent to Europe by the Dutch company was from Mocha; but five years later plantings on Java reached maturity and 90 percent came from Java.

The Dutch East India Company thought that their managed source of supply on Java would allow them to displace Mocha coffee in Asia and control the European price, like the company did for spices. This did not happen because Asians did not like the taste of Javanese coffee and plantings in India, Ceylon, and elsewhere indicated that coffee was a crop that was highly suitable as an exchange commodity for peasant cultivators in tropical highlands. Multiple sources of supply guaranteed competitive prices and competitive prices guaranteed that coffee consumption would increase because the central governments of western Europe encouraged its importation. Like tea, it was highly taxed because it could not be grown in Europe. By 1800 coffee was a significant beverage in Europe.

After the very expensive conquests of Portuguese coastal warehouses in India and Ceylon in the 1650s and 1660s, the managers of the Dutch East India Company halted armed expansion because the only way to earn adequate profits from these warehouses was to reduce military expenditures. This meant peaceful trade. From 1640 to 1700 the Dutch East India Company was immensely profitable because of its dominant position in Indian commerce and commercial hegemony in the Indies (centered in Jakarta).

The accomplishments of Dutch expansion in India and the Indies during the second half of the seventeenth century were: 1) fragmenting and neutralizing the Portuguese commercial empire in the orient; 2) becoming the largest European trader in India; 3) forcing the English to withdraw from the Molucca spice trade; 4) appointing resident advisors (indirect rulers) to an increasing number of sultans and chieftains in the Indies who were advised, on pain of assault on their palaces, to cease internecine warfare because it was bad for business; 5) forcing most Indonesian sultans to trade only with Dutch merchants or indigenous merchants licensed by the Dutch; 6) turning the Java and Banda seas into Dutch lakes by licensing most indigenous merchants engaged in inter-island trade; 7) becoming the only European merchants in Japan.

The first and second English-Dutch wars (1652-1654, 1665-1667) did not affect India or the Indies. They were naval wars that were fought in Europe and the Americas. In North America, New Amsterdam was captured in 1664 and became New York, which consolidated English dominance of colonial commerce along the eastern coast of North America. In return, the English ceded their warehouse in the Banda islands to the Dutch. By the beginning of the eighteenth century, however, abstention from armed intervention in India became a self-defeating policy because the Dutch did not adequately protect their trade during the slow disintegration of the Mughal empire that preceded the death of emperor Aurangzeb in 1707.

ENGLISH COMMERCIAL EMPIRE

In the initial years of entry into Indian commerce, the largest warehouse of the English East India Company was at Surat, in the northwest corner of India (north of Bombay). Surat was the principal maritime city of the Mughal empire. It was well located to export locally manufactured products (mainly cotton textiles) to Persia, Arabia, and down the Malabar coast of India.

The English and Dutch East India companies were intense competitors for Indian commerce but were united in their desire to reduce Portuguese commerce. In 1622 a joint assault by English ships and a Persian army captured Ormuz from the Portuguese. Thereafter, the English controlled a substantial part of the Arabian and Persian trade. A consequence of evicting the Portuguese from the Persian gulf trade was greatly increased English trade into the Mediterranean. English policy was to reduce the amount of Portuguese and Dutch spices that were carried overland from the Persian gulf to the Levant. English ships then delivered spices to Mediterranean cities from London where they had been carried by ships from India. The principal losers from this reorientation of trade were Venetian merchants trading into the Levant.

In dealing with the Mughal empire, however, the English were better diplomats than the Dutch. In 1624 the Mughal emperor granted English merchants freedom of movement throughout the empire and the power to license all Mughal ships engaged in coastal trade. The English mobilized indigenous merchants to extend their trade inland and, at the same time, greatly reduced Portuguese control of Indian coastal trade. The Portuguese fought back, but in 1625 a combined Dutch/English fleet defeated a Portuguese fleet. The intense Dutch competition and Portuguese opposition to the expansion of English commerce in India stretched the resources of the English East India Company. In 1623 the company withdrew its factor from Japan and concentrated its resources in India.

In order to survive Dutch competition in the 1640s and 1650s, the English factor at Surat had to seek new markets and slow Dutch expansion. Another powerful incentive to expand trade was three years of famine in north India around 1630 that greatly reduced the amount of cotton textiles produced for export. In order to slow Dutch expansion on the Malabar coast, the English factor at Surat negotiated a private truce with the Portuguese at Goa. After the successful revolt of the Portuguese from Spain in 1640, the English and Portuguese governments signed a treaty (1642) that ended hostilities; and 10 years later, under the government of Oliver Cromwell, the English obtained the right to trade in Portuguese enclaves worldwide, except Macau. Thereafter, in India, English and Portuguese armed forces cooperated to reduce Dutch hegemony in Indian commerce.

After the north Indian famine of the 1630s, the English company established warehouses at Basra and several locations in Arabia. Ships were also sent to Bengal where several warehouses were established, but none prospered. The Bengal trade was abandoned in the 1650s. There was, however, one winner. In 1639, a warehouse was established at Madras where there was a harbor without commerce. Its attraction was an extensive hinterland where cotton was grown and textiles were produced in substantial quantities. In addition, it was firmly governed by a rajah who wanted revenue from trade, and the English offered better terms than the Dutch.

The English East India Company barely survived the 1640s, and in 1650 was on the edge of bankruptcy. The primary reason for its financial difficulties was the English civil war (1642-1646). In a desperate attempt to acquire money that parliament refused to appropriate, king Charles I licensed independent merchants to trade into India, thereby circumventing the company's monopoly of making all voyages between England and India. Independent traders left England with silver coins and bullion, plus cargoes of iron implements, naval supplies, and ordinance. The ships then traded in the ports of India and the Indies for a year or more and returned with cargoes of items that had a European market. Independent merchants made little contribution to maintaining resident factors and warehouses in ports where they sold items manufactured in England and purchased return cargoes. Their licenses exempted them from paying fees to use the company's facilities. A good measure of the weakness of the company in the 1640s was the ratio of annual voyages to the Indies. For every seven voyages made by the Dutch, the English sent only three, and English ships usually returned with lower value cargoes.

A second reason for the poor performance of the English East India Company in the 1640s was the lure of colonization in Virginia, Massachusetts bay, and especially the Caribbean islands where sugar was produced. These markets were closer to home and although profits margins from sugar, tobacco, potash, and wood products like barrel staves and headings and ship timbers were lower than the Indian trade, they were more assured because voyages were of shorter duration and better protected by the royal navy.

In the second half of the seventeenth century, many countries in Europe tried to gain a share of commerce in India and the Indies by chartering monopoly companies. Denmark, Sweden, France, Ostend (Flemish), and Prussia all tried, but these countries lacked navies and a network of regional merchants that could assemble cargoes at competitive costs. Their commerce was small. Even the Portuguese (1628) tried to supplant crown licensing by incorporating an East India Company, but vested interests in Goa and bad management bankrupted it in 1633.

After 1650, the English East India Company began continuous growth because both Cromwell and king Charles II supported the company's monopoly privilege. By the mid-1660s, it was clear that the most effective means of managing and protecting commerce to the Indies was a monopoly corporation that had very close ties to a central government that was willing to invest in a navy to protect long distance merchants. The government of Oliver Cromwell (in 1657) forced the reorganization of the East India Company into a joint stock company. A joint stock company meant that all voyages financed by the company were at the expense of all stockholders instead of, as in the past, various stockholders having different percentages of different voyages.

Between 1658 and 1688, the company completed 404 voyages to the Indies but the Dutch continued to control the largest portion of Indian trade. The English, however, were slowly increasing their share, especially in cotton textiles. Cotton textiles came in two principal varieties: luxury cloth for sale in Europe and rough cloth to trade for pepper and spices in the Indies, and to sell to planters in the Americas to clothe slaves who cultivated sugar and tobacco. The English specialized in luxury textiles that were marketed in Europe and the Dutch preferred coarser textiles to exchange for spices. The Dutch were slow to recognize the rapidly increasing European market for cotton textiles, especially for calicos, because of their concentration on the highly profitable spice trade.

In the 1660s, English trade with Manila became permanent. An average of three voyages per year sailed from Madras to Manila. English ships were excluded from this trade but ships owned by English regional merchants were leased to Portuguese merchants who had entry. The principal items involved in the Manila trade were cotton textiles that were exchanged for Mexican and Peruvian silver coins. Madras was also the port for transshipping highly profitable pepper to Europe after it arrived from Benkulen, Sumatra. Between 1660 and 1680, Portuguese commerce in India became an English protectorate. Similar commercial cooperation in Europe helped reduce Spanish power in Europe and allowed Portugal to concentrate its commerce in Brazil, particularly for sugar cultivation.

During the 1660s and 1670s English commerce in India was increasingly concentrated at Madras and Bombay. Return cargoes were acquired from English regional merchants operating in the Indian ocean, the Indies, and the South China sea in ships that never returned to England. In fact, a high percentage of their ships were built in India and a high percentage of the crews were indians or other asians. Indigenous merchants operating in the interior supplied substantial quantities of commodities for export. Regional and indigenous merchants were more efficient in procuring return cargoes because they had better information from their agents. Company employees were most efficient in assembling and loading cargoes for return voyages to England.

In the 1660s and 1670s, the company's directors allowed virtual free trade from its enclaves at Bombay and Madras to most ports in India and the Indies. The company did not try to license (tax) indigenous merchants in order to help pay the costs of maintaining their enclaves. Enforcement of licensing was too expensive. Instead, company policy was to encourage all commerce in order to assemble cargoes for the return voyages of its ships. This was strong encouragement for company employees to engage in regional trade in order to assemble cargoes and, in the process, earn private fortunes. The result of the company's free trade policy in the Indian ocean was the rapid financial integration of English regional merchants and indigenous merchants (Hindu, Muslim, Armenian) and other European merchants (Portuguese, Dutch, French) who traded between all Indian ports and to Arabia, Persia, the Indies, and China. In practice English regional merchants and indigenous merchants shared the profits of assembling cargoes for return voyages.

English regional merchants remitted their profits to London by keeping the holds of company ships filled. The best way to quickly fill a ship was to accept commodities on consignment from regional merchants. When these commodities were sold in London, the company subtracted transportation and transaction costs and transferred the remaining funds to the accounts of regional merchants.

The increased numbers of English regional merchants after 1660, and the network of trade they developed, coupled with their complex business relationships with other European merchants and indigenous merchants on land and sea, was why the company steadily increased its profits from Indian commerce. These profits were large enough so that by the beginning of the eighteenth century the company's resident factors could contemplate increasing the number of enclaves they directly governed. The directors in London did not consider this an attractive option but the slow disintegration of the Mughal empire was making the assumption of governance increasingly necessary if the company's commerce was to survive.

The decline of the Mughal empire was slow. It began in the mid-1670s, when Gerald Aungier, the factor at Surat, wrote to the company's directors in 1677, "The times now require you to manage your general commerce with your sword in your hands." [9] Aungier took his own advice. In 1669, he moved the company's Indian headquarters to Bombay and located his warehouses on an inshore island that he fortified. The under-utilized harbor at Bombay had been acquired from the Portuguese in 1662 as part of the dowry of king Charles II's Portuguese queen. It was leased to the East India Company in 1668. Aungier and his successors made it into the English equivalent of the Portuguese enclave at Goa and the Dutch enclave at Jakarta.

Aungier organized the company's first professional infantry, cavalry, and artillery units. Christian eurasians with Portuguese names staffed the infantry and artillery units. In addition, company employees were organized into a militia unit that could perform field service in an emergency. He also stationed a heavily armed cruiser in Bombay harbor, supported by smaller armed ships that his successors organized into the Bombay marine. This small flotilla was available to protect English and indigenous merchant ships, suppress piracy, and carry troops to protect warehouses whenever there was a breakdown of local political order. Within ten years of the fort's completion, equitable taxation to maintain army and naval units to protect commerce, attracted a very large heterogeneous community of merchants.

The third major base for the company's India trade (after Bombay and Madras) was Calcutta, where a fortified warehouse was built on a vacant riverbank in 1692. It rapidly became a city because the Ganges river was used by indigenous merchants and company employees to extend commerce deep into the interior. The principal exports from Calcutta's hinterland were cotton textiles, rice, silk thread, raw cotton, saltpeter, sugar, and indigo. Fine cotton textiles, silk thread, indigo, and saltpeter preferentially went to Europe, while raw cotton, sugar, rice, and coarse cotton textiles were marketed by regional merchants around the periphery of the Indian ocean and eastward.

The most obvious indication of the declining power of the Mughal empire was its increasing inability to enforce peace among the feudal aristocrats who governed peripheral provinces. There were increasing conflicts among them and between dynastic claimants that forced company factors to protect the hinterlands of their enclaves if their commerce was to survive. They did this by using the military and naval forces at their disposal to: 1) intervene between contending warlords who were fighting to control a provincial fragment of the Mughal empire; 2) intervene between contending claimants who sought to rule breakaway provinces. Successful claimants would pay for military assistance supplied by company troops by assigning revenues to the company from a local tax district. The purpose of intervention was to establish domains of peace where commercial relations between indigenous merchants (operating in the interior) and English merchants (living in coastal cities) could conduct business under predictable conditions. Only within peaceful domains could peasant labor be mobilized to produce sufficient amounts of food grains and cotton textiles for export, with the textiles having weights and patterns desired by European buyers.

Parallel with increasing Indian commerce was increasing trade with China. The first tea arrived in England in 1664 and after 1665 the tea trade with China rapidly increased in volume and profitability. By 1685, the intermittent tea trade at the port city of Canton became permanent because there was a sustained demand in both England and Europe. One of the great attractions of the tea trade was that it did not require an expensive fortified enclave to procure cargoes. The trade, however, was highly competitive because Chinese authorities allowed equal entry of all European ships, which meant that interlopers had free entry to purchase tea that could be smuggled into England. By 1690 company ships were sailing directly to Canton and returning with cargoes consisting mostly or entirely of tea; and it was packed in lead or tin lined chests to preserve its aroma and flavor.

Dutch and Portuguese merchants were slow to see the possibilities of tea as a beverage of mass consumption by Europeans. This oversight occurred in spite of merchants being acquainted with tea from the earliest years of imperial commerce: Dutch merchants at their factory at Nagasaki, Japan and from resident Chinese merchants in Jakarta; and Portuguese merchants from their residence in Macau. The tea the Dutch initially imported into Europe came from Canton to Jakarta in Chinese junks. It was more expensive than tea exported directly from Canton and it did not preserve its quality on long voyages because it was packed in bamboo reinforced crates.

Between 1728 and 1734, the Dutch East India Company sent ships directly to Canton from Europe but this voyage was discontinued in favor of sending one or two ships a year from Jakarta to Canton and from there to Europe. The Dutch company wanted a supply directly under their control, like they had for spices and coffee. They did this by inducing peasants on Java and Ceylon to cultivate tea as their exchange commodity. Nonetheless, the Dutch missed the opportunity to be the principal supplier of tea to Europe when consumption was growing at an explosive rate. The missed opportunity is measured by the amount of tea the Dutch imported, compared to the English. Between 1720 and 1730, The Dutch company imported 3.3 million pounds and the English 8.9 million pounds. By 1785, the tea trade accounted for about half of the profits of the English East India Company, even though there was a much larger volume of commodities coming from India than there had been in 1700. [10]

Although, the volume of Indian trade rapidly increased after 1660, it was a small part of England's maritime trade. In 1688, the year of the Glorious Revolution, only about 5 percent of England's maritime trade was with India, the Indies, and China; 35 percent was with North

America and the Caribbean, and 60 percent was with Europe and the Levant. Much of the European trade, however, was re-exports of tobacco, sugar, tea, and cotton textiles. Because of the high value of cargoes from the east and the high taxes these items paid when they entered England, the Indian trade was of more importance to the English treasury than indicated by the small number of annual voyages.

The Glorious Revolution is the dividing event in English commercial policy because it confirmed the previous 50 years of economic development. Many historians and most economists have not fully understood that this is the significance of deposing king James II. Like other kings who attempted to rule by divine right, his priority was to pursue dynastic ambitions, not to increase national commercial wealth. The English crown was offered to William III of the Netherlands because he understood that the first priority of his reign was protecting and promoting commerce. This was the same political economy that governed his tenure as king of the Dutch. Like the political economy of the Dutch during the previous 100 years, English domestic and foreign policies during the eighteenth century would be governed by considerations of commercial advantage.

Parliament ratified William's kingship because he accepted the power of parliament to make commercial policy, levy all taxes, and appropriate all tax revenues. Parliamentary supremacy insured that future wars would be approved by parliament and would be fought for commercial advantages in the European and global markets, not for dynastic or religious purposes. King William and his successors would be chairmen of the board who would preside over the full commercialization of English culture

After the revolution many London merchants hoped that parliament would cancel the monopoly charter of the East India Company and legalize independent traders. During the confrontations between James II and parliament, the king had supported the East India Company monopoly because he could acquire loans from it without parliamentary approval. Parliamentarians supported independent traders. With parliamentary acquiescence, independent traders ignored the East India Company's monopoly during the reign of James II and in the immediately following years. The issue simmered until 1692 when the company forfeited its charter because it failed to pay a tax that parliament levied on monopoly companies. In January 1694, the House of Commons resolved that all English merchants had a right to trade into the Indies. By this time, however, independent traders and the managers of the monopoly company realized that profitable trade in the Indies depended on an accommodation. The Indian trade could not be sustained without coordinated political, military, and commercial policies in England and India. Free trade would seriously jeopardize England's increasing commercial advantages in India.

Parliament gave direction to commercial policies in 1698 by passing a charter that merged the old East India Company and all independent merchants into a new monopoly company strong enough to challenge Dutch commercial hegemony in India and survive the increasing anarchy of the disintegrating Mughal empire. Only stockholders in the new company could trade between England and India but shares of stock were readily available for purchase. In return for a monopoly of Indian trade, the new company had to loan the central government 2.0 million pounds sterling, and an additional 1.2 million in 1708. Coincident to rechartering the East India Company in 1698 was the permanent acquisition by parliament of the power to grant charters of incorporation to business corporations.

Viewed from London, the English commercial empire that grew at an accelerated rate in the last half of the seventeenth century became an increasing source of political and military strength. The foundation of this strength was taxing commercial wealth. The four principal sources of tax revenue were: 1) rents and excises; 2) European trade; 3) colonial trade to North America and the Caribbean; 4) long distance commerce to India, the Indies, and China. These revenues were used to enlarge the navy and train and equip armies that could be deployed in Europe and elsewhere. Leonard Gomes summarizes:

After the Restoration (1660) England rose to a position of commercial leadership based on a flourishing export trade in the cheaper, lighter new draperies—mixed fabrics and coloured cloth—mainly to Iberian and Mediterranean markets. To this was added a growing volume of trade in re-exports mainly of colonial goods promoted by the Navigation Acts and various protective measures. By the end of the seventeenth century London succeeded to the role of Amsterdam as the leading entrepot. [11]

In the revolutionary settlement of 1688, the landed aristocracy no longer had preponderant influence in defining domestic and foreign policies. This, however, was not an issue in the settlement because the rapid increase in commercial wealth during the previous 50 years had changed the interest of landowners. Political power no longer depended on the number of peasants they could mobilize to fill the ranks of an army. Political power now depended on money incomes, and the most reliable sources of income were rents that commercial cultivators (yeomen, farmers) paid to landowners; and profits from commerce and artisan manufactories. The common political denominator among landowners, merchants, and artisan manufacturers were policies that facilitated the acquisition of money incomes. During the reigns of William and Mary (1689-1702), money incomes, not land ownership, became the principal arbitrator of political influence and social status.

The interests of rural landowners, artisan manufacturers, and city merchants merged. Second and third sons and daughters of rural landowners married the sons and daughters of merchants, especially if merchants bought enough agricultural land to be called an estate. This social interchange operated whether rural landowners were aristocrats or gentry, and whether marriage partners were the children of rich maritime merchants, successful cloth merchants, or manufacturers of glass bottles or iron hinges.

The new aristocracy in eighteenth century England was an aristocracy of money; and how the money was earned was immaterial. City and rural money had equal weight and this equality translated into domestic and foreign policies that were designed to increase all forms of money incomes. The five principal sources of incomes were: 1) rental incomes to owners of agricultural and city land; 2) profits from maritime commerce; 3) profits from domestic commerce; 4) profits from the production of manufactured items of common consumption (textiles, iron implements); 5) profits from improved overland and marine transportation.

The new aristocracy of money strongly believed that energetic persons ought to be encouraged to earn profits and have their wealth protected by contract law because the skills and innovations they applied to agriculture, commerce, and manufacturing increased national welfare. In return for policies that encouraged the acquisition of private wealth, the owners of this wealth consented to high taxation during the wars for commercial advantage that England fought in the seventeenth and eighteenth centuries.

NOTES

1. Ronald E. Seavoy, *Famine in Peasant Societies*, 24-25.
2. John H. Parry, *The Age of Reconnaissance*, 32.
3. John H. Parry, *The Age of Reconnaissance*, 20.
4. Bailey W. Diffie, George D. Winius, *Foundations of the Portuguese Empire*, 229.
5. Holden Furber, *Rival Empires of Trade*, 3.
6. Clarence H. Haring, *Trade and Navigation Between Spain and the Indies*, 8.
7. Holden Furber, *Rival Empires of Trade*, 33.
8. George D. Winius, Marcus P. M. Vink, *The Merchant-Warrior Pacified*, 13.
9. Holden Furber, *Rival Empires of Trade*, 93.
10. Kristof Glamann, *Dutch-Asiatic Trade, 1620-1740*, chapter 11
11. Leonard Gomes, *Foreign Trade and the National Economy*, 30.

REFERENCES

Axelson, Eric. *Congo to Cape: Early Portuguese Explorers*, New York, Barnes and Noble, 1973

Blomquist, Thomas W. "Commercial Associations in Thirteenth-Century Lucca," *Business History Review*, Vol. 45, 1971

Boxer, Charles R. *The Dutch Seaborne Empire, 1600-1800*, New York, Knopf, 1965 (chapters 1, 2, 4, 7)

Boxer, Charles R. *Francisco Vieira de Figueiredo: A Portuguese Merchant Adveturer in South East Asia, 1624-1667*, Gravenhage, Martinus Nijhoff, 1967

Boxer, Charles R. *The Portuguese Seaborne Empire, 1415-1825*, New York, Knopf, 1969

Boxer Charles R. *Jan Compagnie in War and Peace, 1602-1799: A Short History of the Dutch East-India Company*, Hong Kong, Heinemann Asia, 1979 (chapters 1, 2)

Braudel, Fernand. *Civilization and Capitalism 15ᵗʰ-18ᵗʰ Century*, New York, Harper Row, 1984

Carlos, Ann M., Stephen Nicholas. "Giants of an Earlier Capitalism: The Chartered Trading Companies as Modern Multinationals," *Business History Review*, Vol. 62, 1988

Cipolla, Carlo M. *Guns, Sails, and Empires: Technological Innovation and the Early Phases of European Expansion, 1400-1700*, Manhattan, Kansas, Sunflower University Press, 1985 (reprint of 1965 edition)

Davies, Kenneth G. *The Royal African Company*, New York, Atheneum, 1970 (reprint of 1957 edition) (chapters 1, 2)

Diffie, Bailey W., George D. Winius. *Foundations of the Portuguese Empire, 1415-1580*, Minneapolis, University of Minnesota Press, 1977

Disney, Anthony R. *Twilight of the Pepper Empire: Portuguese Trade in South west India in the Early Seventeenth Century*, Cambridge, Harvard University Press, 1978

Fieldhouse, David K. *The Colonial Empires: A Comparative Survey from the Eighteenth Century*, New York, Delacorte Press, 1967 (chapters 1, 2, 3, 4)

Foster, William, ed. *The Embassy of Sir Thomas Roe to the Court of the Great Mogul 1615-1619: As Narrated in His Journal and Correspondence*, Nendeln/Liechenstein, Kraus Reprint, 1967 (reprint of 1899 edition)

Foster, William, ed. *The Journal of John Jourdain, 1608-1617: Describing His Experiences in Arabia, India, and the Malay Archipelago*, Nendeln/Liechtenstein, Kraus Reprint, 1967 (reprint of 1905 edition)

Foster, William, ed. *The Voyage of Sir Henry Middleton to the Moluccas, 1604-1606*, London, Kraus Reprint, 1990 (reprint of 1943 edition)

Furber, Holden. *Rival Empires of Trade in the Orient, 1600-1800*, Minneapolis, University of Minnesota Press, 1976

Glamann, Kristof. *Dutch-Asiatic Trade, 1620-1740*, Copenhagen, Danish Science Press, 1958

Gomes, Leonard. *Foreign Trade and the National Economy: Mercantilist and Classical Perspectives*, New York, St Martins Press, 1987 (chapters 1, 2)

Hale, John R. *Renaissance Exploration*, New York, Norton, 1968

Hanna, Willard A. *Indonesian Banda: Colonialism and Its Aftermath in the Nutmeg Islands*, Philadelphia, Institute for the Study of Human Issues, 1978

Haring, Clarence H. *Trade and Navigation Between Spain and the Indies in the Time of the Hapsburgs*, Cambridge, Harvard University Press, 1918

Keay, John. *The Honourable Company: A History of the English East India Company*, New York, Macmillan, 1991

Morison, Samuel E. *The European Discovery of America: The Southern Voyages, 1492-1616*, New York, Oxford University Press, 1974

Parry, John H. *The Establishment of the European Hegemony, 1415-1715: Trade and Exploration in the Age of the Renaissance*, New York, Harper Torchbooks, 1961 (reprint of 1949 edition)

Parry, John H. *The Age of Reconnaissance*, New York, Mentor Books, 1964

Penrose, Boies. *Travel and Discovery in the Renaissance, 1420-1620*, New York, Atheneum, 1971 (reprint of 1952 edition)

Phillips, Carla R., William D. Phillips. *Spain's Golden Fleece: Wool Production and the Wool Trade from the Middle Ages to the Nineteenth Century*, Baltimore, Johns Hopkins University Press, 1997 (chapters 4, 5, 9, 12)

Pike, Ruth. *Enterprise and Adventure: The Genoese in Seville and the Opening of the New World*, Ithaca, Cornell University Press, 1966

Prakash, Om. *The Dutch East India Company and the Economy of Bengal, 1630-1720*, Princeton, Princeton University Press, 1985

Ringrose, David R. *Transportation and Economic Stagnation in Spain, 1750-1850*, Durham, Duke University Press, 1970 (introduction, chapter 1)

Russell-Wood, A.J.R. *A World on the Move: The Portuguese in Africa, Asia, and America, 1415-1808*, Manchester, Carcanet Press, 1992

Schurz, William L. *The Manila Galleon*, New York, Dutton, 1959 (reprint of 1939 edition)

Seavoy, Ronald E. *Famine in Peasant Societies*, Westport, Greenwood Press, 1986 (chapter 1)

Verlinden, Charles. *The Beginnings of Modern Colonization*, Ithaca, Cornell University Press, 1970

Wills, John E. *Pepper, Guns and Parleys: The Dutch East India Company and China, 1622-1681*, Cambridge, Harvard University Press, 1974

Winius, George D., Marcus P. M. Vink. *The Merchant-Warrior Pacified: The VOC (The Dutch East India Company) and Its Changing Political Economy in India*, Delhi, Oxford University Press, 1991 (parts 1, 2)

2

COMMERCE AND TAXATION IN ENGLAND IN THE SEVENTEENTH AND EIGHTEENTH CENTURIES

SOURCES OF TAX REVENUE

The first substantial tax records in England date from about 1275. They are of export-import taxes and they were farmed. Tax farmers paid the crown a fixed sum of money in return for the legal right to collect a specific tax, or to collect a bundle of taxes from a specific seaport. Tax farmers were favorites of the monarch or were merchants or bankers to whom the king owed money. In thirteenth century England the usual farmers of export-import taxes were bankers from Florence and Lucca.

From the first records of taxation, English monarchs had the authority to levy export taxes on wool, sheep pelts (woolfells), leather, and import taxes on wine. These were prerogative revenues that belonged to the king without reference to parliament. Parliament levied two types of taxes: land and export-import. The export-import taxes were usually five percent of their value, measured by weight (tunnage and poundage). At the beginning of a monarch's reign parliament usually granted the king the use of tunnage and poundage taxes for his lifetime. In theory these taxes were levied to build warships to protect merchant ships and pay for the use of commandeered merchant ships during wartime. In practice export-import taxes were part of the general revenue at the disposal of the king, therefore, revenues from taxing commerce were a means of centralizing power in the monarchy at the expense of the feudal aristocracy. The monarchs of England had a vested interest in increasing maritime trade because they had full use of export-import taxes for their lifetimes.

From these revenues and revenue from royal estates and feudal dues, reigning monarchs were expected to pay for the peacetime expenses of the central government. Taxes levied by parliament were intermittent subsidies for limited amounts of money for a limited number of years in order to pay extraordinary expenses. War was the most common extraordinary expense. The need to levy these taxes was the usual reason for calling parliament into session. During the sixteenth century, the principal sources of crown revenue were taxes on land, personal property, exports-imports, polls, shares of church revenue, and an assortment of feudal dues that produced unpredictable amounts of money.

When Elizabeth became queen in 1558, parliament confirmed revenues from export-import taxes and other customary revenues for her lifetime, as had been done for preceding monarchs. Elizabeth had a compelling interest in increasing long distance maritime commerce because, in the sixteenth and seventeenth centuries, this source of revenue was an opportunity to create an empire of long distance commerce to compete with the Spanish and Portuguese empires that were still in skeletal form. During her reign there was almost continual war with the united monarchies of Spain and Portugal and by encouraging investments in all varieties of long distance commerce by armed merchant adventurers, she could not only increase her revenues but also reduce the revenues of the Spanish monarchy.

Queen Elizabeth (1558-1603) was acutely aware of the increased revenue available from increased trade. Among the long distance trading companies she chartered (with monopoly privileges) were the Muscovy Company (1566) trading into Archangel in northern Russia, the Eastland Company (1579) trading into the Baltic, the Levant Company (1581) trading into present day Lebanon, the Barbary Company (1585) trading into north Africa, the Guinea Company (1588) trading along the west coast of Africa, and the East India Company (1600) trading into the Indian Ocean and beyond. James I continued her policy by chartering Virginia Companies in 1606 and 1609, the New-foundland Company in 1610, and Massachusetts Bay and Bermuda companies in 1615. Later in the seventeenth century the Providence Island, Royal African, and Hudsons Bay companies received charters from the king. These charters were supplemented by land grants to individuals who contracted to settle populations in the Carolinas, Maryland, Maine, and Pennsylvania. The reciprocal of these grants was that the English government would use the royal navy to protect the commerce and coastal settlements of these colonies. All settlers would produce some export commodities that could only be marketed in England where they would be taxed on arrival.

Like her predecessors, Elizabeth farmed the collection of export-import taxes. In London the farm was in the hands of competent persons but collectors in the outports were often favorites and just as often there was little attention to detail by the persons who were deputized to collect it. During the later years of her reign she tightened the procedures for collecting export-import taxes in order to increase her revenues without having to ask parliament to levy taxes. In 1586 her lord treasurer published a book of rates that standardized taxation for various categories of exports and imports, with alien merchants paying higher rates than English merchants. Additional regulations governed the procedures for collecting export-import taxes. Ship captains engaged in European trade posted bonds to ensure payment of fines if they were convicted of smuggling; and procedures were defined for examining cargoes and conveying funds to the treasury. At the end of her reign there was a proposal to update the rate book in order to rank taxable items on their value instead of their weight. The new ratebook was not compiled until 1608 in the reign of James I.

During the reign of Elizabeth and until the Long Parliament in 1641, English taxes were medieval in form and content, even though the feudal basis of local and national governments had largely disappeared. The continuation of medieval forms of taxation into the mid-seventeenth century was an anachronism because neither the central government's bureaucracy nor parliament had changed policies for collecting taxes on the very substantial increase of commercial wealth that had occurred in the previous 100 years. Most of

England's new wealth came from increased per capita food production and increased amounts of artisan manufactured items, particularly woolen textiles that were produced for sale on anonymous markets. The persistence of a feudal tax structure meant that crown revenues declined relative to the increase in commercial wealth. Stated another way, the new commercial wealth of the sixteenth and seventeenth centuries was lightly taxed.

Taxation was the key issue in the contest between parliament and the attempts of the last three Stuart kings (1625-1688) to become autocratic rulers. A large percentage of persons who could vote (landowners and merchants) objected to Charles I's (1625-1649) use of prerogatives, dispensations, monopolies, ships writs, and compulsory loans (benevolences) to increase the crown's revenues without the consent of parliament. A second source of increased revenue was the increase in maritime commerce during his reign, coupled with a new book of rates that was promulgated in 1635. Increased maritime commerce and increased import-export tax rates increased crown revenues to 350,000 pounds sterling per year, which further increased to about 500,000 pounds in 1641. These revenues were collected during the 11 years (1629-1640) when Charles I governed without calling parliament into session.

A high percentage of merchants engaged in maritime trade, and especially commercially motivated landowners who earned increasing incomes from higher rents paid by yeomen and farmers, objected to arbitrary taxation and autocratic governance. They wanted all taxes and appropriation defined by statute law. In the Petition of Right (1628) parliament insisted that the king accept its taxation policies and that he conduct foreign relations in conformity with parliament's wishes. Charles I objected because he believed that monarchs possessed autocratic power by divine right. He began and led a civil war (1642 to 1646), and was defeated and beheaded.

During the civil war parliament began remodeling the fiscal system because more and predictable revenue was needed to pay the new model army that defeated the king's levies. The new model army was made up of volunteers who were paid for their services, unlike the royalist army that was largely composed of agricultural laborers mobilized from the estates of landowning aristocrats, often without their consent and often with little chance of being paid. The greatest innovation of the civil war was the excise tax of 1643 that parliament levied on many items produced and consumed within England. French and Dutch governments had been levying excise taxes for many years. In the regions of England controlled by royalist troops, king Charles also levied excise taxes on a similar number of locally produced and consumed items.

The Commonwealth parliaments (1649-1658) put the collection of export-import and excise taxes in the hands of a commission consisting of members of parliament. Parliament also simplified the tax base by abolishing feudal dues and ending the practice of taxing the clergy as a separate status group. After the restoration of the monarchy in 1660, neither feudal dues nor taxation of church revenues could be revived. The restoration was, therefore, the occasion for systematizing taxation and putting it on a solid bureaucratic foundation. It began with the Great Statute. Its purpose was to make revenues more predictable and adequate for peacetime governance. It contained an updated ratebook for taxing export-import items and codes that defined procedures for evaluating taxable items and for collecting taxes on them.

Following medieval precedent, parliament granted king Charles II (1660-1685) and his successor James II (1685-1688) the use of export-import taxes for their lives. In return for revenue equivalent to discontinued feudal dues, Charles II accepted revenue from excise taxes on beer, ale, cider, liquor, tea, coffee, and chocolate that were consumed in public houses. These taxes were almost exact copies of the excise taxes passed by the Commonwealth parliaments. Charles II put the collection of export-import taxes at farm because of his urgent need for money. The tax farm was managed by a syndicate of London bankers and merchants who provided the king with a fixed annual income for an agreed number of years. Any revenue collected in excess of the money they lent to the king belonged to the farmers. On an expanding tax base, tax farmers could enjoy substantial incomes.

In 1671, the collection of export-import taxes was nationalized because tax farmers had difficulty making profits due to wartime disruptions of commerce and royal dispensations on import taxes as part of the king's foreign policy. A bureaucracy was created to collect the tax. Collection was delegated to a Board of Customs Commissioners. The commissioners converted the deputies of the last tax farm into salaried civil servants. In 1683 the bureaucracy was expanded to collect excise taxes that were rapidly increasing in yield. Because the revenue from these taxes belonged to the king for his lifetime the king initiated bureaucratization in order to increase the efficiency of collection and the amount of revenue at his disposal.

After the Glorious Revolution (1688) the five principal sources of revenue were excise, export-import, poll, land (rent) taxes, and borrowing. During peacetime only two taxes were collected: export-import and excise. These taxes were sufficient to conduct peacetime government. They belonged to the king and were expended at his discretion. In 1688 the central government had revenues of 1,812,000 pounds sterling. Fifty-five percent came from export-import taxes and 45 percent from excise taxes and miscellaneous sources. There were no land or poll taxes because they were levied only for extraordinary purposes—usually war. England was at peace.

The leaders of Glorious Revolution acted on consensus. They welcomed William and Mary as monarchs because they accepted parliamentary supremacy as defined in the Declaration of Rights (1689). By far the most important section in the Declaration of Rights was that parliament had the authority to levy all taxes and appropriate all revenues. This fiscal power was institutionalized during the following 22 years of almost continuous warfare. In this situation parliament had to meet every year to find ways of acquiring needed revenue by taxation and borrowing. The distinction disappeared between the monarch's personal revenue and additional revenue needed for extraordinary purposes. The need for revenue:

was so great that every source of revenue was strained and no distinction between ordinary and extraordinary was possible. The distinction came to mean nothing more than the difference between the revenue sufficient for one year and the increase required in the next, for which taxes had to be found. [1]

The accession of William and Mary meant that English resources would be mobilized to defend the independence of the Netherlands from sustained attacks by the French. England was at war with France until 1697. Like Charles II and James II, parliament granted William and Mary the lifetime use of excise taxes but not export-import taxes. If this revenue was combined with excise revenues, William and Mary could conduct peacetime governance with minimal reference to parliament. Parliament decided that export-import taxes were to be appropriated to the king's use for four years, and thereafter reviewed before being renewed.

Parliament also consolidated and updated the navigation acts in 1696 and, in the same year, established a Board of Trade to supervise colonial commerce and recommend policies to increase revenues and reduce smuggling. From its inception the board's principal concern was commerce with the American and Caribbean colonies. It was very efficient at collecting information from: 1) agents (lobbyists) that most colonies had in London; 2) merchants engaged in colonial trade; 3) imperial officials appointed by the English government. The board acted as the principal advisor to the secretary for state of the southern department who managed colonial policy. At the end of the Seven Years War (1763) the board recommended taxing commerce in America as a means of transferring some of the enormous expenses of the war to the Americans who had gained great advantage by the annexation of Canada and the removal of the French threat to its northern and western borders. More on the consequence of the Seven Years War later in the chapter.

Poll taxes were very unpopular, even though different amounts were collected from persons according to the amount of property they owned. During the reign of Charles II they had been levied in 1660, 1666, and 1677. Their great attraction was ease of collection that translated into a near instant source of revenue. After the Glorious Revolution and subsequent wars with France, poll taxes were collected in 1689, 1690, 1692, 1693, 1694, 1697, and 1698. Their unpopularity was such that no poll taxes were levied after 1698.

The tax on city land and arable land was really a tax on rents; and it was levied by landowners themselves in the many units of local government they controlled. There was no uniformity of assessment. Parliament levied the tax and apportioned it among the cities and counties on the basis of the estimated fiscal needs of the central government and the ability of landowners to pay, a procedure that had operated since 1334. Local assessments were made on the assumption that a tax of one shilling to the pound (5 percent) would yield a fixed amount of revenue. Depending on the immediate needs of the central government, the tax rate was one, two, three, or four shillings to the pound for one, two, three, or four years.

Its great strength was that it was collected without opposition because the landowners who controlled local governments made a committee of their number responsible for apportioning and collecting it. During the nine years of war with France (1689-1697) and the War of Spanish Succession (1702-1713), the need for revenue escalated beyond previous experience. The land tax evolved into an annual tax with the rate varying according to military needs. At the beginning of the War of Spanish Succession, the expenditures of the central government were 5 million pounds sterling per year and by the end of the war they were 15 million annually.

Parliament experimented with many taxes to obtain the needed revenue. For example, in 1695 glassware was taxed. It was reduced by half in 1698 and abolished in 1699 "as vexatious and troublesome to levy and collect, of small advantage to the crown, and calculated, if continued to lessen the produce of the coal duty by more than the revenue it would produce." Coal was the fuel used in glass furnaces and the coal tax was easy to collect because a high percentage of coal went to places of consumption in ships or wagons, and a standardized measure (chaldron) was used after the coal was on the surface. Furthermore, the glass tax would "hinder employment of great numbers of poor and endanger the loss of a beneficial manufacture to the kingdom." [2] In the years following its repeal the production of glassware rapidly increased.

An equally important source of revenue was the ability of the central government to borrow. The Bank of England greatly increased the ability of the English government to borrow money because all loans to the central government were consolidated into one debt (consols). The consolidated debt was paid from the total revenues collected by the central government instead of allocating the revenue from a specific tax to repay a specific loan. The ability to pay interest on the consolidated debt was dependent on an increasing volume and value of domestic manufacturing and maritime commerce, and the ability to collect taxes on it.

The governor of the Bank of England showed that a much larger national debt was possible, not only because money for investment was available from landowners and merchants, but also because these persons considered government bonds a safe investment as long as tax revenues were sufficient to pay the annual interest. Sustaining the credit of the central government required high peacetime tax rates. Annual meetings of parliament became necessary to decide what products or services could bear taxation, assess the rate of taxation that could be collected without overt opposition, and what rates would yield maximum revenues.

After 1700, parliamentary leaders understood with greater clarity that the ability of landowners to pay taxes on rents and the ability of the general population to pay excise taxes on items of domestic consumption depended on increasing the volume, value, and variety of artisan manufacturing and maritime commerce. Especially, this meant increasing exports, and especially exports of manufactured items. The best way to make English exports more competitive in overseas markets was to end export taxes. In 1700 they were ended on woolen cloth, grain, and breadstuffs and in 1721, they were ended on all manufactured items. They were, however, retained on raw materials that were used by artisans to manufacture high value items for export. Export taxes were retained on alum, bars of lead and tin, coal, leather, baled wool, and undyed woolen cloth. For example, if bars of tin were made into pewter cups or bowls for export, they were not taxed; or if woolen cloth was dyed it paid no export tax because domestically produced alum had been used to set the dyes.

In order for the lord treasurer to devote full time to the political economy of taxation and appropriation, the treasury was put into commission in 1710. The first lord of the treasury was responsible for making the budget and the other lords administered the details of tax collection, payments to government contractors, and the salaries of persons on the civil list.

Establishing the civil list was, in many respects, the second most important result of the Glorious Revolution. It created a bureaucracy that was loyal to national welfare because persons were paid from national revenues appropriated by parliament. Appointments to jobs on the civil list did not end patronage but merit was increasingly used as a principal qualification. This was especially important in tax collection. The Board of Customs Commissioners became civil servants, not the king's servants. Better qualified personnel developed bureaucratic procedures that made essential government services predictable and efficiently administered. Persons on the civil list considered government employment to be a lifetime career rather than a reward for political service.

The long tenure of Robert Walpole as first lord of the treasury (1721-1742) was based on his ability to maintain a majority of members of parliament who supported his policies of taxation, borrowing, and appropriation. His ability to maintain a parliamentary majority in fiscal matters made him the first, or prime minister of the king. The king was forced to seek his counsel because he was responsible for making an annual budget that would be approved by a majority of members of parliament, especially a majority in the House of Commons where all fiscal legislation originated.

Walpole's political and fiscal skills were required to finance England's wars because, between 1700 and 1763, there were 30 years of war. Financing current wars and paying for past wars was extremely expensive. Borrowing paid for a large part of these wars. In 1702, the national debt was 12.8 million pounds sterling. In 1763, at the end of the Seven Years War (1756-1763), it was 132.1 million pounds. "The Seven Years War was far the most costly. The total bill was 82 million. About 60 million of this was added to the debt." The war of American independence was even more costly. At its end in 1783 England's debt was 245 million pounds. [3]

How did England sustain this debt without inflation? The primary reason was that taxable wealth was increasing faster than tax rates enacted by parliament. Other reasons were the ability of the Bank of England to convert short term borrowing into long term debts that had low interest rates. The Bank of England was incorporated in 1694 to be the fiscal agent of the central government. This was a monopoly privilege that rapidly evolved into a central bank, where the bank's governor became the prime minister's principal advisor on financial policies. In its capacity as a central bank, it became the lender of last resort to the government by its ability to mobilize savings from the commercial sector in order to supply the wartime needs of the government.

When the bank's charter of incorporation came up for renewal in 1708, it had become the manager of the national debt. It performed this function because it used its capital and deposits to purchase government bonds (consols). The two largest monopoly companies did the same. The East India Company invested a large part of its profits in consols and all of the capital of the South Seas Company (incorporated in 1710) was invested in consols. The South Seas Company engaged in no trade. Instead it became a holding company for government bonds. In 1714 these three monopoly corporations held a majority of the national debt of 36.1 million pounds, and continued to be the principal source of funds to about 1735. After 1735 they could not supply enough funds to sustain government spending. Other sources of revenue had to be found.

Middling-sized landowners wanted to provide annuities for their widows or for their children so that their land would not be sold at their death in order to divide money among heirs. They wanted their landed estates to remain intact and under the management of one of the heirs. These investors usually purchased bonds through the office of a county banker. Walpole did everything possible to keep land taxes (rent taxes) low, even in times of war, and his successors did the same. During the American war of independence when there was an accelerating need for revenue, the rent tax supplied only 20 percent of the national revenue. The low rent tax created a pool of capital that was available for investment in consols and new manufacturing technologies. At the same time Walpole and his successors rapidly increased the number of excise taxes that were preferentially paid by the working and middle classes.

Other principal investors in consols were London and county banks that converted some of their deposits into interest bearing reserve funds that would ensure liquidity during emergencies. Another group of investors was foreign businessmen, mainly Dutch and French, who wanted a safe deposit for some of their capital. Consols were so attractive an investment that interest rates on 75 percent of the national debt could be lowered to 3 percent (from 4) in 1749. By about 1770, foreigners owned approximately 25 percent of the national debt.

The permanent national debt was a political asset. Government bonds were a safe investment for persons and businesses to conserve capital until put to other uses, and bondholders were committed to supporting government tax policies that preserved the value of their bonds. The prevention of inflation (that depreciated the value of bonds) required high peacetime taxes so that the central government had sufficient tax revenue to pay the annual interest. Between 1713 and 1785, on average, about 40 percent of annual revenues were required to service the national debt; and at the end of the American war it was 66 percent of total revenue. Investors had little desire to engage in panic selling on receipt of bad economic or political news as long as: 1) tax revenues were known to be sufficient to pay the annual interest; 2) there was no inflation; 3) the bonds had a market value; 4) Bank of England banknotes (paper currency) received from the sale of consols could be converted to gold coins on demand; 5) interest income from consols was not taxed; 6) consols could be used to pay taxes. Investors were further protected because the monopoly corporations (the largest bondholders) could not sell them because their continued profitability depended on favorable government policies.

The American war (1776-1783) followed by the Napoleonic wars (1793-1814) vastly increased the need for revenue. Much of it came from new taxes on luxury items: riding horses, carriages, cards, male and female servants, private coaches, public cabs, and wills (inheritance). In addition a tax was levied on houses with annual rents of more than 5 pounds sterling and on retail shops with annual rents of more than 4 pounds; and taxes were increased on domestically distilled liquor (gin, whisky) but always in a fine balance between increasing revenue, preventing excessive consumption, and reducing the amount of illegal distilling. None of these taxes could have been paid unless there was no inflation and no overt opposition to their collection. Levying and collecting these taxes depended on a steady per capita increase in both agricultural and manufacturing productivity and an efficient tax collecting bureaucracy.

It is impossible to overemphasize that the full commercialization of English society was the basis for England's ability to wage European wars and, at the same time, acquire an empire of governance in India and a colonial empire in North America. Above all, full commercialization meant the commercialization of agriculture. In the second half of the seventeenth century agriculture was the leading sector in the commercializing process, and it continued to be the leading sector until the end of the eighteenth. The full commercialization of English society made England a first rank European power; and the failure of Spain to commercialize agriculture and artisan manufacturers was responsible for Spain's decline to a second rank European power. [4]

COMMERCIAL AGRICULTURE

Commercial agriculture began in England when the demesne land of royal estates had to be managed. Like the collection of taxes, demesne land was farmed. Demesne farming on royal estates began early in the fourteenth century and was rapidly applied to the estates of feudal landholders. In order to rent demesne land, farmers had to pay more money (rent) than feudal landholders acquired from the sale of harvests produced by the unpaid labor services of resident peasants (villeins) who held their subsistence sized cultivation units in customary (copyhold) tenure. Copyhold tenure obligated landholding households to perform unpaid labor to cultivate demesne land, in addition to the labor required to cultivate their cultivation units.

As long as peasants held land in copyhold tenure they could control their labor expenditures. In practice this meant cultivating food grains by performing subsistence labor norms on their cultivation units and on demesne land. The subsistence labor norms they performed on their cultivation units produced subsistence sized harvests in normal crop years, seasonal hunger in poor crop years, and privation in consecutive poor crop years; and harvests from demesne land were always less than from the peasantry's cultivation units.

The rent that the crown received from farming demesne land exceeded the value of the harvests produced by the unpaid labor services of copyholders because farmers hired servants of husbandry (usually for one year) to perform the labor of cultivation. Servants of husbandry were usually the unmarried children of copyholding peasants. They usually lived with the yeoman or farmer and he supervised their labor. Supervised labor produced larger harvests than the unsupervised labor of copyholders. Rents paid by the farmers of the demesne land of royal estates were higher than the money received from the sale of harvests produced by the unpaid labor of copyholders. High money rents were an incentive for all feudal landholders to farm their demesne land.

Farmers of demesne land were usually village or city merchants who leased demesne land and then leased cultivation rights to manor bailiffs or upper strata peasants who owned draft animals, plows, harrows, and other cultivation implements. These men became yeomen cultivators. They supervised labor of servants of husbandry or they worked beside them in the field to insure that they performed commercial labor norms. The labor they performed was often inefficient but it was more than resident copyholding peasants performed on their cultivation units or performed on demesne land.

The main source of social security of farmers and yeomen cultivators was the money incomes they earned by selling harvests on anonymous markets. The food crops they grew were purchased by artisan manufacturers, city residents, or were exported. Their incomes varied with their ability to supervise paid laborers to produce larger harvests. Earning money incomes from the sale of harvests on anonymous markets is commercial agriculture.

By about 1450, farming demesne land was the usual practice; and some landholders had begun to convert copyhold tenure into leasehold tenure. English landowners began the process of tenure conversion by residing on their estates and using the powers of local government, which they controlled, to induce/coerce peasants to convert copyhold tenure (customary tenure, subsistence tenure) to leasehold tenure. In the process, landowners charged money rents. The conversion of copyhold tenure into leasehold tenure, where land use required paying money rents; and then seeking to maximize money rents, transformed feudal landholders into commercially motivated landowners. Tenure conversion was often accompanied by consolidating scattered cultivation strips into contiguous holdings (fields) and enclosing (fencing) them.

There was a bewildering variety of copyhold tenures on English manors in the sixteenth and seventeenth centuries because copyhold tenure was defined by customary law that was peculiar to a single manor, group of manors, or a unit of local government. Historical antecedents made customary law extremely local and extremely variable. It was difficult to evict copyholders because their claim to land use was recorded on a manor roll. Customary law recorded on the manor roll granted them a hereditary claim to land use, but households occupying land in leasehold tenure could be evicted for failure to pay rents. Some form of coercion was usually required to induce tenure changes by copyholders, but without changed tenure there would be no per capita increase in the production of food grains for market sale.

The only way households holding land in leasehold tenure could acquire the money to pay rents was to increase production of crops for market sale or become paid laborers (servants of husbandry) on demesne land. Peasant households that failed to pay their rent were evicted. They became landless cottagers, often living in hovels on the edges of communal grazing land (village commons), who usually performed enough intermittent paid labor in normal crop years to avoid privation. If a village common was unavailable, evicted peasants were forced to perform continuous paid agricultural labor in order to pay the rent for a cottage and to purchase food. If they refused to perform continuous paid labor they were evicted and became vagabonds or sturdy beggars.

In the conversion process landowners had the silent cooperation of the monarchy and strong cooperation from the national courts if tenure changes were contested. The direction of decisions by the judges of the national courts in the sixteenth and seventeenth centuries was strongly in the direction of simplifying tenure. Agricultural land would be occupied by the same tenures that governed urban occupancy: freehold by landowners who paid money taxes and leaseholders (tenants) who paid money rents. After commercially motivated landowners extinguished copyhold tenure they could change land use from cultivating subsistence food grains to cultivating the most profitable crops, or producing the most profitable commodity (wool).

The confiscation of monastic lands in 1536-1539 and their subsequent sale to merchants, yeomen, and farmers accelerated the commercialization of English agriculture because the new owners were determined to make their investments profitable. The first english language manuals on how to improve cultivation practices were published a few years after confiscation. Their purpose was to instruct landowners how to produce larger harvests for market sale in order to increase their money incomes.

In *Utopia* (published in 1516), Thomas More (now a Roman Catholic saint) defended the subsistence social order that was governed by a feudal aristocracy who lived in symbiosis with the peasantry. He castigated the profit seeking landowners of Tudor England because they were enclosing their land, evicting peasants, and converting grain fields into pastures to graze sheep in order to produce wool. Grazing sheep were eating the subsistence livelihoods of peasants (sheep eating men) and evicted peasants were forced to seek other means of livelihood that obligated them to perform commercial labor norms. In Utopia, slaves perform most labor. For Thomas More the principal social evil of medieval European culture was profit seeking landowners, not slavery.

Evicted peasants in Tudor England had three options. They could migrate to villages or cities and perform paid labor, they could remain in rural areas and become artisan manufacturers, or they could become vagabonds. The number of vagabonds was a reflection of fewer households making commercial labor inputs into cultivation on land leased to farmers who then leased land to yeomen cultivators who supervised paid laborers. Unneeded agricultural laborers were evicted because households remaining on the land performed more per capita labor. The political records of the reign of Elizabeth are bursting with concerns and alarms about the number of enclosures, rural depopulation, and the number of vagabonds.

In 1575 justices of the peace in all counties were authorized to spend tax money to establish houses of correction where vagabonds could be confined and made to perform useful labor. The labor they usually performed was spinning wool or linen thread or, alternatively, performing heavy labor improving roads. In 1597 parliament made a clear distinction between the deserving and undeserving poor. All parishes were to tax landowners and appoint overseer of the poor to distribute funds to the deserving poor. Overseers were authorized to apprentice the children of the deserving poor at ages 11 to 14. An accompanying statute authorized flogging vagabonds.

The crown encouraged (or did not actively oppose) enclosing common grazing land (intakes) within village boundaries. The better management of enclosed land increased wool production that yeomen weavers converted into cloth. Much of the cloth was exported and export taxes enriched the treasury. In the sixteenth and seventeenth centuries wool and woolen cloth were the largest exports of England and the largest source of export taxes.

Alternatively, intakes from village commons, formerly used for subsistence grazing, could be used to increase butter and cheese production by grazing milk cows on pastures planted in nutritious grasses. Better livestock management also meant building shelters to protect them from winter storms and feeding them during the winter with forage crops grown for that purpose.

During the seventeenth century increasing numbers of commercially motivated landowners who resided on their land began making innovations in food crop cultivation. By the second half of the seventeenth century numerous manuals had been published urging landowners to plant new crops and how to increase yields of customary crops. The four most obvious innovations were: 1) enclosure; 2) substitution of horses for oxen in plowing and harrowing; 3) planting pastures in nutritious grasses and clover to feed more livestock; 4) planting forage crops that were harvested to feed horses and other live-stock during the winter. Horses were stronger than oxen and could pull plows faster and thus plow more land in one day, provided they were adequately fed during the winter with hay, silage, oats, or root crops so they were strong enough to pull plows in the spring.

The new forage crops were turnips, potatoes, clover, and alfalfa that were planted on fields that were formerly fallow. The new field practices used animal manure as fertilizer, crop rotation (up and down husbandry) and, beginning about 1710, the adoption of more efficient agricultural implements. Profit seeking landowners required tenants to use the new practices by inserting them into the 14 to 21 year leases they made to yeomen and farmers. Landowners were also urged to survey their land, usually preparatory to enclosure, which would be followed by digging drainage ditches and building access roads for carts and wagons.

The two most important innovations, however, were less visible. They were tenure change and the performance of commercial labor norms by paid laborers who were supervised by yeomen and farmers. By super-vising paid laborers, without any other innovations, yeomen and farmers substantially increased both per capita and gross yields of food and for-age crops compared to peasants who cultivated copyhold land that was in scattered strips in open fields. The unseen results of larger labor inputs were more harrowing, earlier planting, denser sowing of seeds, intensive weeding, timely harvests, and reduced areas of fallow land.

The increased harvests of the seventeenth and eighteenth centuries were available for sale to weavers, cutlers, potters, blacksmiths, coal miners, ship carpenters, seamen, and commercially employed city residents. In the seventeenth century, most artisan manufacturers lived in rural areas or in villages where food was available to feed them. Yeomen weavers owned their looms and many cutlers owned one or more water powered grinding wheels located in millhouses; and potters and blacksmiths owned shares in a kiln or forge where the fuel was coal. Like yeomen cultivators, artisan manufacturers owned their own tools and measured their social security by money incomes earned by producing products for sale on an anony-mous market.

The increasing number of artisans practicing these skills in the seventeenth century was clearly related to the availability of food for sale in all crop years. Food availability was a strong inducement for displaced peasants and the second sons of yeomen cultivators and merchants to become artisan manufacturers. Sale of the items they manufactured on anonymous markets gave them sufficient money incomes to purchase sufficient food, clothing, and housing to enjoy a standard of living in excess of subsistence; and if they were steady workers, they could live in comfort.

English agriculture was largely commercialized by 1650. By about 1660 the invisible changes, particularly less fallow land and increased labor inputs, had sufficiently increased per capita yields of food grains so that assured food surpluses were produced in all crop years, and in most crop years there was an exportable surplus. The best evidence for the advent of commercial food production is the 1663 parliamentary statute that legalized the practice of aggregating local grain surpluses and storing them until merchants could sell them for acceptable prices—wherever that might be. In other words, food grain became a commodity that English merchants could sell anywhere in England, or export if overseas prices were high. In political terms, the 1663 statute meant that the central government no longer had to concern itself with local food shortages in poor crop years because merchants always had sufficient stores available for transportation to places where prices were high, but not at starvation levels.

After 1630, landless households that rejected performing commercial labor norms had a fourth option. They could immigrate to the North American colonies as indentured servants where, at the expiration of their indentures, they could claim land on the frontier and resume subsistence cultivation. Evicted peasants seeking subsistence opportunities were a high percentage of immigrants to the North American colonies during the seventeenth and early eighteenth centuries. They preferentially immigrated to Virginia, Maryland, and other southern colonies.

The availability of the assured food surplus was confirmed in 1670 when parliament allowed English and foreign merchants to export food grain regardless of local prices, provided they paid the export tax. This policy was reconfirmed in 1673 when parliament passed a statute (in effect for five years) that paid bounties to grain exporters if the domestic price of grain was below a minimum price. These statutes ended the central government's control over food grain exports that had been in effect since 1204 when exports of food grains were prohibited unless licensed by the king.

In 1689 a new statute reinstated the subsidy for grain exports. "Contemporary evidence on the reasons for passing the law is rather meagre. It seems to have been one of the measures of minor significance which was lost sight of in the stirring events following the Glorious Revolution." [5] Whatever the reasons for its lack of controversy, the 1689 subsidy for grain exports reflected three highly beneficial developments in the previous 50 years: 1) England produced an assured food surplus to feed an increasing percentage of its population that was employed as artisan manufacturers or as paid laborers; 2) the production of wheat (the best breadstuff) steadily increased; 3) grain exports steadily increased to 1750 and averaged about 10 percent of domestic production.

Unregulated food grain exports could not have become a policy without the assurance that enough food grains would be harvested in poor crop years to feed England's population; and that the distribution system was sufficiently efficient to transport food grains to districts with deficient harvests. Commercial food production and an adequate transportation infrastructure made the statutes of 1663, 1671, 1673, and 1689 non-controversial.

In 1700 London was the largest city in Europe with a population of 550,000. This was one-tenth of the population of England, but there was no difficulty in supplying the city with food. After 1700 the annual surplus of food grains had two effects: 1) the population increased; 2) an increasing percentage of the population was engaged in non-agricultural employment. A principal reason for population increase was a decline in the death rate. Better nutrition was a principal cause for increased longevity. A second cause of population increase was earlier marriages because incomes were sufficiently high to establish a family; and because affordable food was available to feed them. Finally, food availability removed a major barrier to industrialization.

The situation changed in the 1750s because of increased non-agricultural employment and urbanization. Urban laborers were prone to riot when high bread prices threatened their improved diet of more wheat bread and fresh meat than they consumed in the past. During the previous 50 years meat had become a common item in their diets because part of the larger harvests of grain and forage crops were used to fatten cattle, sheep, and hogs. These animals were slaughtered throughout the years instead of the subsistence practice of the autumn slaughter in order to salt, pickle, smoke, or dry meat because peasants did not grow enough forage crops to feed all of their livestock during the winter. Livestock that remained were usually greatly weakened by spring because they grazed on the meager grasses and weeds growing on fallow ground or in common pastures.

In normal crop years in the mid-1750s, domestic production of food grains matched domestic consumption. In poor crop years there were excessive price increases. From 1756 to 1759, exports of food grains were prohibited and in 1764 all import duties were removed from wheat. The corn law (food grain law) of 1773 attempted to ensure the availability of fair priced breadstuffs. It allowed food grains to be imported if the price of domestically grown grain exceeded a price that was thought to be fair to landowners and city consumers.

Conversely, if the price of domestically grown grain was thought to be too low to provide an adequate income to landowners, a bounty was paid for grain exports. There was also a provision that imported food grains could be stored in bonded warehouses in port cities to ensure a supply of fair priced bread for city residents. The corn law of 1773 was a political balancing act. It was designed to encourage landowners to cultivate more fallow land and make additional improvements to increase per capita yields. At the same time, it tried to ensure that city residents had an assured supply of bread at affordable prices.

Another measure of increased commercial wealth in the seventeenth century was the ability of landowners to pay the rent tax without difficulty. During the seventeenth century, rents were increasing on land leased to farmers and yeomen. As the size of harvests increased, the tax became a smaller proportion of the incomes of resident landowners who actively managed the cultivation practices of tenants. Low taxation of agricultural land continued until the constitutional settlement of 1689 placed all taxing power in parliament. Thereafter, during the nine years of war with France (1689-1697), following William and Mary's accession to the throne, all taxes were increased because the war greatly reduced revenues from export-import taxation. The peacetime tax rate was two shillings per pound sterling (10 percent of rental income), but it doubled during wartime.

After the return of peace in 1697 (Treaty of Ryswick), parliament immediately reduced the tax to two shillings on each pound of rental income. The two shilling tax rate was calculated to produce one million pounds sterling of annual revenue. The War of Spanish Succession (1702-1713) produced the same tax rate as the previous war. In 1702, before the outbreak of hostilities, the revenues of the English government were 4,250,000 pounds sterling and expenditures were 3,223,000. Only 23 percent of the peacetime revenue came from the rent tax. Excise taxation shifted more of the cost of peacetime government to persons employed as wage laborers and artisan manufacturers. This policy became permanent during the rest of the eighteenth century.

Low land (rent) taxation, coupled with enclosures, encouraged rural landowners to make large investments in aggregating scattered cultivation strips, fencing fields, adopting more efficient agricultural implements, practicing crop rotation, and applying animal manure as fertilizer. The principal means of enclosure in the eighteenth century was private statutes passed by parliament. Private statues to legalize enclosures were not new, but their frequency greatly increased during the eighteenth century. They became a dynamic part of the economic development policies of England until enclosure was complete in the mid-nineteenth century. The number of enclosures statutes passed by parliament began from a very low base.

1700-1720	-	9
1720-1740	-	68
1740-1760	-	194
1760-1780	-	1066
1780-1800	-	793 [6]

Enclosure was always followed by increased per capita labor inputs that were essential for the efficient use of improved cultivation implements. The effects of increased labor inputs, improved cultivation practices, and improved implements were larger harvests and affordable food prices for the working and middle classes. It is obvious, but seldom recognized by economists, that the assured food surplus produced during the second half of the seventeenth century and thereafter was the most important capital contribution to increasing the commercial wealth of England. Furthermore, the availability of food at affordable prices for persons who were full-time paid laborers eased the political tensions that always accompany the social dislocations of industrialization.

By 1760, in several districts in England, factories were part of the rural landscape. In them, wage laborers operated water powered machinery to produce an increasing variety of items of common consumption. The advent of factories defines the beginning of the industrial revolution; but factories did not become highly visible until after 1780 when James Watt's steam engine was used to power machinery in factories located in cities. England's leadership in the most visible forms of new wealth (factories, cities, maritime commerce, ability to keep armies supplied in the field) would not have occurred without the production of an assured food surplus.

LITERACY

Increasing literacy contributed to England's competitive advantage in a way that cannot be accurately measured. In the sixteenth, seventeenth, and eighteenth centuries England almost certainly had a higher percentage of functionally literate persons than Spain, Portugal, and France. Functionally literate persons were those who could read and write english and do mathematical calculations with sufficient ability to conduct private and public affairs in the commercial sector of English society. Lawrence Stone documents the rapid increase in functional literacy after the reformation and David Cressy estimates that by about 1600 something less than one-third of adult

English males could read (at various competencies), but not necessarily write. Other authors estimate that up to two-thirds of adult males in London were functionally literate, but literacy in rural areas was much lower because there was less commercial activity.

The relatively high rate of functional literacy in England was the result of the reformation that weakened or destroyed many of the feudal institutions of English society. It helped break the link between feudal landholders living in symbiosis with an illiterate peasantry that Thomas More strongly defended in *Utopia*. For More, feudal aristocrats would support the hierarchical church and the hierarchical church would support the feudal aristocracy; and both aristocracies would govern England to conserve a social order with minimal commerce because Utopians did not use money.

Before the reformation the literacy that was taught in villages, monasteries, and chantries was "closely embedded in the ecclesiastical structure." Teaching was done by clergymen in order to train children to participate in the mass. Secular education was concentrated in market towns and cities and was for the children of the governing elite and principal merchants. After the dissolution of the monasteries and chantries, teaching functional literacy greatly increased and went strongly in the direction of secularization. In the post-reformation social order, "laymen were the chief benefactors, there was a new interest in teaching methods, a wide development of facilities, and the main trend was the bringing of the school into the market place."[7] All persons who participated in monetized commerce knew that literacy was the fundamental commercial skill. Literacy acquisition was further promoted by the Church of England and especially by dissenters, so that persons could read the book of common prayer and the bible in english.

Functional literacy in english was taught in parish or village schools in order to prepare the children of yeomen and farmers to manage the marketing of crops or to market artisan manufactured products. After the reformation, parish clergy were the usual teachers in rural and village parishes in order to supplement their incomes (benefices). Functional literacy was also taught by itinerant teachers (often dissenters) who established elementary schools (petty schools) wherever they found a suitable building and sufficient numbers of parents will-ing to pay. Alternatively, literacy was taught in he homes of literate women (dame schools). Unlike pre-reformation teachers, both the parish clergy and other elementary teachers taught what parents wanted taught. It was functional literacy in english. The principal reasons parents wanted their children to be literate was to qualify them for apprenticeships to artisan manufacturers or to merchants or storekeepers, or as domestic servants in wealthy households.

Often, commercially motivated landowners or successful storekeep-ers in a village endowed a parish or village school with the rent from a small parcel of cultivated land or from a village building. These small endowments provided enough money to pay the fees for a small number of children from the households of tenant cultivators, agricultural laborers, or artisan manufacturers whose parents saw the advantage of literacy for their children. Endowed schools were called free schools. After learning to read english, pupils were given highly variable amounts of instruction in writing (on expensive paper) and in arithmetic, which was usually called learning to cast accounts. The number of elementary schools teaching only functional literacy rapidly increased during the late sixteenth and early seventeenth centuries—at the same time that commercialized agriculture was being imposed on a reluctant peasantry.

One of the few studies of teaching functional literacy in post-refor-mation England is Foster Watson's *The English Grammar Schools to 1660*. The small number of studies of elementary education con-trasts to the numerous studies of grammar school (teaching latin), and an even larger number of studies of the universities. Most grammar schools were located in market villages, and after the reformation they were frequently endowed by local landowners. Pupils usually entered at the elementary level where they were taught the alphabet and how to read and write english. As soon as they were competent readers of english, by about the age of 10 or 11, they began to learn latin, which became the principal purpose of instruction to the age of 14 to 16.

Learning latin classics had little relationship to commercialized agri-culture or to business. The people who were creating much of the

new wealth in England (commercially motivated landowners, artisan manufacturers, merchants, town and city shopkeepers, clerks, and local government officials) were little interested in learning latin, but they had to be
functionally literate in english because it was necessary for conducting
business and government. Functional literacy was also essential for technicians engaged in transforming artisan manufacturing into factory production during the industrial revolution, yet the extent of functional literacy
and how it was used has received minimal investigation by British historians.

Most young people not destined for a life of commerce did not learn arithmetic. . . .
English public schools like Eaton and Harrow did not offer any instruction in
arithmetic until well into the nineteenth century. Nor did Oxford and Cambridge
include arithmetic in their curriculums. . . . Arithmetic became solidly identified
with mercantile life. [8]

In 1699 the Church of England contributed to increasing functional literacy in cities when a group of London philanthropists organized the Society for Promoting Christian Knowledge (SPCK). They
urged local businessmen, like themselves, to organize charity schools
in their parishes to teach functional literacy to the children of displaced peasants (paupers) who had migrated to cities. A high percentage of urban migrants were illiterate and performed menial labor
because they had no choice. They had exactly the same status as displaced peasants in contemporary peasant nations who migrate to cities. If
their children were to be employable in urban commerce above a menial
level, they had to be literate. In the curriculum devised by the SPCK,
functional literacy could be taught in four years if competent teachers conducted classes, but it often took five or more years, depending on attendance.

The primary purpose of charity schools was to train the children to
be apprentices but there were three related purposes. 1) Pupils were
catechized according to the doctrines of the Church of England. 2)
They were taught respect for persons in authority and obedience to
the existing social order. 3) They learned simple manual skills, like
knitting, or spinning woolen or linen thread that yeomen could weave
into cloth. Thread produced by child labor was of inferior quality but
when woven into cloth it clothed the pupils; and spinning taught chil-

dren the habit of laboring every day and performing commercial labor norms. The habit of commercial labor norm coupled with literacy made graduates of charity schools into excellent recruits for apprentice training.

Charity schools were not usually controlled by clerics. Trustees were usually the businessmen who founded the schools and continued to fund them. Most contributors came from middle class merchants and tradesmen. They knew exactly what should be taught and the discipline that had to be imposed on the children of displaced peasants to make them employable. The trustees of most urban charity schools composed "a scheme of instruction for boys and girls from about the age of seven to twelve or fourteen years" coupled with the necessity of retaining children in attendance by a "never-ceasing endeavor . . . by personal appeal . . . to induce the parents to co-operate in the education of their children." [9]

The alternative, favored by most illiterate parents, was menial labor by their children for a few pennies a day in order to contribute to household subsistence. The few pennies they earned were appropriated and often converted into drunkenness and other forms of parental indolence. In contemporary Mexico City Oscar Lewis defined this behavior as the culture of poverty; and in contemporary U.S. cities this behavior defines the underclass. Charity schools were designed to overcome the indifference to literacy by evicted peasants who had been forced to migrate to cities.

Charity schools were most successful in London where there was an insatiable demand for literate persons who would perform commercial labor norms. The success of charity schools was also attributable to a large and growing number of middle class merchants and tradesmen who were available to fund them. By 1750, England had the highest rate of functional literacy in Europe. There is no question that the high rate of functional literacy was one of the principal propellants of the industrial revolution that was beginning to gain momentum at mid-century. [10]

In 1799, 100 years after the organization of the first charity schools, there were 179 in London with 7,108 pupils. These pupils probably comprised 10 percent of the elementary school enrollment in the city.

In other cities in England, they were less successful in finance and management; and in rural areas they failed because large number of children were employed in agriculture, coal mining, and textile processing. Landowners and owners of these labor intensive businesses wanted immobile laborers, and illiteracy reduced social and geographic mobility.

Dissenting academies had their origin in the Act of Uniformity (1662) passed by the parliament that restored Charles II to the throne. It evicted parish clergymen installed during Cromwell's protectorate if they refused to accept the doctrines and hierarchical organization of the Church of England. The act required all teachers in parish schools and grammar schools to be communicants of the Church of England, and be licensed by the bishops in the dioceses where they lived. Many of the evicted clergy founded dissenting academies. Their primary function was to train dissenting clergymen because dissenting students no longer had entry to universities. The usual age of entry was 15 to 17 and the usual course of study was four years.

The dissenting academies and Scottish universities of the seventeenth and eighteenth centuries were very receptive to the new learning of science, medicine, and technology while they continued to train clergymen for dissenting and presbyterian congregations. They accepted students without reference to religious preference and taught the new skills because they were essential for business. Reception of the new learning helped make technologically backward Scotland a leading participant in the industrial revolution.

Reception of the new learning in dissenting academies and the Scottish universities had its origins in Calvin's rejection of hierarchical authority in church governance. The principal effect of rejecting hierarchical governance was a mental attitude that was receptive to innovation, especially technical innovations that could improve the material welfare of individuals. Calvinists generally agreed that a favorable reception of innovation began with the adoption of commercial social values, often called the protestant ethic. In practice, the two fundamental innovations were: 1) the performance of commercial labor norms; 2) education curriculums designed to teach functional literacy that could be applied to commercial opportunities.

When state surveillance of dissenters was relaxed after 1725, many dissenting academies grew in size and endowments and acquired a firmer institutional basis. Their curriculums were often influenced by discussions in London coffeehouses where fellows of the Royal Society and their associates met and exchanged the results and implications of the experiments they conducted. Many persons who participated in these discussions became teachers in dissenting academies for a few years and brought with them a desire to prepare graduates to undertake practical applications of the new learning. They were, therefore, sympathetic to businessmen who wanted to develop the technology of steam power or apply chemistry to business opportunities, or underwrite further scientific experiments. In England, the essential commercial and technical skills needed for propelling the industrial revolution (accounting, navigation, land surveying, and skills related to civil engineering and architecture) were often taught in dissenting academies. By 1750 dissenting academies had strongly deemphasized teaching latin and just as strongly sought to prepare graduates for careers in business.

The new learning taught in dissenting academies is contrasted to the fossilized curriculums of English grammar schools and universities. The English universities virtually ignored science, medicine, mathematics, geography, and modern languages because learning latin was thought to be the best preparation for service in government, the church, law, and education, but not in business. The concentration on learning latin classics in grammar schools and universities was a strange form of education in a nation that was rapidly becoming the world leader in commerce and industry.

During the sixteenth, seventeenth, and eighteenth centuries there were six obvious trends in education and commerce: 1) the percentage of literate persons in the general population increased; 2) the increase was directly related to the commercialization of British society; 3) that generated sufficient incomes for landowners, merchants, and artisan manufacturers to support fee paying elementary schools in most parishes and endow grammar schools in many market towns;

4) almost all elementary schools, grammar schools, and academies were controlled by the laity; 5) the curriculums of elementary schools focused on teaching functional literacy in english that could be applied to commerce; 6) English universities, under clerical control, ignored most of the new learning and its linkage to commerce.

POLITICAL ECONOMY OF MERCANTILISM

The monarchs of nations facing the Atlantic ocean saw great opportunities in promoting and protecting long distance commerce because substantial tax revenues would make them less dependent on feudal landholders for revenue. The geographic discoveries of the sixteenth and seventeenth centuries were a strong incentive to create empires of commerce by: 1) establishing fortified warehouses on the peripheries of existing principalities and empires; 2) imposing imperial governance wherever indigenous cultures were politically and militarily weak; 3) establishing colonies on vacant land.

By 1700 the central governments of European nations that promoted long distance commerce were groping for a set of policies that could give coherence to the increase of commerce that had taken place during the previous 200 years. Mercantilism was the strategy of economic development that guided the commercial policies of the governments of England, France, Portugal, and Spain during the eighteenth century. Mercantilism had three objectives. The first was to maximize the production of artisan manufactured items for export and, in the process, acquire the skills of banking, insurance, and shipping required for imperial commerce. The second objective was to minimize the purchase of manufactured items from foreign nations and encourage (often with subsidies) domestic production of desirable products. The third objective was to encourage national monopoly corporations that traded into distant regions to import commodities that could be highly taxed and, at the same time, earn high profits for merchants.

During the sixteenth century long distance imperial commerce was a small part of the trade of Spain, Portugal, England, France, and the

Netherlands. It had, however, a huge importance because three com-modities had very high profit margins: pepper from India, spices from the Indies, and the bullion looted from the Aztecs and Incas. During the seventeenth century the importance of long distance commerce increased because it: 1) supplied European nations with an increasing variety of commodities that were not produced in European nations (tea, coffee, tobacco, cotton textiles); 2) supplied products that could be profitably exported to other nations; 3) provided larger markets for manufactured items produced in European nations; 4) accumulated precious metal in order to pay for past and future wars.

The ultimate purpose of the mercantile system was to maximize the acquisition of gold and silver bullion that could be minted into precious metal coins (specie). Specie was the most flexible and durable form of money and spending it was the most efficient way to build cities, expand commerce, and mobilize the material and human resources to wage war. Put another way, specie was the most efficient means of paying for wars to displace rivals in imperial commerce or to implement dynastic ambi-tions. Mercantile doctrine claimed that European nations that used specie to encourage and protect imperial commerce would become rich. The unstated alternative was that nations that waged wars for dynastic pur-poses would become poor.

Dutch commercial policies were not mercantilist, and the Dutch became rich. Dutch commercial policies were designed to encourage Dutch merchants to participate in markets wherever they existed or could be created, not to supply the small Dutch domestic market, nor accumulate bullion to wage war. The governing elite of the Nether-lands did not fight wars to enhance dynastic ambitions, promote true religion, or acquire precious metals as loot. The Dutch fought Euro-pean wars only when they had little choice. After 1567 they had little choice because they declared independence from Spain and adopted the Calvinist variety of reformed Christianity. Almost continual war-fare followed until Spain finally recognized Dutch independence in 1648 (Peace of Westphalia).

Without independence the Dutch could not have promoted all forms of commerce to their advantage, particularly long distance commerce.

The principal propellant for increasing Dutch commerce was money earned from commerce that was converted into credit that was extended to customers. The Dutch learned from Genoese and Florentine bankers that credit was the best way to attract and hold customers; and the English learned this business strategy from the Dutch. "The essence of much of the so-called mercantilist literature was to commend a programme of deliberate imitation of the Dutch, combined with policies to protect the nascent economy from the effects of their powerful competition." [11]

The great advantage of English maritime commerce, compared to the Dutch, was that it operated in four regions: 1) Europe; 2) the Mediterranean; 3) India and China; 4) North America and the Caribbean. In the last quarter of the seventeenth century the increased volume of long distance commerce produced a rapid increase in export-import revenues; and during the eighteenth century the volume and profitability of long distance maritime commerce helped make England a major European power. At the same time the decline of revenues from long distance commerce helped reduce Spain to a second rank European power.

The next section focuses on the policies that the English government used to encourage maritime commerce during the seventeenth century and how the revenues derived from taxing it helped England become a first rank military power in the eighteenth century. Many of the policies implemented by the English were borrowed from other European nations and many of the innovations made by English policy makers were copied, more or less successfully, by European nations that actively promoted maritime commerce.

TAXATION OF MARITIME COMMERCE

All monarchs from Elizabeth to William and Mary, including the government of the Commonwealth, sought to increase the volume of maritime commerce to the advantage English merchants, bankers, and shipowners, and especially to the advantage of the treasury. The policy of encouraging maritime commerce in order to increase tax revenues was not accidental. Increased maritime commerce resulted from: **1)** three Anglo-Dutch wars: 1652-1654, 1665-1667, 1672-1674;

2) navigation acts; **3)** the inability of Spanish artisans to produce enough items to supply its domestic and colonial markets, and the inability of Spanish peasants to grow enough food to feed Spain's urban population; **4)** London replaced Amsterdam as the principal entrepot of Europe.

1. The Anglo-Dutch wars were designed to replace Dutch ships as the principal carriers of European maritime commerce and help London overtake Amsterdam as the largest entrepot and banking center of Europe. The first two wars were largely naval and were fought in Europe. They had little effect in India and no effect in the Indies. In the third war the Dutch had to defend their borders from invasion by king Louis XIV of France who wanted to annex Dutch commercial wealth to France. England, under king Charles II supported France for commercial advantages. In return, Louis XIV supported Charles II's ambition to rule with autocratic powers in order to duplicate the autocratic rule of France.

In the War of the League of Augsburg (1689-1697) and the War of Spanish Succession (1702-1713), England and the Netherlands were allies. The war was fought to prevent the domination of western Europe by France and reduce French competition in long distance commerce. The great lengths of the wars, continual French assaults on Dutch borders, and English navigation laws weakened the ability of Dutch commerce to compete with the English for the carrying trade of Europe. Likewise, the English East India Company steadily increased its competitive advantage over the Dutch East India Company for the profits of Indian commerce. By 1715 the Dutch were, in large part, junior partners of the English in European and Indian commerce; and they had a greatly reduced presence in American commerce. The Indies, however, remained a Dutch preserve.

2. The first Navigation Act (1651) was framed by the Council of Trade, a committee established in 1650 by the first parliament of the Commonwealth. Prior to its passage, proclamations by monarchs and statutes passed by parliament had:

experimented with regulations of trade inward, outward, and coastwise, in the colonies and at home; with the size, master, crew, ownership, and cargo of ships; with the enactment of preferential tariffs, and the grant of bounties. By a process of trial and error it had gradually exhausted the possibilities, until eventually it stumbled upon a formula which was to supply protection to shipping and ease of administration. [12]

The Navigation Act of 1651 was clearly written. It applied only to imports and it equally affected English and foreign merchants. Imports had to come directly to England from the nation where they were produced but could be carried by English ships or the ships of the exporting nation. This provision was aimed directly at the Dutch. It prevented Dutch ships from carrying generalized cargoes to England, composed of products assembled in Amsterdam from European nations, India, the Indies, or America because these products did not originate in the Netherlands. The purpose of this provision was to promote London as an entrepot at the expense of Amsterdam and encourage English shipowners to carry more of England's maritime commerce.

An additional provision required long distance commerce from Asia, Africa, and America be carried only in English or colonial owned ships. This provision was designed to exclude Dutch ships from trading with England's American and Caribbean colonies. Enforcement of these provisions provoked the first Anglo-Dutch war. The steady increase in the size of the royal navy after the restoration of Charles II (1660) was a necessary corollary of the navigation act of 1651 because the increased commerce contemplated by the acts required increased protection.

After Charles II was restored to the throne, he refused to accept statutes passed by Commonwealth parliaments. This forced the restoration parliament to revise the Navigation Act on the basis of nine years of experience in its administration. The Navigation Act of 1660 allowed any product produced in Europe, except for an enumerated list, to be imported from any place in any ship. Enumerated items, however, had to be imported in English owned ships (but not necessarily English built) or in the ships of the nation that produced the items. There was also a short list of colonial commodities (sugar, tobacco, cotton, indigo, and other dyestuffs) that had to be imported directly into England in English or colonial owned ships. These commodities were just beginning to be produced in quantity in the American and Caribbean colonies but they had great potential for increased production. Increased imports of them would increase revenue from taxing them, and this would benefit the treasury.

An amendment in 1663 required that all manufactured products exported to the American colonies had to originate in English ports and be carried in English or colonial owned ships. Furthermore, two-thirds of the crew had to be English, Irish, or colonial. North American commerce, like commerce from India, the Indies, and China would be a monopoly for English (and colonial) merchants; and the cargoes they carried would be mostly of English origin or be assembled in English ports. Parliament passed the last Navigation Act in 1696. It strengthened and regularized the operations of the earlier acts and contained regulations for governing the rapidly growing volume of North American and Caribbean trade. Its operation was monitored by the Board of Trade whose principal function was to recommend policies to govern North American and Caribbean commerce.

3. There was an unrelenting decline in Spanish power from the end of the sixteenth and during all of the seventeenth centuries. It was the result of the dynastic ambitions of Spain's governing elite that were unrelated to commerce. The decline was cumulative because of the neglect of domestic industry and commerce. After 1600, imperial commerce stagnated relative to the size of the empire because the revenues of the central government were insufficient to fund European wars, defend imperial commerce, and encourage commercial development at home and in the American colonies. With stagnation of long distance commerce came Spain's decreasing ability to maintain its status as a first rank military power in Europe. After 1600 Spain was continually on the edge of bankruptcy.

The enervating policies pursued by Spanish monarchs were: 1) almost continual European wars using vast amounts of precious metal money to try and reverse the reformation; 2) attempts to protect monopoly trade to the Americas by the merchants of Seville; 3) failure to actively promote weaving of woolen cloth and the manufacture of iron implements by Spanish artisans using abundant Spanish wool and iron ores; 4) failure to encourage feudal landholders to commercialize food production; 5) failure of colonial governors in the Americas and the Philippines to mobilize the labor of indigenous peasants to produce export commodities.

Compared to England, Spanish agriculture in the seventeenth and eighteenth centuries was largely subsistent. Commercial agriculture was concentrated in the production of wine, vinegar, olive oil, salt, and livestock (wool). Minimal amounts of food crops were produced by the Spanish equivalent of English yeomen cultivators. The failure of Spanish landowners to commercialize agriculture (failure to produce assured food surpluses) became glaringly apparent as early as 1580 when Spain became dependent on food grains imported from the Baltic. What made the failure glaringly apparent was that the grain was carried to Spain in Dutch/Flemish ships while the Dutch were at war with Spain. Dependency on imported food persisted through the seventeenth and eighteenth centuries and made seasons of hunger into recurrent events.

Likewise, the inability of Spanish artisans to produce all of the manufactured items needed at home and in the American colonies meant that a considerable portion of these items had to be purchased from England and elsewhere in Europe, and they were carried to Spain in Dutch and English ships. Mexican and Peruvian silver was used to pay for them. These policies strongly contributed to increasing the revenues of the Dutch and English governments.

4. By the beginning of the eighteenth century the navigation acts had helped England increase its share of an increased volume of European and North American commerce. By 1720, London replaced Amsterdam as the principal entrepot and banking center of Europe. The revenue generated by increased trade, particularly re-exports of American and Indian commodities, helped defray the costs of building and maintaining the royal navy that was responsible for protecting English maritime commerce.

The rest of the chapter focuses on increased manufacturing in England during the eighteenth century and the concomitant increase in long distance commerce. These two developments help explain how the English commercial empire in the eighteenth century evolved into an empire of governance in the nineteenth century.

COMMERCIAL EXPANSION IN THE EIGHTEENTH CENTURY

During the first three-quarters of the eighteenth century British exports of manufactured items steadily increased, and after 1775 they accelerated. Woolen textiles were the dominant item but they steadily declined as a percentage of total exports of manufactured items. The reciprocal of stagnant exports of woolen textiles was increased exports of metal implements. Increasingly they went to America in exchange for raw materials.

In 1700 the total value of exports of manufactured items was 3.8 million pounds sterling. Woolen textiles accounted for 79 percent and 90 percent went to continental Europe. Of the 21 percent of other manufactures, 55 percent were exported to continental Europe. Seventy-five years later exports of British manufactured items had increased 220 percent to 8.5 million pounds sterling. Woolen textiles accounted for 49 percent and had about the same value as in 1700, but only 62 percent went to continental Europe.

In 1700 America and Africa took 12 percent of the total exports of manufactured items (including woolen textiles). In 1775 America and Africa took 43 percent, with most of it going to America. Much the same happened in the Indian and Chinese trade but on a much smaller scale. India and China took 2.8 percent of England's total exports of manufactured items in 1700 (including woolen textiles) and in 1775 they took 7.5 percent. The commodities imported from India and China could not have been acquired by the sale of manufactured products because local artisans supplied local needs. Most of the funds to purchase commodities in India and China came from profits earned in regional trade and from exporting silver coins.

The most striking change in the export of manufactured products was the increasing percentage of non-textiles. In 1700 non-textiles accounted for 21 percent of English exports of manufactured items but in 1775 they accounted for 50 percent. Four developments are hidden in these statistics: 1) a large part of the increased exports of manufactured items were metal implements; 2) export of these items to America and Africa increased 773 percent; 3) continental Europe was the destination of 82 percent of all manufactured items (including woolen textiles) in 1700 but in 1775 only 42 percent went to Europe because; 4) European nations were attempting to become self-sufficient in the same items that were manufactured in England for export. The success of the mercantile policies of European nations forced British merchants to seek new long distance markets. They found them in India, China, the Caribbean, and especially in North America.

During the eighteenth century the number and volume of commodities entering Europe from India, the Indies, and China steadily increased. [13] English merchants garnered a disproportionately large amount of the increased long distance commerce because London merchants and bankers could supply credit and because artisan manufacturers were able to supply increasing amounts of low cost iron implements, especially to the North American colonies.

So rapidly was American expansion proceeding after mid-century that . . . the process of industrialization in England from the second quarter of the eighteenth century was to an important extent a response to colonial demands. . . . I have taken it for granted that these were nearly all manufacturers. In the iron and brass industries and all the metal working crafts dependent on them, colonial demands made an important supplement to those of the growing homemarket. [14]

IMPERIAL COMMERCE

This section focuses on Indian commerce because: 1) India was one of the places where English and French commercial rivalry was settled by armed conflict. 2) Political anarchy in India was an opportunity for the English to convert their empire of commerce into an empire of governance, as the Dutch were doing in the Indies. 3) The potential for future commerce with India was very great if peace could be imposed on feudal warlords; and if Indian merchants could be protected so they could mobilize peasant labor to produce export commodities.

During the 30 years of European peace following the Peace of Utrecht (1713), the English East India Company increased its trade and profitability. Its fundamental political interest was the maintenance of monopoly trade; and this was protected by friends in parliament. Profitability came from two sources. The first was a steady increase in Indian trade. The second was the receipt of feudal taxes in districts and principalities where the company established imperial governance.

When cotton textiles first found a market in Europe about 1670, there was insufficient production in India to satisfy demand. The primary market for Indian textiles was the Indies where they were exchanged for pepper, cloves, nutmeg, and mace. As long as the principal market was the Indies, Hindu weavers, operating within the Hindu Caste System, produced sufficient cotton textiles to satisfy demand. Silver coins were used to pay weavers. The development of global trade in cotton textiles pierced the shell of the non-monetized self-sufficiency of peasant villages where the Hindu Caste System governed labor norms. Villagers now had a source of money that could be used to purchase food grains in years of privation, or pay money taxes instead of levies of one or more cloths that was the customary form of taxing weavers.

Indian merchants wholly controlled the interior trade in cotton textiles. They made advances of silver coins (supplied by the English) to village weavers and conveyed accumulated cloth to the coast. Production of cotton textiles, however, was unpredictable because the Hindu Caste System preserved subsistence labor norms. Its operation was an inherent restraint on increasing textile production for export because, after village needs and tax obligations were satisfied, many weavers declined to produce an extra cloth for money, even if raw cotton was available.

A second hazard to predictable trade was the vulnerability of Indian merchants to extortionate taxation while conveying cloth to the coast. Merchants were vulnerable because they were members of a caste with a low social status in the Hindu Caste System, regardless of their wealth. Their low status gave all levels of feudal rulers the right to levy unpredictable taxes and escheat their estates upon their death in order to satisfy a rajah's, sultan's, or emperor's need for money. Escheated wealth could include the houses where they lived and their warehouses, if they had one. Within the caste structure of Indian society the inheritance of commercial wealth was precarious.

Extortionate taxation and the threat of escheatment made it difficult for Indian merchants to accumulate working capital in order to fund increased production of cotton textiles.

As the Mughal empire began its slow disintegration after 1670, the greed of tax collectors could be restrained only at its center. When a European market developed for cotton textiles after 1670, a rapid increase in production was more easily achieved in the hinterlands around Surat where Mughal governance was strongest. Villages of Muslim weavers were established that subsisted on food purchased on credit from the East India Company. This was the same strategy devised by the Dutch for spice producing villages in the Moluccas. These villages were partially dependent on rice imported from Java and Thailand by the Dutch East India Company. In India, the English and Dutch companies supplied raw cotton and some or most food grains for weavers, and Muslim merchants supervised textile production in villages mainly devoted to weaving.

In Hindu provinces, the rapid growth of the European market for cotton textiles was a huge incentive for the English East India Company to rapidly increase production. This was difficult within the constraints of the Hindu Caste System. Company servants in Madras and elsewhere borrowed the practice of the Surat factor. They established villages where residents planted larger cotton crops and wove cotton textiles for export. In return, the company supplied weavers with food grains and additional raw cotton that was imported from Surat and elsewhere. These villages operated outside the subsistence restraints of the Hindu Caste System; and as long as the company could maintain peace, supply food grains and raw cotton, enough textiles were produced to satisfy European demand.

Peace, however, was difficult to maintain. In the years before the death of emperor Aurangzeb in 1707, Indian merchants operating in the interior became increasingly vulnerable to arbitrary taxation. After his death, the position of Indian merchants and their client weavers were under increasing stress because feudal warlords began fighting over pieces of the crumbling empire.

The measure of increased commerce from India after the Treaty of Utrecht (1713) was the number of annual voyages originating from

England. In 1717 there were approximately 100. Ten years later there were 150. The increase in regional traders after 1713 was even more dramatic. Increasing numbers were employees of the East India Company or employees who had retired or resigned. The company allowed its employees to engage in private trade because they served the company's interest. Regional traders assembled cargoes for return voyages, often with commodities acquired by smuggling voyages into the Dutch sphere of influence in the Indies. By about 1740 English regional traders outnumbered the regional traders of all other European nations operating in the Indian ocean and beyond.

In the India trade, the fortified warehouse at Calcutta slowly increased in importance based on exchanging silver coins for cotton textiles, saltpeter, and indigo. After 1740, the head factor at Calcutta gained the power to directly govern and collect land taxes from an enclave surrounding the fort where the warehouses, homes, and offices of European and Indian merchants were clustered. The power to collect a land tax was the first incidence of a policy that would transform the English commercial empire in India into an empire of governance.

The French entered the India trade about the same time as the English and Dutch. The first French voyage was in 1601, and in 1642 the first French East India Company was organized. The French crown subscribed a major portion of the capital in order to use the company as an instrument of foreign policy. Trade languished because of domestic religious conflicts; the management's reluctance to allow its employees to engage in regional trade; failure to fully participate in the China trade, and a continuing attempt to colonize Madagascar. There were several French East India Companies and all of them received nearly continuous subsidies.

In spite of financial weakness and mismanagement there was a continuing French presence in the Indian ocean. French presence was put on a sustaining basis by settling the island of Mauritius in 1721 and establishing a principal warehouse at Pondicherry in the 1670s. Mauritius was converted into a giant sugar plantation cultivated by African slave labor similar to what had been done on West Indian islands, and Pondicherry was a source of cotton textiles.

While England and France were fighting the War of Austrian Succession (1740-1748), English and French factors in India maintained a truce in order to carry on business as usual. Equilibrium was broken in 1744 when both nations sent fleets and regular army troops to India. Royal warships of both nations captured merchant ships and regular army units captured warehouses. In 1746 a unit of the French army, supported by sepoys (Indians trained to fight as European infantry) marched north from Pondicherry and captured Madras. Both the English and French East India Companies had mercenary armies composed of sepoys led by European officers, supported by field artillery and cavalry, and stiffened by units of European infantry when they were available. Both companies sought to create spheres of influence on the wreckage of the Mughal empire. Although Madras was restored to the English in 1749, its capture introduced a new variable in the political economy of Indian commerce.

In south India, in several principalities during the 1740s and 1750s, there were frequent dynastic disputes. Contending claimants made bids to use company troops to secure the throne. Governors of English and French enclaves were willing to use European troops while they were in India. The purpose of company intervention was to secure governance of a territory that successful claimants assigned to them. Governance gave the company the right to collect land taxes in sufficiently large amounts to repay the costs of using its troops. The power of governance also included the right to mobilize peasant labor to produce increasing quantities of export commodities, particularly cotton textiles.

For the French East India Company, acquisition of the right of governance would supply more revenue than was earned by trade. The means of acquiring this revenue was using sepoys, stiffened by French troops, to enlarge directly governed enclaves. The opportunistic acquisition of the power of governance by English and French governors was a sure source of future conflict. The French were the first to act. In 1749, their intervention was decisive in a dynastic dispute near Pondicherry. As a reward, they were granted tax collecting power in a territory that more than doubled the area of the French enclave. Thereafter, there was continual intervention by English and French military units in dynastic disputes whenever there were opportunities.

Early in the Seven Years War (1756-1763), often called the Great War for Empire, proxy warfare by company troops became direct conflict. Bengal was the focus of this conflict because, from the enclave at Calcutta, the English East India Company had extended its trade far into the interior to secure export commodities. Both English and Dutch merchants operated warehouses at Patna to supervise the production of saltpeter that was barged down the Ganges River to Calcutta and Chinsura for export.

Company factors, private English merchants, and Indian merchants who were engaged in interior trade needed protection from extortionate taxation whenever the rajah of Bengal needed revenue. In order to protect its commerce the company did everything possible to reduce taxation on its merchants because unpredictable taxation added costs to commodities that would not be sold for six months to a year (until they arrived in England).

In 1756 the rajah of Bengal needed additional revenue and levied a lump sum tax on the governor of Calcutta. After much negotiation the rajah refused to compromise and the company refused to pay. The rajah assaulted and captured Calcutta. In the past, the company would have paid an indemnity to regain possession of its warehouses. This time, however, the company chose to use force to regain possession because force was available. A squadron of the royal navy brought British troops and units of the company's troops north from Madras where they were engaged in reducing French influence among rajahs hostile to the commercial policies of the company.

The French had encouraged the rajah of Bengal to limit the company's commerce beyond the boundaries of the Calcutta enclave. They sent a small contingent of regular army troops to encourage him to act. In 1757, at the battle of Plassey (north of Calcutta), a mixed army of British and company troops defeated the army of the rajah of Bengal. In that battle the company had 600 European troops, 50 sailors borrowed from warships at Calcutta, 2,100 Madras sepoys, and 171 men serving 12 pieces of artillery. The artillery was manned by Christian Eurasian topasses. The rajah of Bengal had approximately 35,000 poorly trained, poorly armed, and poorly led infantry. Senior officers were mounted on elephants and were easy targets. The rajah's levies were supported by approximately 15,000 cavalry armed with lances and swords and stiffened by 53 pieces of artillery operated by Indians but with 50 French soldiers who directed fire.

Robert Clive, who commanded the company's army, probably had the advantage. In the previous 15 years the huge numbers of untrained and poorly led levies mobilized by rajahs had proven vulnerable to highly mobile units of disciplined, well armed, and competently led infantry supported by field artillery operated by Indians trained to European levels of skill. In these battles, as well as the battle of Plassey, the company's army had the benefit of subversion gained by bribing the nominal allies of the rajah. Clive had reasonable confidence his army could defeat the incoherent levies of the rajah. The principal danger was a mass charge by the rajah's army that would overwhelm Clive's army. This, however, was unlikely because of poor leadership and poor motivation. Clive won the battle and five days later entered the undefended capital and placed his nominee on the throne of Bengal.

In return the company was assigned tax revenues from three large districts in order to pay the costs of the war, and the company was granted the right of governance to an enlarged territory (6,680 square kilometers) around Calcutta. The company was also granted a monopoly in the production of saltpeter that squeezed the Dutch out of their share of this highly profitable export. After 1780 when the Dutch government sided with the Americans in the American war of independence, the company acquired the remaining Dutch coastal warehouses that had not been captured by Indian rajahs.

In the eight years following Plassey, conditions in Bengal were unsettled because the company did not have the military capability to impose peace. Peace in Bengal required time because the company had to defend Bengal's borders from invasions by rajahs of bordering principalities. The second necessity was preventing the resurgence of the French, which was accomplished with great effort and equally great French ineptitude. Pondicherry was captured in 1761 but the Treaty of Paris (1763), that ended the Great War for Empire, returned it to France along with several other warehouses. The French military was limited to a few troops at Pondicherry; and in 1769 the French East India Company was dissolved. The French attempt to establish an empire of governance was dead. From 1763 onward French commerce in India, like Portuguese and Dutch commerce, was by permission of the English East India Company.

In the same year as the battle of Plassey, an Afghan army plundered Delhi and the Mughal empire became an empty shell. The emperor survived but without power because he did not have a territorial tax base. What remained of his prestige could be bought or coerced from him by rajahs who were hostile to the practice of the company's employees selling passes to Indian merchants that the company claimed exempted them from unpredictable transit taxes when entering or leaving their domains on the way to the coast.

Drift changed to purpose in 1765 when Robert Clive returned to Bengal with the title of governor and president of the council. He had the authority to appoint a management committee of four, all of whom were his nominees. They were committed to defending the borders of Bengal, restoring internal order, regularizing the collection of taxes, and putting the government of Bengal on a firm institutional basis. Thereafter, the power of the company, based on its mercenary army, would be used to create commercial opportunities in bordering princely states. The principal interest of the company was predictable taxation of all trade within the principalities bordering Bengal in order to maximize the amount of commodities produced for export. This policy conflicted with the principal interest of rajahs. They wanted to continue taxing merchants with no rules except their immediate fiscal needs.

Rajahs in the bordering principalities accurately assessed events in Bengal. They clearly recognized that the company's commercial and political policies were long-term threats to their personal rule. They saw the post-Plassey weakness of company governance as an opportunity to drive the company back into its enclave of Calcutta. By doing this they could appropriate the revenues that were going to company employees who sold passes to Indian merchants so they could bypass most transit taxation.

Governing Bengal would not be easy because the company did not have enough personnel, and a high percentage of them were venal, sometimes in the extreme. After securing Bengal's borders, the most important reform was reducing extortion by the company's employees and Indian feudal officials. The first thing Clive did was put a puppet on the throne of Bengal. His accession was legitimatized by an endorsement from the Mughal emperor who had become a client of the company. The company appointed all of the rajah's principal ministers, especially the minister responsible for collecting taxes, and forced the rajah to disband his palace guard so that the funds used for its upkeep could be used to support the company's troops that guarded Bengal's borders. The puppet rajah disguised the company's acquisition of the power to govern. Customary taxes continued to be collected in customary amounts by the rajah's agents, but the agents were under new management.

The acquisition of Bengal's customary tax revenues was the most important long-term result of the battle of Plassey. The company's exclusive use of customary tax revenues was the foundation for imperial governance because tax revenues were much larger than commercial profits; however, the company's profits also increased after imperial governance was firmly established. Increased trade and increased profits were directly related to the company's ability to enforce internal and external peace, levy predictable taxes, and protect the accumulation of commercial wealth by Indian merchants.

When Clive returned to India in 1765 the company was purchasing approximately 350,000 pounds sterling of commodities produced in Bengal. Ten years later purchases exceeded one million pounds. Clive would have liked company employees to collect Bengal's tax revenues but there were two impediments: 1) not enough honest company employees; 2) if foreigners became tax collectors this would indicate that the company was a conqueror instead of a commercial organization. Clive recognized that the company's power in Bengal was fragile and its power of governance had to be disguised as much as possible.

Clive's first task was to stop the practice of company employees taking gifts to expedite the commerce of Indian merchants. This was not easy because company personnel considered employment to be a license to get rich in exactly the same way that Indian feudal rulers used political power to get rich. The principal weakness of company governance was low salaries. Their low salaries were augmented by building working relationships with Indian merchants. In the process they acquired export commodities that filled the holds of company ships on their return voyages.

The key reform for putting company governance on a solid foundation was higher salaries. Company employees engaged in commerce had to perform full-time business duties and those who performed civil duties had to devote all of their energies to governance. High salaries would attract men of ability from Britain and convert the government of Bengal into a solid bastion of power that could be used to expand commerce (and governance) into the interior as opportunities occurred. The separation of governing personnel from business personnel was the beginning of a professional civil service that was essential for governing India as British hegemony expanded beyond the borders of the enclaves at Calcutta, Madras, and Bombay.

Clive also had to deal with the military. The first step was removing their opportunity for plunder. Officers threatened revolt. Clive met them head-on. Any officer who resigned while stationed at a border post where the threat of invasion was constant was relieved of command, court-martialed, and put aboard ships that took them from Bengal. Clive also redressed a continuing complaint of officers and men. Personnel wounded in battle had no incomes after they recovered and were found unfit for duty. A pension fund was established to provide for their welfare and for the welfare of wives and children of men killed in battle. In 1767 Clive returned to England.

After Plassey (1757), India became an English sphere of influence. English hegemony was the opportunity for the company to create an empire of governance by the judicious use of armed force, diplomacy, bribery, and partnerships with indigenous merchants. In the next 50 years, the ability of English and company troops to impose peace on warring rajahs institutionalized a commercial sector that reached far into the interior instead of being confined to coastal enclaves.

The company used two strategies to enforce peace: 1) imperial governance (direct governance); 2) installation of resident advisors for feudal rulers (indirect governance). Imperial governance was by a central government that resembled European central governments. It had salaried civil servants and an appointed governor who served on good behavior. More importantly, money taxes were collected by civil servants and deposited directly into treasuries. The primary use of tax revenues was to build infrastructure facilities that encouraged commerce, including paying professional soldiers to defend frontiers and professional policemen to maintain civil order.

Indirect governance allowed feudal rulers to retain jurisdiction over customary law that affected religious customs (Hindu Caste System), rural land tenure, cultivation practices, and village governance. Resident advisors had jurisdiction in all military and commercial matters, and some aspects of criminal justice. If feudal rulers did not follow the advice of resident advisors, they were deposed.

After the establishment of imperial peace in Bengal, indigenous merchants became junior partners of English merchants who monopolized exports. The reciprocal was that English merchants became junior partners of indigenous merchants who conducted most of the interior trade. They assembled a high percentage of the food grains, cotton textiles, and other commodities that were exported to Europe and Asian destinations. They also supplied the food grains that fed Calcutta and peripheral villages of weavers.

In principalities that had a resident advisor, he was usually a large private trader who was also a company employee; and if a small contingent of company troops was quartered near the rajah's palace, officers often devoted most of their energies to trade. These company officials were the funnel through which an increasing volume of commodities reached Calcutta for export. Resident advisors and military officers used the power of their offices to exempt themselves from the rajah's internal taxation, and this exemption was frequently transferred to Indian merchants in return for a gift.

Between 1767 and 1772 Bengal was put in good order; however, contending rajahs in the principalities surrounding Madras were ravaging the countryside. Commerce suffered. In 1772 Warren Hastings was appointed governor of Bengal, but his first order of business was to protect the borders of the Madras enclave. The fiscal resources of Bengal were insufficient. He requested a loan of one million pounds sterling from parliament. The loan was granted but it was accompanied by the Regulating Act of 1773 that established the supremacy of parliament in company affairs. After 1773, the British government was, in many ways, a resident advisor to the company in the same way that the company forced resident advisors on Indian rajahs in order to enforce compliance to its commercial policies.

The same act appointed Hastings as governor-general with authority over the councils of Bengal, Madras, and Bombay. Hastings's authority over the councils of Madras and Bombay was difficult to enforce because circumstances required his presence in Bengal. The Regulating Act of 1773 did, however, centralize commercial, political, and military policies in India but it was up to Hastings to make it operational. In Bengal Hastings ended the fiction of indirect rule by creating a civil service that implemented direct governance. He did this in spite of great opposition by the Bengal council. Hastings believed that an honest and efficient government was the fundamental responsibility of imperial governance, as well as being necessary for the continued presence of the company in India.

At the same time he was enforcing reforms in Bengal, he had to deal with protracted warfare in the south. By 1784, warfare in the south was reduced but the principalities bordering Madras were not completely pacified. He resigned in 1785 and returned to England. Hastings's accomplishments were substantial. He built an institutional framework that made it possible to transform company governance into imperial governance.

A parliamentary statute in 1784 facilitated the transformation. Although it strengthened the power of the board of control to make commercial and political policies, the governor-general was granted autocratic power to overrule the board of control as well as the governors of Bengal, Madras, and Bombay if it was necessary to protect the company's interest. This authorization was a license for future governor-generals to expand imperial governance as opportunities occurred. The expansion that occurred in the next 20 years was often indistinguishable from personal ambition.

By 1786, a high percentage of the production of export commodities in the principalities bordering Bengal was in the hands of private British merchants, resident advisors and their Indian partners, and military officers and their Indian partners. During the period of geographic expansion after Plassey (1757), and the appointment of Charles Cornwallis as governor-general of India and commander-in-chief of Bengal in 1786, the company gradually changed its focus from earning commercial profits to tax collection. Bengal was the model for the extension of imperial governance in India because the increased commerce that resulted from peace was the essential condition for increased tax revenues.

Cornwallis was a nominal servant of the company but in fact he conducted wars that were approved by the British government because he commanded six regiments of the king's infantry and one of cavalry, plus the company's troops. In past wars the king's troops had fought as the auxiliaries of company troops. Under Cornwallis the roles were reversed. Michael Edwardes describes the transition. "So the Indian empire began. Unformed, casual, but hardly accidental, it was constructed with mixed motives and powered by personal and commercial profit." [15]

Cornwallis's administration was the beginning of effective imperial governance.

After 1786 the Governor Generals were usually men with British military and political experience but no previous knowledge of India. . . . [They] were completely beyond the reach of Indian aspirants for influence. By contemporary standards the service they headed was a highly professional administrative corps, whose generous salaries attracted well-educated young men of high social standing. Although Indian agency at lower levels was still essential for the running of the government, the ethos of the higher ranks of the service had become firmly British. [16]

Cornwallis decisively suppressed corruption by company employees but in return for bureaucratic honesty, salaries were increased. Persons entrusted with governance were preferentially British expatriates, especially in the revenue department. They came directly from Britain with no previous exposure to the corrupting influences of Indian feudal governance. The task of new senior administrators was to make the government of Bengal honest and efficient in fiscal affairs and, in the process, raise sufficient revenues to expedite commercial expansion elsewhere in India. The increased honesty and efficiency of the Bengal government, coupled with secure borders and internal peace, was a strong incentive to invest in new buildings.

A sensitive indicator of the security of commercial wealth was the availability of institutional credit. After 1786, the two banks in Calcutta (Bank of Calcutta, Bank of Bengal) began large scale lending for building construction, but they also lent to Indian and private British merchants who conducted an increasing volume of trade in cotton textiles. Other sources of commercial growth were increased production of saltpeter, indigo, opium, and raw cotton. Much of the raw cotton went to weaving villages near Calcutta but increasing amounts went to China, that was also the destination of most of the opium.

Indigo was produced in interior districts. It replaced the indigo that Britain formerly imported from several west indian islands and the southern colonies of North America before the war of independence. American production of indigo had been subsidized, and the subsidy ended after independence. So did production. Indian production was not subsidized and it was of higher quality because it was produced by free labor instead of the slave labor used in America.

Cornwallis also inherited a simmering war in the principalities bordering Madras, which became threatening after England and France resumed warfare (Napoleonic wars). Rajahs hired French officers to train their troops to use muskets and artillery in the same disciplined way they were used by European armies. When Cornwallis returned to England in 1795, the principalities of central India were actively contesting British hegemony in commerce, not only those bordering Madras but also where British advisors to feudal rulers were weakly established.

In this situation, the governor-general could interpret defense of the company's interest as requiring armed intervention in bordering principalities. This was an opportunity for ambitious governors to take what actions were necessary to protect company commerce. Company directors were not happy with hostilities but they accepted the governor-general's decisions as long as warfare did not seriously reduce profits.

Richard and Arthur Wellesley were sent out in 1798 to impose peace. Richard was to govern and Arthur was to conduct military operations. Arthur Wellesley was hugely successful in judging the opportunities where the armed forces at his disposal could be used to maximum effect. He not only imposed peace in districts surrounding company enclaves but, by 1804, had imposed peace on a large part of the rest of India by defeating all of the armies of the rajahs who contested imperial governance. When the Wellesley brothers returned to England, only Punjab had the political cohesion to contest further expansion of imperial governance.

Both the company's directors and the English government were flustered by the Wellesley brothers success. The company was not prepared to take advantage of the commercial opportunities that were in its grasp, and the English government was distracted because it was using most of its resources to defeat Napoleon in Europe. The military success of Arthur Wellesley in India was good reason to recall him in 1805 so that his skills could be used in Europe.

Richard Wellesley left behind a militarized civil administration because it was the only workable means of collecting taxes in insecurely held principalities. Its principal purpose was to raise sufficient revenue to pay the armed forces that had been used to expand the area of imperial governance, a policy that the company's managers in Bengal had consistently implemented after Plassey. Between 1761 and 1804 more than 40 percent of all tax revenues were used to keep an army in being.

Richard Wellesley's successor, Lord Minto (1807-1813), had two priorities: consolidation of imperial governance in insecurely held principalities and peaceful borders. A treaty with Punjab secured peace that lasted 30 years. The framework of government established by Minto was based on building a bureaucracy that was governed by laws, and levying taxes that were known in advance and honestly collected. This would be the model for governance in colonies that Britain acquired later in the nineteenth century.

The Indian merchant community strongly approved of imperial governance because it imposed peace, regularized taxation, and encouraged the expansion of commerce. It also established courts of law to enforce written contracts and protect the ownership of real property.

The transfer of English commercial law to India equally protected merchants in all ethnic communities, and allowed them to accumulate the working capital needed to expand commerce. It also encouraged indigenous merchants to invest in real property in cities because urban land was converted to freehold tenure. Contract law and legal protection of real property was the opportunity for Indian merchants to become rich; and for their children to inherit their wealth.

Ian B. Watson summarizes why Indian merchants favored the commercial policies of the East India Company and approved the transformation of company governance into imperial governance.

What was crucial was that the English offered the Hindus both a commercial and a socio-cultural alternative which was very evident in the identification of the Hindu bankers with the English. . . . What was to prove radical in the relationship was the assimilation within Indian commercial thought of the totality of the English commercial ethic, and notions toward the security under law of enterprise and property. [17]

British rule was secure enough by 1813 so that when the company's charter came up for renewal, it was stripped of its monopoly of trade between India and Britain, but it retained its monopoly of trade with China for an additional 20 years. After 1833, it ceased being a trading company.

In the 20 years after the end of the Napoleonic wars, imperial governance continued to expand as opportunities occurred, but there was no overall pattern. In principalities where imperial governance was firmly established, revolutionary economic changes occurred. One of the most important was the decline in the demand for hand woven cotton textiles for sale in Europe and the Indies. The export market collapsed because, after 1815, mechanically woven cloth using raw cotton from the United States was cheaper than Indian textiles and available in larger quantities.

As the company's commercial activities declined, indigenous merchants rapidly increased the scale and scope of their activities. By 1833, they were sufficiently influential so that the company reduced inland transit and export taxes and equalized import taxes on items carried in English and foreign owned ships. Indigenous merchants conducted almost all of the internal trade that resulted from imperial peace; and indigenous brokers assembled a high percentage of commodities for export.

Both indigenous and British merchants were avid for improved transportation into the interior. By 1850 a strong beginning had been made in building trunkline roads, railroads, and establishing steamboat transportation on rivers. Likewise, both indigenous and export commerce was encouraged by establishing modern commercial banks (banks of deposit) that lent to merchants on the basis of good character and a history of making deposits from previous business transactions. These banks also issued paper currency, a more flexible form of money than specie. By 1850 the company had evolved into an imperial government that managed an empire of commerce.

Three interest groups were the scaffold of imperial governance: 1) the army; 2) the Indian commercial community; 3) the bureaucracy. A minuscule number of British officials and businessmen staffed senior government positions and managed export commerce. In 1852 there were only 6,000 European males in India (exclusive of the military) and the company employed 2,000. The Indian commercial community was totally dependent on the honesty and efficiency of imperial governance for its prosperity. "There was, in fact, a profound identity of interests between the newly-emerging Indian middle classes and the British mercantile community, and this was to have political consequences."[18]

When the mutiny occurred (1857), the Indian commercial community strongly supported preservation of imperial governance because:

The revolt of 1857 originated in the reaction of a conservative, tradition-loving section of Indian society to the modernizing zeal of their British conquerors. As the British consolidated their power in India, they also seemed to be intent on reforming Indian society both morally and politically. In creating a rational and efficient administration, they threatened much of the traditional order. Princes and landowners, the principal representatives of that order, felt themselves under sentence of extinction.[19]

COLONIAL COMMERCE

Although the events that created the Indian empire were more dramatic, the principal source of increased long distance commerce in the eighteenth century was the North American and Caribbean colonies. The purpose for settling Caribbean islands and the North American mainland was to create an empire that was a source of raw materials and a captive market for products manufactured in England. This objective is different from the commerce conducted by the East India Company where the principal objective was the acquisition of high value products that could be highly taxed when they entered England. Items acquired in India were largely purchased with silver coins. In contrast, the raw materials imported from America were largely low value and purchased using bills of exchange (credit) supplied by London merchants and banks.

The American colonies (Caribbean and mainland) could not have been established without the willingness of the English government to go to war to protect them. The necessary naval protection was expensive; therefore, from the beginning, the English government mandated that all colonial trade must be with England or among English colonies, and be done in English or colonial owned ships. Exceptions were made for some colonial products like dried and salted fish and breadstuffs that England did not need. These commodities could be marketed outside of imperial commerce.

Manufactured products coming from England were the other side of colonial commerce. All of the charters and proprietary land grants that authorized settlements in America explicitly stated that raw materials from the colonies would pay import taxes when they entered England and that exports to the colonies would pay export taxes when they left England. Later legislation prohibited foreign ships from trading with the colonies, which had been difficult to enforce as long as the Dutch had a colony at New Amsterdam. This drain on tax revenues ended in 1664 with the capture of New Amsterdam and renaming it New York.

To acquire a clear understanding of English colonial policy, it is above all essential to know . . . . what compensating advantages it expected to derive from American possessions in return for the responsibilities it assumed in sanctioning the movement. To the extent that the colonization of America was an act of the English state, it was fundamentally an economic movement. [20]

In 1700, the North American market consisted of approximately 300,000 persons but by 1775, it was approximately 2.5 million. During these 75 years the value of North American and Caribbean commerce increased from 250,000 pounds sterling to 4 million. Trans-Atlantic trade was between one-sixth and one-third of all British maritime commerce. Navigation laws had habituated Americans to trade with England, but it was a habit that was mutually advantageous.

Colonial merchants had substantial advantages by participating in imperial commerce: 1) equality of English and colonial merchants in trans-Atlantic commerce; 2) access to credit from London merchants and banks; 3) protection of colonial merchant ships by the royal navy; 4) an assured market for colonial raw materials (although, the number of enumerated articles that could only be shipped to England was sometimes an irritant); 5) English manufactured products were cheaper and of better quality than manufactured products from other European nations; 6) English and North American merchants equally participated in carrying sugar from Caribbean islands to England; and bringing slaves from Africa to the Caribbean and North America; 7) a substantial market for North American foodstuffs developed on Caribbean islands where slave labor produced sugar; 8) an equally large market developed in England and the Caribbean islands for wood products, particularly barrel staves and headings; 9) bounties were paid for cultivating, processing, and exporting indigo and hemp, and for manufacturing and exporting bar iron; 10) tobacco imports into England from Spanish colonies were prohibited; 11) tobacco cultivation in England was suppressed for the benefit of colonial producers; 12) American fisherman had equal access with English fishermen to the fisheries off of Nova Scotia and Newfoundland; 13) a large measure of self-government allowed colonial legislatures to control land distribution in order to reward men who defended the frontiers, or to sell land in order to supplement tax revenues.

The availability of arable land also attracted many displaced peasants (coming as indentured servants) who immigrated to North

America to escape having to perform full-time paid labor. They came in search of subsistence opportunities because land on the frontier was abundant and cheap (or free if they performed military service). Colonial governors were anxious to increase the number of frontier settlers because they created a buffer zone to repel indian attacks.

British advantages were: 1) increasing revenues from taxing colonial imports; 2) cheap raw materials for artisan manufacturers; 3) an enlarged market for products manufactured by British artisans; 4) a reservoir of trained seamen who could be mobilized during war; 5) colonial shipwrights who built ships for sale to British merchants at highly competitive prices; 6) defending the land frontiers of continental colonies was the responsibilities of colonial governments, not the British treasury.

After the Glorious Revolution the governance of the American colonies evolved without a plan. The power of the British government was conspicuously present in wartime because army and naval units came and went with the vicissitudes of warfare in North America and the Caribbean. These units fought only European armies and navies. In peacetime they disappeared because the almost exclusive interest of parliament was trade between Britain and the colonies. As long as trade increased without interruption and without complaint, the English government did little to disturb the flow.

From the earliest settlements, the political economy of the north Atlantic commercial empire evolved into a federal empire. The British government conducted foreign affairs and defended the maritime frontier; and behind the naval shield colonial legislatures governed and taxed their citizens with few restraints by parliament. The Board of Trade disallowed colonial legislation only when it threatened the interests of British merchants. The board was particularly vigilant in disallowing colonial statutes that authorized the payment of debts to British merchants with inflated paper currencies that were intermittently issued by colonial governments.

The great cost of the Seven Years War (1756-1763) was an incentive for parliament to seek to transfer some of its cost to the American colonies. In 1765 parliament levied a stamp tax on many types of legal and commercial documents. Enumerated documents could not be admitted as evidence in courts without a stamp affixed to them. The colonial stamp tax was a variation of a similar tax that had been collected in England since 1694. It was not a large source of revenue but it was a steady source because it was difficult to avoid.

The North American colonies unanimously objected because it was a tax imposed within their borders. From the beginning of settlement colonial legislatures were responsible for all internal taxation and, more broadly, for all taxation on the American side of the Atlantic ocean. The Americans had no objection to paying taxes on American products when they entered Britain. They recognized that this revenue was essential for the defense of imperial trade and for other services provided by Britain.

If Americans lived in a federal empire, which is how trans-Atlantic commerce operated, then the stamp tax was a threat to the taxing power of colonial legislatures. By extension, it was also a threat to American political liberties because the power to tax is the foundation of the power to govern. The stamp tax could not be collected without the cooperation of Americans, and it was not collected. Two strategies forced its repeal. Violence forced the resignations of all persons who were appointed to collect it; and there was a serious decline in exports of manufactured products to the colonies. After its repeal, parliament did not concede the power to Americans to conduct all of their internal affairs. Instead, it passed the Declaratory Act (1766) that defined parliament's claim to imperial governance. The act categorically stated that parliament had the power to enact statutes that applied to the American colonies in all cases whatsoever. Parliament considered the trans-Atlantic commercial empire to be unitary with parliament exercising unrestrained power of taxation and governance whenever expedient.

Parliament immediately implemented its claim to imperial governance. In 1767 it passed the Townshend Revenue Act to supply a projected shortfall in revenue because the rent tax had been reduced in England. It taxed a small number of items when they entered the colonies. Walpole's repeal of most export taxes in 1721 meant that it was expedient to collect export taxes on the American side of the Atlantic. Again, the Americans objected because it was a tax that colonial legislatures had not levied. Opposition was so intense that American merchants lost control of the process of protest. Politicians were increasingly interpreting parliamentary intransigence to American commercial interests as justifying rebellion.

In all colonies the principal elected leaders encouraged the organization of committees of inspection (or riot) in port cities to prevent British manufactured products from being landed. Enforcement was highly effective. British exports to the mainland colonies declined from 2.1 million pounds sterling in 1768 to 1.3 million in 1769. In 1770, parliament repealed the Townshend taxes except on tea. It was retained and lowered, and the East India Company was authorized to ship tea directly to the American colonies.

As a result, the inventories of tea in the warehouses of American merchants lost much of their value and future profits from tea would be nonexistent because control of the tea trade was transferred to a monopoly corporation. Parliament's taxation policies in general, and its manipulation of tea taxation in particular, indicated to American merchants that their equality of participation in trans-Atlantic commerce was not being protected. In Boston (December 1773), waterfront workers supervised by their daytime foremen, took tea from the holds of three ships and dumped it into the harbor. The response of parliament was to close Boston harbor to commerce as of June 1, 1774 (Coercive Acts); and it would remain closed until the Massachusetts legislature compensated the East India Company for its loss. The Coercive Act strangled the commerce of Boston merchants.

American political leaders responded with the spontaneous assembly of the continental congress. It met in April 1774 for the purpose of seeking an accommodation with parliament on American terms. If parliament refused to recognize the federal structure of the trans-Atlantic empire and protect American commercial interests within it, then Americans would be forced to undertake full retaliatory action in order to preserve self-government. The continental congress urged Americans to cease purchasing British products, and in order to stop imports it authorized the organization of committees of enforcement in all port cities.

Parliament refused to repeal the Coercive Acts and, thereby, refused to recognize the federal structure of the trans-Atlantic empire of commerce. Instead, it acted on the assumption that responsibility for regulating trans-Atlantic commerce and promoting imperial prosperity belonged exclusively to parliament. A high percentage of American politicians, merchants, and colonial residents refused to concede this power to parliament because it was obvious to them that American commercial prosperity and self-government would not prosper under rules made in a legislature where Americans had no representation. Parliament would always favor policies that disproportionably benefited British merchants. When a satisfactory accommodation was not forthcoming, armed conflict began in April 1775 and did not end until the United States became independent in 1783.

NOTES

1. William C. Kennedy, *English Taxation, 1640-1799*, 25.
2. Stephen Dowell, *A History of Taxation and Taxes in England*, Vol. 2, 56.
3. Charles H. Wilson, *England's Apprenticeship*, 313-314.
4. John Brewer, *The Sinews of Power*, chapters 4, 5.
5. Donald G. Barnes, *A History of the English Corn Laws from 1660-1846*, 11.
6. John R. Plumb, *England in the Eighteenth Century*, 82.
7. Joan Simon, "Was There a Charity School Movement? The Leicestershire Evidence," in Brian Simon, ed. *Education in Leicestershire, 1540-1940*, 65.
8. Patricia C. Cohen, *A Calculating People: The Spread of Numeracy in Early America*, 26.
9. Mary G. Jones, *The Charity School Movement*, 46.
10. Carlo M. Cipolla, *Literacy and Development in the West*, 79, 86-90, 102, Appendix 1.
11. Charles H. Wilson, *England's Apprenticeship*, 361.
12. Lawrence A. Harper, *The English Navigation Laws*, 33.
13. Ralph Davis, "English Foreign Trade, 1700-1774," in Walter E. Minchinton, ed. *The Growth of English Overseas Trade in the Seventeenth and Eighteenth Centuries*, 108.
14. Ralph Davis, "English Foreign Trade, 1700-1774," in Walter E. Minchinton, ed. *The Growth of English Overseas Trade in the Seventeenth and Eighteenth Centuries*, 106.
15. Michael Edwardes, *British India, 1772-1947*, 25.
16. Peter J. Marshall, *Bengal: The British Bridgehead*, 101.
17. Ian B. Watson, *Foundation for Empire*, 276.
18. Michael Edwardes, *British India, 1772-1947*, 91.
19. Michael Edwardes, *British India, 1772-1947*, 149.
20. George L. Beer, *The Origins of the British Colonial System*, 25-26.

REFERENCES

Armytage, W.H.G. *Four Hundred Years of English Education*, Cambridge, Cambridge University Press, 1970 (chapters 3, 4)

Ball, J. N. *Merchants and Merchandise: The Expansion of Trade in Europe, 1500-1630*, New York, St Martins Press, 1977

Barnes, Donald G. *A History of the English Corn Laws from 1660-1846*, New York, Crofts, 1930 (preface, chapters 1, 2, 3)

Basye, Arthur H. *The Lords Commissioners of Trade and Plantations: Commonly Known as the Board of Trade, 1748-1782*, New Haven, Yale University Press, 1925

Beer, George L. *The Origins of the British Colonial System, 1578-1660*, Gloucester, Mass., Peter Smith, 1959 (reprint of 1908 edition)

Brewer, John. *The Sinews of Power: War, Money and the English State, 1688-1783*, New York, Knopf, 1989

Bridenbaugh, Carl. *Vexed and Troubled Englishmen, 1590-1642*, New York, Oxford University Press, 1968 (pp 315-326, 332-339)

Charlton, Kenneth. *Education in Renaissance England*, London, Routledge and Kegan Paul, 1965 (chapter 9)

Chartres, John, David Hey, eds. *English Rural Society, 1500-1800*, Cambridge, Cambridge University Press, 1990 (chapters 2, 3, 5, 14)

Cheong, Weng E. *The Hong Merchants of Canton: Chinese Merchants in Sino-Western Trade*, Richmond, Surrey, Curzon, 1997 (introduction, chapter 1)

Cipolla, Carlo M. *Literacy and Development in the West*, Baltimore, Penguin Books, 1969

Clough, Shepard B., Charles W. Cole. *Economic History of Europe*, Boston, Heath, 1952

Cohen, Patricia C. *A Calculating People: The Spread of Numeracy in Early America*, Chicago, University of Chicago Press, 1985

Cressy, David. *Education in Tudor and Stuart England*, New York, St Martins Press, 1976 (introduction)

Cressy, David. *Literacy and the Social Order: Reading and Writing in Tudor and Stuart England*, Cambridge, Cambridge University Press, 1980

Dickson, Peter G. M. *The Financial Revolution in England: A Study in the Development of Public Credit, 1688-1756*, London, Macmillan, 1967

Douglas, Roy. *Taxation in Britain Since 1660*, London, Macmillan, 1999 (chapters 1, 2, 3, 4)

Dowell, Stephen. *A History of Taxation and Taxes in England from the Earliest Times to the Year 1885* (2 volumes), London, Longmans Green, 1888 (vol. 1, chapter 1, part 2, sections 1, 2; chapter 2, parts 2, 3; chapter 3, part 2; vol. 2, books I, II)

Edwardes, Michael. *British India, 1772-1947: A Survey of the Nature and Effects of Alien Rule*, London, Sidgwick and Jackson, 1967 (part 1)

Edwardes, Michael. *Plassey: The Founding of an Empire*, London, Hamilton, 1969 (chapter 13, 17, 18)

Fisher, Michael H. *Indirect Rule in India: Residents and the Residency System, 1764-1858*, Delhi, Oxford University Press, 1991

Furber, Holden. *Rival Empires of Trade in the Orient, 1600-1800*, Minneapolis, University of Minnesota Press, 1976

Galenson, David W. *White Servitude in Colonial America: An Economic Analysis*, Cambridge, Cambridge University Press, 1981 (chapters 1, 2, 3, 4, 5)

Gomes, Leonard. *Foreign Trade and the National Economy: Mercantilist and Classical Perspectives*, New York, St Martins Press, 1987 (chapters 1, 2)

Gras, Norman S. B. *The Evolution of the English Corn Market: From the Twelfth to the Eighteenth Century*, Cambridge, Harvard University Press, 1915 (chapter 5, section 2; chapter 8, sections 7, 8)

Greene, Jack P., ed. *Great Britain and the American Colonies, 1606-1763*, New York, Harper and Row, 1970

Harper, Lawrence A. *The English Navigation Laws: A Seventeenth-Century Experiment in Social Engineering*, New York, Columbia University Press, 1939 (chapters 3, 4, 5, 19)

Houston, Robert A. *Literacy in Early Modern Europe: Culture and Education, 1500-1800*, London, Longman, 1998

Jack, Sybil M. *Trade and Industry in Tudor and Stuart England*, London, Allen and Unwin, 1977

John, Arthur H. "English Agricultural Improvement and Grain Exports, 1660-1765," in Donald C. Coleman, Arthur H. John, eds. *Trade, Government, and Economy in Pre-Industrial England*, London, Weidenfeld and Nicholson, 1976

Jones, Eric L., ed. *Agriculture and Economic Growth in England, 1650-1815*, London, Methuen, 1967 (chapters 2, 6)

Jones, Mary G. *The Charity School Movement: A Study of Eighteenth Century Puritanism in Action*, Hamden, Conn., Archon Books, 1964 (chapters 1, 2, 3), (reprint of 1938 edition)

Kennedy, William C. *English Taxation, 1640-1799: An Essay on Policy and Opinion*, London, Bell, 1913 (chapters 2, 3)

Kerridge, Eric. *Agrarian Problems in the Sixteenth Century and After*, London, Allen and Unwin, 1969

Kranzberg, Melvin, Carroll W. Pursell, eds. *Technology in Western Civilization: The Emergence of Modern Industrial Society, Earliest Times to 1900*, New York, Oxford University Press, 1967 (chapters 7-17)

Lawson, John. *Medieval Education and the Reformation*, London, Routledge and Kegan Paul, 1967

Lewis, Oscar. *Five Families: Mexican Case Studies in the Culture of Poverty*, New York, Wiley, 1962 (Gutierrez Family)

Marshall, Peter J. *Bengal: The British Bridgehead: Eastern India, 1740-1828*, Cambridge, Cambridge University Press, 1988 (chapters 3, 4)

Marshall, Peter J. *Trade and Conquest: Studies on the Rise of British Dominance in India*, Aldershot, Variorum 1993

Minchinton, Walter E., ed. *The Growth of English Overseas Trade in the Seventeenth and Eighteenth Centuries*, London, Methuen, 1969

More, Thomas. *Utopia*, Harmondsworth, Penguin Books, 1965 (pp 46-47)

Newton, A. P. "The Establishment of the Great Farm of the English Customs," *Transactions of the Royal Historical Society, Fourth Series*, Vol. 1, 1918

Parker, Irene. *Dissenting Academies in England: Their Rise and Progress and Their Place Among the Educational Systems of the Country*, New York, Octagon Books, 1969 (reprint of 1914 edition)

Parry, John H. *The Establishment of the European Hegemony: 1415-1715*, New York, Harper Torchbooks, 1961 (reprint of 1949 edition) (chapters 7, 8, 9, 10)

Plumb, John H. *England in the Eighteenth Century*, Baltimore, Penguin Books, 1965 (reprint of 1950 edition)

Plumb, John H. *The Growth of Political Stability in England, 1675-1725*, Baltimore, Penguin Books, 1969

Price, Jacob M. "Transaction Costs: A Note on the Merchant Credit and Organization of Private Trade," in James D. Tracy, ed. *The Political Economy of Merchant Empires*, Cambridge, Cambridge University Press, 1991

Price, Jacob M. "The Imperial Economy, 1700-1776," in Peter J. Marshall, ed. *Oxford History of the British Empire: The Eighteenth Century*, Vol. 2, Oxford, Oxford University Press, 1998

Seavoy, Ronald E. *Famine in Peasant Societies*, Westport, Greenwood Press, 1986 (chapters 1, 2)

Seavoy, Ronald E. *The American Peasantry: Southern Agricultural Labor and Its Legacy, 1850-1995, A Study in Political Economy*, Westport, Greenwood Press, 1998 (chapters 7, 12)

Seavoy, Ronald E. *Subsistence and Economic Development*, Westport, Praeger, 2000 (chapters 1, 2, 3, 6)

Simon, Brian, ed. *Education in Leicestershire, 1540-1940: A Regional Study*, Leicester, Leicester University Press, 1968 (chapters 1, 2, 3)

Simon, Joan. *Education and Society in Tudor England*, Cambridge, Cambridge University Press, 1966 (chapter 15)

Stone, Lawrence. "The Educational Revolution in England, 1560-1640," *Past and Present*, No. 28, 1964

Thirsk, Joan. *The Rural Economy of England*, London, Hambledon Press, 1984 (chapters 6, 9, 11, 12, 19)

Watson, Foster. *The English Grammar Schools to 1660: Their Curriculum and Practice*, Cambridge, Cambridge University Press, 1908 (chapters 8, 9, 10, 11)

Watson, Ian B. *Foundation for Empire: English Private Trade in India, 1659-1760*, New Delhi, Vikas Publishing, 1980

Wilson, Charles H. *England's Apprenticeship, 1603-1763*, New York, St Martins Press, 1965

3

INDUSTRIALIZATION AND IMPERIALISM

IMPERIAL IMPULSE

There is a revolutionary difference between nineteenth century imperialism and the imperialism of the preceding three centuries. Nineteenth century imperialism was impelled by the technological power that was available to industrial nations and the vacuum of power that existed in all subsistence cultures. In the second half of the nineteenth century imperial governance could be imposed on all subsistence cultures worldwide if industrial nations were willing to expend the money. Most of the nations with an ability to impose imperial governance were in western Europe. Industrialization had produced unimaginable amounts of new wealth in Britain, and this wealth was easily converted into political power by Britain and other industrial nations that had efficient central governments. New colonies would be sources of desirable raw materials and markets for a limited variety of manufactured products, as well as being visible artifacts of national wealth and power.

The industrial revolution in England had three roots: 1) the chartering of many monopoly corporations by queen Elizabeth in the late sixteenth century to trade into distant regions; 2) the assured food surplus from commercial agriculture (after the second half of the seventeenth century) that fed increasing numbers of artisan manufacturers; 3) the application of steam power to manufacturing and transportation after 1780 when the Bolton and Watt high pressure steam engine became operational and was adapted to producing rotary motion. After the end of the Napoleonic wars (1815) industrialization visibly accelerated when steam engines were applied to power machinery used in textile production, iron smelting, iron fabrication, coal mining, railroad transportation, and ship propulsion.

In the 99 years after 1815, all of the nations of western Europe struggled to catch up to Britain by applying British inventions and technologies and by greatly increasing educational budgets to teach functional literacy so that workers could learn new skills. As soon as sufficient revenues were available, the central governments of western European nations organized primary school systems funded by tax revenues that required compulsory attendance to the age of 12 or 13 years. By 1850, several continental nations had equaled England's rate of functional literacy of about two-thirds of adult males.

The rate of functional literacy in England had stagnated for 100 years, so that by 1850 continental nations had a reservoir of functionally literate males needed for commercial and industrial employment. This reservoir of literacy helped initiate and sustain the industrialization of continental European nations in the same way it had sustained industrialization in England. By 1880, several nations of western Europe had, to a greater or lesser extent, commercialized agriculture and built industrial bases comparable to England's. Like England they had the capability of projecting their political and commercial ambitions beyond their European borders. This projection was either within existing spheres of influence (Britain in India, the Netherlands in Indonesia), or within new spheres of influence created by their ability to overwhelm feudal and tribal governments anywhere in the world.

IMPERIAL ACQUISITION

During the nineteenth century imperial governance, protectorates, and treaties intruded global commerce into all of the world's subsistence cultures. Governing elites in subsistence cultures were powerless to reject participation. If they resisted the penalty was extinction. The indigenous governing elites that survived empire building participated in global commerce on terms offered by imperial nations. This was the only response that would avoid the imposition of imperial governance.

After industrial nations established imperial governance, seven policies guided commercial relations with colonies. These policies were not always applied with equal vigor in all colonies at all times, but they explain some of the principal reasons for acquiring colonies, as well as explaining how governors hoped to make colonies economically self-supporting. The seven policies were: 1) imports into colonies had to come from the mother country and, generally, had to be produced there; 2) commodities exported from colonies had to go to the mother country; 3) the mother country used tariffs to give preference to colonial commodities in domestic markets; 4) ships transporting commodities to and from colonies had to be owned and operated by domestic corporations; 5) colonies were forbidden to produce manufactured items that might compete with products manufactured in the mother country; 6) only citizens of the mother country were permitted to conduct export businesses in colonies; 7) trade was often, but not always, in the hands of monopoly corporations. [1]

By 1914, almost all of the subsistence cultures in the world were governed by industrial nations. Europeans had settled on or annexed 84 percent of the land area of the earth. Only Iran, Afghanistan, Ethiopia, Thailand, China, Tibet, and the Ottoman empire avoided annexation. The industrialized nations of Europe recognized that the Ottoman empire was in its death throes because its feudal government had not initiated policies to induce industrialization. It survived because European nations could not agree on how to divide its dependencies after it was dismembered. China was in a similar situation. It survived because it was too big to be incorporated into the commercial empire of a single industrialized nation. Instead, several industrial nations established coastal enclaves to capture interior trade, as the British had done in India during the eighteenth century.

After colonies were acquired the principal purpose of imperial governance was to extend commerce into interior peasant villages. The most important accompaniment of commercial intrusion was a rapid increase in the number of monetized exchanges. Three less visible practices accompanied monetization: 1) increasing amounts of commodities were produced for sale in anonymous markets; 2) large amounts of paid labor were mobilized to initiate and sustain the production of export commodities; 3) paid laborers, whether voluntary or corvee, were induced or forced to perform commercial labor norms, usually to build infrastructure projects. One of the essential skills of colonial governors was the ability to co-opt indigenous merchants or attract commercially motivated immigrants to be village storekeepers or traveling merchants in the interior. These persons were the agents of global commerce. They were the essential link between illiterate peasants who produced exchange commodities that were sold (for money of account) so they could purchase manufactured products made in factories in the mother country.

Monetized markets were acceptable to peasants in newly acquired colonies because there were favorable terms of trade for commodities peasants could produce and the manufactured items peasants desired to acquire. Colonial governors often introduced the cultivation of exchange commodity crops because there was a market for them in European nations, or because the merchants of European nations were equipped to distribute them in the global market. Some of the exchange commodities introduced for peasant cultivation were peanuts in French west Africa; cocoa in English west Africa; tea and coffee in Kenya; coffee and cotton in Uganda; sisal and coffee in Tanzania; sugarcane in Natal province, South Africa; tea, coffee, and rubber in Ceylon; rubber and oil palms in Malaysia; and coffee, tea, tobacco, and rubber in Indonesia. Peasants grew these commodity crops on plots of land near their dwellings or they were grown on plantations (agricultural factories) owned and managed by Europeans who used paid peasant laborers to perform commercial labor norms to cultivate and harvest them.

If the indigenous governments of newly acquired colonies were feudal or tribal, advisors were appointed to guide their conduct. Resident advisors exercised broad powers to end internecine warfare, maintain civil order, and expand commerce. Garrisons of indigenous troops with European officers usually supported them. No indigenous populations in subsistence cultures were granted self-government; although, colonial governors and resident advisors usually had a group of local notables who they consulted.

I omit discussion of Australia, Canada, New Zealand, and South Africa. From their inception, the British government conceded varying degrees of self-government to these colonies because European settlers carried commercial social values and the supporting political and commercial institutions with them. European settlers were acutely aware that maximized commerce was essential for their survival and prosperity. Likewise, this chapter omits discussion of the Spanish colonies in the Americas where European settlers secured self-government by wars of independence. These semi-subsistence nations could not be annexed to the empires of industrialized European nations without costly and protracted military campaigns.

The overwhelming superiority of western European nations in the technologies of armaments, transportation, communication, finance, and disciplined armies made the conquest of most subsistence cultures easy and cheap. Conquest was so cheap that there was minimal opposition to imperial expansion from domestic electorates or other interest groups in western European nations. Colonies were cheaply acquired because spheres of influence were defined in Europe by agreements among the political leaders of industrial nations. There were no armed conflicts between European nations in the competition to acquire colonies in subsistence cultures.

Otto von Bismarck, chancellor of Germany, organized the West African Conference in 1884 in order to elevate Germany from a minor colonizing nation into a competitor with England and France for annexing territory in subsistence cultures. Bismarck recognized that there was a power vacuum in most of sub-Saharan Africa and in other remote places, and that Germany could acquire colonies there. Above all, acquisition had to be without conflict. This meant that territorial acquisitions were excluded from places where a European nation already had consuls. Almost always, this was in coastal enclaves where a European nation exercised some form of local governance to protect the commerce of its merchants.

The immediate effects of the conference were small. England, France, and Portugal recognized Germany's claim to establish imperial governance in the Namibian desert (Angra Pequena), Togoland, Cameroon, Tanganyika, Zanzibar, and part of the north coast of the island of New Guinea (north of Australia), where German trading corporations had a tenuous presence. Its longer term effect was to precipitate a scramble to annex African territory from the coast inward by establishing sufficiently strong colonial governments to end the endemic tribal and feudal warfare that hindered or prevented the expansion of commerce into the interior.

Who benefited from colonial acquisition? The principal beneficiaries were trading companies established in coastal enclaves. Frequently, they were converted into chartered monopolies and granted the power to govern a specific territory in order to protect their interests (and a national interest). [2] Business interests were supplemented by Christian missionaries, anti-slavery crusaders, mineral prospectors (especially for gold), geographic explorationists, and commanders of punitive military expeditions into the interior. All of them had an interest in pacifying the interior and all of them had sympathetic friends in policy making positions in the central governments of European nations. All of these persons recognized that industrialization had created a power vacuum that was waiting to be filled by energetic men who were supported by the resources of European central governments. These persons were at the leading edge of the expansion of European commerce and their initiatives could induce vacillating governments to ratify local initiatives of pacification (and the cost of imperial governance) as long as costs were minimal.

A byproduct of imperial governance in sub-Saharan Africa was ending slavery because one of the principal purposes of feudal warfare was to capture slaves in order to transfer agricultural labor from warrior households to slave households. Emancipation could not proceed until internecine warfare ended and imperial governance was established. Michael Crowder cites an estimate made in 1905 by a senior French administrator that there were two million slaves in French west Africa who had been captured by warfare or who were slaves by birth.[3] Only after 1905 was imperial governance strong enough to begin to enforce emancipation; and it was done district by district in order to prevent a precipitous decline in food production. Emancipation was enforced by district police detachments that prevented owners from pursuing slaves when they walked away from their fields.

Emancipation was essential for increasing the production of exchange commodities. Unmotivated slave labor would produce minimum amounts of exchange commodities because all of the benefits went to feudal slaveowners. Many emancipated slaves were settled on vacant land near the headquarters of district officers. There, they could be induced to produce exchange commodities because they would enjoy all of the benefits of the products they produced and sold. They were also reservoirs of laborers who could be mobilized and paid to build infrastructure projects, like trunkline roads or railroad rights-of-way.

Between 1865 and 1900, three additional empire building nations emerged because their central governments had maximized the mobilization of national resources to build industrial bases. They were Russia, Japan, and the United States. The empires they acquired were in regions that were less accessible to western European nations.

Russian imperial expansion was concentrated along its southern border. There were three cogent reasons for imperial expansion: 1) lack of natural borders; 2) unstable Muslim sultanates engaged in predatory warfare to capture peasants to enslave them; 3) the necessity for increasing north-south trade to pay for the construction and operation of railroads that were necessary to sustain conquests and retain possession of annexed territories. At the earliest stage of industrialization (1800-1865) Russia annexed the feudal kingdoms and principalities in the Caucasus, plus a huge expanse of steppe east of the Caspian sea that was thinly populated by a heterogeneous collection of nomadic herdsmen. Between 1865 and 1895 Russia annexed the feudal principalities of Bokara, Khiva, and Kokand along its southern border. These annexations were possible because the central government of Russia had vigorously implemented a policy of industrialization.

Japan was the second nation with a large enough industrial base to acquire a colonial empire. It annexed Taiwan (from China) in 1895 and in 1904 imposed a protectorate over Korea (ahead of the Russians), and then annexed Korea in 1910. The United States annexed Hawaii, the Philippines, Puerto Rico and the Panama Canal Zone, in order to extend U.S. commercial reach in the Pacific; and firmly establish the primacy of American commerce in the Caribbean and Central America.

Until about 1900 the new colonial empires created by industrialized nations in Europe were mostly colored areas on maps. In Africa and elsewhere they were mostly products of "precautionary annexations to preserve commercial opportunities."[4] They did not become commercial assets until tribal or feudal warfare was suppressed, monetized taxation was imposed on the peasantry, a serviceable transportation network was built into the interior, and peasants were induced to increase the production of exchange commodities for sale in export markets.

As soon as possible after acquisition, colonies had to produce taxable exports and become markets for taxable imports in order to generate sufficient revenue so that colonial governments were self-supporting. Thereafter, enough additional revenue had to be collected to build transportation and other infrastructure projects. Exports were essential for making colonies self-supporting, and not be financial drains upon the treasuries of imperial nations. The electorates of industrialized nations would not tolerate excessive financial deficits for the benefit of remote and primitive people.

By 1910, almost all of the British colonies acquired since 1880 were self-supporting. This was an extraordinary accomplishment for colonies in sub-Saharan Africa and southeast Asia where 30 years previously infrastructure facilities were hugely deficient to non-existent. It was doubly extraordinary because the revolutionary social changes that impacted these cultures were initiated and maintained by a minuscule number of resident Europeans. The resident Europeans were civil governors, small garrisons of European soldiers (supplemented by indigenous soldiers and policemen), missionaries, and businessmen. Annual revenues in most colonies were small but, by 1910, they all had treasuries that could allocate funds to create bureaucracies and build infrastructure projects. Funds were available because colonial governance was, in all cases, as cheap as possible in terms of the salaries of civil governors and the garrisons that were necessary to maintain internal peace. [5]

ESTABLISHING IMPERIAL GOVERNANCE

This section focuses on English and French expansion in west Africa. From the beginning of inland penetration, policy makers in Europe and colonial governors realized that seven policies were necessary for success: 1) pacification; 2) some sort of accommodation with the indigenous political and social order; 3) increased production of export commodities; 4) coopting indigenous merchants or inviting strangers to become local agents of imperial commerce; 5) monetized taxation sufficient to put governance on a self-supporting basis; 6) written laws and predictable taxation administered by impersonal bureaucracies; 7) constructing commercial infrastructure projects that indicated an intention to stay.

All imperial governors in Africa (and elsewhere) had to perform these functions and all of them used similar strategies to create central governments and accelerate the intrusion of imperial commerce into the fabric of the subsistence cultures they governed. In the short term, imperial governance destroyed several subsistence institutions (slavery being the most obvious), and in the long term it profoundly modified all the others; however, in the whole period of imperial rule it had minimal impact on subsistence agriculture—the foundation of subsistence cultures.

All European participants in the expansion of imperial commerce in west Africa (governors, district officers, military commanders, merchants) had a vision of the future that gave unity of purpose to their activities, even when their conduct was flawed. They had confidence that they were part of a process of creating a peaceful society where the governing and commercial skills they taught to indigenous persons would create peace and new wealth where none previously existed. The foundation for wealth creation would be honest bureaucrats, predictable government policies, investments in transportation and communication infrastructure projects, and greatly increased literacy.

Like Christian missionaries, colonial administrators at all levels were imbued with a belief that the duties they were performing were part of a civilizing mission; and with the technologies available to them they were helping to create a modern society from a primitive and frequently violent social order. They were fully aware that they were institutionalizing revolutionary social changes that had political, commercial, and religious dimensions; and they implemented this vision, often at considerable risk, even though most of them would derive no personal profit.

Pacification was the first and necessary action to increase commerce, but military expenditures could not be financially exhausting. When the scramble for sub-Saharan Africa began about 1880, penetration into the interior was launched from secure coastal enclaves where export commerce was firmly established. Many of these enclaves had existed for several hundred years where slaves were assembled for shipment to trans-Atlantic destinations. After 1820 these enclaves attracted Christian missionaries and when imperial expansion began after 1860, they became the staging areas for Christian missionary activity into the interior. Missionary activity proceeded, more or less in tandem with the expansion of imperial commerce and governance; and was justified by evangelical Christians as a civilizing mission to abolish slavery at its source.

The animist peoples. . . . were periodically raided by the sultans from the northeast. . . . Most of them were of foreign origin and supported themselves by slave raiding and subjugating by military means the indigenous peoples . . . whom they forced to collect ivory and rubber for the Europeans in exchange for firearms. . . . In these regions (northern Nigeria) approximately ten thousand people still disappeared annually, killed in raids, sold as slaves, or dying on their way to exile. At the end of the century, even though European penetration was still thin on the ground, nevertheless by the very fact of their presence local conditions were profoundly altered. [6]

Coastal enclaves were loosely governed by consuls who were appointed by European governments to protect their merchants. The principal duty of these governments was to collect sufficient taxes to maintain a frontier police force capable of protecting commercial activity in enclaves and peripheral areas. When imperial penetration of the interior began, the coastal enclaves were unaffected. They had already experienced the principal effects of imperial commerce: 1) pacification; 2) monetization; 3) the influence of Christianity that promoted social change; 4) by teaching functional literacy; 5) that created opportunities for literate persons whatever their previous social status. Acceptance of imperial governance was often prepared by literacy taught by missionaries. Many newly literate persons recognized that imperial commerce could be the foundation of an improved social order that could bring large benefits to themselves and their culture.

The inland advance of imperial governance was mostly peaceful; although, politically correct historians emphasize the violence that was occasionally required, especially in the initial stages. The imposition of imperial peace was usually achieved by negotiating treaties of protection with feudal rulers or paramount chiefs who controlled small territories with dispersed populations. These rulers wanted protection from neighbors who made continual raids that kept the boundaries of tribal and feudal governments in constant flux. Warfare was usually nibbling. One or two villages would be assaulted and its inhabitants enslaved, or raiding parties would ambush single persons or small groups of persons and enslave them. Many rulers of these weak governments welcomed imperial protection because it promised to preserve their status as rulers without the risk of being killed or deposed after losing a battle.

The inland expansion of imperial governance was, in fact, a march upcountry. Almost all of the soldiers were Africans trained in the discipline and skills of European infantry. Most of the officers and technical support personnel, and many of the senior non-commissioned officers, were European. These units were stiffened by small units of European soldiers that operated light artillery and machine guns. The armies were small. Even in the largest arenas of activity, like Nigeria and Senegal, there were never more than 6,600 and no more than 3,000 were ever in the field at one time because of great difficulties in supply. Until roads were built and trucks could be used, tsetse flies prevented the use of packhorses or draft animals pulling wagons. Human porters supplied military units when they operated in the interior. At its best, human porters were a tenuous means of supply. The only reliable means of supply was steamboats operating on rivers. As opportunities presented themselves, small military units were used to intimidate rulers to sign protection treaties, or depose rulers who continued to make slave raids or levy transit taxes on merchants crossing their territories. The elimination of all transit taxes was fundamental for encouraging the extension of imperial commerce into the interior.

In the march upcountry there was no clear distinction between the army and police because the suppression of slave raiding was more a police action than warfare, but when warfare was required to depose rulers or stabilize territorial boundaries, the battles were small. Imperial armed forces were seldom defeated. It was not until about 1895 when pacification was complete that African soldiers were separated into police and army units. Infantry units were concentrated in cantonments, usually near port cities, where they could be moved as entire units to troubled areas and deployed as an overwhelming force. During the next 40 years, in large colonies like Nigeria, the infantry was never more than two regiments (6,000 men).

Police units were dispersed as small contingents in villages where district officers or resident advisors made their headquarters. Their principal function was to enforce the collection of taxes. In all subsistence cultures that were incorporated into nineteenth century commercial empires, it was easy to recruit volunteers for infantry or police service from tribes or religions that prided themselves on being warriors. Molding them into nonpolitical enforcers of peace was another matter. This could be a problem when their principal function was helping to enlarge the commercial sector. Most police and soldiers were illiterate but their principal duty was protecting the literate. The best way for them to understand their duties was to teach them literacy and then force them to use literacy in order to learn new skills like the necessity of sanitation, and how to build barracks, drive trucks, and fill out duty rosters. The police and army were highly effective organizations for training persons to use basic commercial skills.

Colonial governors were acutely aware that imperial governance depended on a police/military presence that was nonpolitical. The only way to keep it nonpolitical was sufficient tax revenues to pay them and provide housing and health services. This was the same formula that operated in India and kept the peace after 1857. Governors were equally aware that the military resources at their disposal were small. The small military presence in west African colonies accurately measures their skill in maintaining domestic peace and their ability to expand commercial activity by inducing peasants to produce export commodities.

After pacification, colonial governors had to devise a system of local government that was administered by indigenous persons. In many instances they had to create local governments by creating tribal chiefs (warrant chiefs) to rule a geographic area. Persons who were appointed chiefs did not necessarily have a high political status in the social order they governed. The principal criteria for appointment was a willingness to implement directives from district officers. Their most important duty was inducing monetization in order to collect money taxes.

In many places in west Africa, the coastal trade was monetized by the end of the eighteenth century but monetization was not introduced into many interior villages until the second decade of the twentieth century. Monetization allowed colonial governors to levy money taxes on polls (males 16 to 50 years of age), and on huts. The money peasants acquired to pay poll and hut taxes was frequently acquired by performing paid (corvee) labor building vehicle tracks into peasant villages. This was a principal way that access roads were built and was often the way of introducing monetization. Feudal rulers or tribal chiefs, acting on the advice of district officers, mobilized the necessary labor. Building roads into peasant villages was necessary because they were essential for marketing bulky exchange commodities. Without roads food could not be transported to cities for consumption nor commodities assembled in harbors for export.

District officers were junior appointees from the colonial office. They were usually well educated generalists (history, literature, military) who had little understanding of the subsistence social values that motivated both peasants and feudal rulers, and they had little respect for subsistence labor norms that was the cause of the privation that surrounded them. Whatever their feelings, however, their isolation in an alien culture made them vulnerable. In order to maintain their leadership they had to administer social and economic changes with caution because the police contingents at their disposal were small, and army units were distant from the districts they administered. The orders they gave to tribal chiefs and feudal rulers had to have a reasonable certainty of being obeyed, and they had to be given as authoritative directives rather than as peremptory commands.

The cooperation of indigenous rulers was essential for governance because they retained the power to administer customary law. Customary law applied only to indigenous people, but with several restraints. It could not be used to condone uncivilized conduct (tribal warfare, slavery, mutilation, torture), nor could it subvert colonial political authority, impede the expansion of monetized commerce, or block the construction of infrastructure projects. In these areas of potential conflict, European commercial law superceded customary law. The new jurisdiction of commercial law required colonial governments to establish courts and borrow sufficient written laws from the mother country to administer criminal justice, regularize the collection of money taxes, and enforce commercial contracts.

In west Africa and elsewhere, indirect rule was an expedient policy that was used to initiate the intrusion of imperial commerce into subsistence cultures. At the same time, it was a means of accommodating imperial governance to subsistence institutions. Colonial governors and district officers were forced to concede communal control of land use and labor expenditures to village councils because there was insufficient force to do otherwise.

The long-term cost of indirect rule was high because feudal and tribal rulers had a vested interest in preserving the subsistence social order and their places in it. The easiest way for them to preserve their authority was to preserve as much customary law as possible. They had little interest in actively accelerating commercial growth because bureaucrats would diminish their authority at every opportunity as the revenues of central governments increased; therefore, they had little desire to induce increased per capita production of export commodities. Even if district officers were inclined to push commercial development it had to be done by cajoling rather than by coercion; and most district officials were not inclined to push for increased production of export commodities any harder than colonial governors pushed them to increase tax revenues.

In all subsistence cultures, monetization is essential for increasing the volume and value of trade. Monetization is not commercialization but it introduces a standard measure of value. It enables adult peasants to calculate the terms of trade for the purpose of reducing labor expenditures. Peasants could compute how much labor was required to grow exchange commodity crops in order to acquire sufficient money to purchase manufactured items they desired.

The most desired items were textiles and edged steel tools of greater durability than handicraft items that required continual replacement. Money was acquired by producing exchange commodities (for export) or by performing paid labor in sufficient amounts to acquire target sums of money. After a target sum was acquired they ceased laboring. The acquisition of a limited number and variety of manufactured items allowed peasants to improve their subsistence welfare. Once a household's subsistence needs were satisfied, any increase in the production of exchange commodities was due to increased population rather than increased per capita production.

Monetization and the cultivation of exchange commodity crops did not disrupt the fundamental social value of peasants: subsistence food production by minimal expenditures of agricultural labor. Amounts of agricultural labor performed by adults remained the same because much of the labor for cultivating exchange commodity crops could be transferred to children. Transferring agricultural labor to women and children (or slaves) is the subsistence compromise that I defined in *Famine in Peasant Societies*.

The peasant concept of the good life is the minimum expenditure of physical labor. When applied to food production, peasants attempt to grow enough food to last until the next harvest with the minimum expenditure of labor, on the assumption that every year will be a normal crop year. This defines the subsistence compromise. [7]

The subsistence compromise assumes that a fixed amount of per capita labor per year will produce sufficient food to feed all village residents at an acceptable level of nutrition. Peasants know that all crop years are not normal but they willingly risk seasons of hunger in poor crop years and famine conditions in consecutive poor crop years in order to preserve subsistence labor norms. Any labor in excess of this fixed amount is unnecessary and indolence is the proper use for time after subsistence needs have been satisfied.

Colonial governors had to accommodate governance to this reality because they could not commercialize food production with the resources available to them. By default, they became protectors of subsistence institutions. From their perspective, accommodation with the subsistence social order was a policy that made the commercial sector an appendage of the subsistence sector unless commercial projects, like mines or plantations, were inserted into the subsistence social order.

In spite of hugely deficient revenues, and the weakness of imperial governance, all colonial governors sought to strengthen the power of central governments as soon as possible after pacification. Bureaucracies were the best institution to do this, but they are expensive and their growth was always constrained by small revenues. As bureaucracies slowly grew in size and efficiency, the authority of tribal chiefs and feudal rulers steadily declined because they were not allotted budgets (treasuries), and were denied the power to levy money taxes. Tax funds could not be entrusted to them because they were illiterate and had little understanding of impersonal bureaucratic administration, and no concept of accounting for expenditures. They were, however, usually paid salaries as the means of coopting their services.

By 1940, most tribal chiefs and feudal rulers had greatly reduced power. Experienced administrators, however, knew that their governing function had been preserved too long because they were the principal cause for the failure to increase per capita production of export commodities. Indirect rule, however, was retained beyond its usefulness because it was cheap and because it dampened the peasant unrest.

INSTITUTIONALIZING IMPERIAL GOVERNANCE

The previous section examined the process of establishing imperial governance. This section examines how imperial commerce and governance were institutionalized in the subsistence social order. Four institutions were required to increase commerce in nineteenth century empires: 1) central governments strong enough to enforce peace; 2) monetized taxation; 3) infrastructure facilities that were essential for encouraging the production of export commodity crops; 4) schools to teach functional literacy (often in a European language) so that new skills could be learned and applied by indigenous persons who became full time salaried employees in business and government.

Central Governments: The permanency and efficiency of imperial governance and the expansion of imperial commerce required bureaucratic institutions. The scope and effectiveness of imperial governance proceeded as fast as tax revenues could pay the salaries of bureaucratic personnel. Bureaucracies routinized impersonal government so that persons of merit could be recruited and promoted. A department of political affairs (native affairs) was usually one of the first to be established. Its function was to appoint warrent chiefs and other customary rulers, and supervise their performance. As imperial governance became firmly established, bureaucracies became the means of gradually reducing their authority.

As more revenues became available additional departments were formed to: 1) recruit and train a police force and an army; 2) supervise the building of railroads, trunkline roads, and port facilities, and manage their operation; 3) establish schools and manage their operation; 4) establish an agricultural service, usually to improve the cultivation of export crops; 5) attract banks to provide institutional credit; 6) establish hospitals and manage public health services; 7) establish a postal service.

Monetized Taxation: Monetization of the interior began with coins of small denominations. As effective imperial governance was established in the interior, monetized taxation and monetized commerce proceeded together. Paper currency was not generally acceptable in peasant villages until an access road had been built and there was a resident storekeeper or a traveling merchant who visited at regular intervals. Only after 1920 was paper currency acceptable in these villages because, previously, there were not enough people who could read printed numbers and have confidence that paper money could be used to purchase manufactured items and pay taxes.

The collection of money taxes was the first step in compelling peasants to increase per capita labor expenditures. In west Africa the monetization process often began with paid corvee labor to build trunkline roads. Subsequent payments of money taxes had to be enforced if households failed to acquire sufficient money by growing an exchange commodity crop or delegating a household member to migrate to where paid labor opportunities were available. Tax collection was done by village headmen and the money transferred to the district officer when he made an annual or semi-annual visit to each village in his district. If a household failed to pay its taxes, the police detachment that always accompanied him burned the huts of delinquent households. Peasants had to be taught that money taxation was permanent.

The second step was collecting money taxes in all crop years, even in the poorest crop years when hunger might be severe. Collecting money taxes in all crop years was essential for economic development because taxation was the source of a high percentage of funds used to build infrastructure projects, pay police, and pay bureaucrats. Collecting money taxes in poor crop years usually provoked resistance if a household's exchange commodity was a portion of their food crop. The most visible form of resistance was peasant rebellions.

Money taxation was also the entering wedge of literacy because any money in excess of sums needed to pay taxes could be used to purchase manufactured items from traveling merchants or village storekeepers. Illiterate peasants understood the use of literacy because traveling merchants and village storekeepers kept written records of the money that client households had available to purchase manufactured items. The use of money of account required literate merchants and storekeepers.

Infrastructure Construction: Increased bureaucratic governance was necessary before the newest technologies of the day could become operational. After about 1900 railroads were the principal technology available to accelerate inland penetration of imperial commerce and consolidate imperial governance. By the end of WWII (1945), in British west Africa (Nigeria, Ghana, Sierra Leone) there were 4,366 kilometers of trunkline railroads and 4,389 kilometers in French west Africa (Senegal, Ivory Coast, Guinea). A high percentage had been built before 1914. After WWI (1918), fewer railroads were built because roads were much cheaper to build and a much more flexible means of access to peasant villages.

Railroads required large capital investments to build and large numbers of literate persons to operate. The construction of railroads and port facilities required centralized governments to underwrite the capital costs. They also had to mobilize the labor necessary to build them as well as to train indigenous persons to operate and maintain them. All the capital to build railroads had to come from Europe and it was not usually forthcoming unless European governments guaranteed repayment of construction bonds. Guaranteeing repayment of bonds was required because most railroads built into the interior were built ahead of demand. Railroads built into the interior could never be sure that peasants would produce enough export commodities to pay construction and operating costs unless a large part of the traffic came from large commercial projects like mines or plantations. It was, therefore, strongly in the interests of colonial governors to induce or coerce peasants to produce much larger quantities of export commodities as soon as railroads or roads were operational.

Large amounts of credit were needed to purchase commodity crops when they were harvested and transported to the coast for export. Only banks could supply this credit. The creation and allocation of institutional credit was a largely invisible accompaniment to highly visible infrastructure projects like railroads, warehouses, and dock facilities. Most institutional credit was allocated to European businesses and colonial governments. Institutional credit, however, was the smallest portion of the credit needed to market commodity crops after subsistence cultures were incorporated into European commercial empires.

Most credit was supplied by village storekeepers or traveling merchants. During the course of a year, they extended it to households that planted commodity crops. It was subsistence credit; and it required no collateral because peasants had no collateral. The credit was in the form of money of account. In return for receiving manufactured items on credit, households had to sell their exchange commodities (an export crop or a portion of their food crop) for less than market value to the storekeeper who supplied manufactured items. The conjunction of monetized taxation, road building, and the availability of subsistence credit were strong inducements (mixed with compulsion) for peasant households to cultivate commodity crops in order to acquire desirable manufactured items and pay money taxes.

Literacy: "Literacy is the fundamental skill of commercial cultures." [8] But what type of literacy? Imperial governors, merchants, and Africans clearly recognized two types of literacy: functional and educational. During the whole era of colonial rule, both types of literacy were concentrated in cities or where imperial commerce and governance extended into the hinterland. Bureaucratic departments of government and businesses needed clerks. Clerks had to be functionally literate. Functional literacy is defined as persons "who can perform all activities for which literacy is required. Functional literacy enables persons to use reading, writing, and arithmetic calculations to perform labor that is for their benefit and that also contributes to their community's welfare." [9]

In the nineteenth century functional literacy was the literacy taught in rural schools in European nations and the United States. Schooling ended at the age of 13 or 14. In the United States it was called a common school education. Common schools taught literacy that was appropriate to rural and small town employment. Its purpose was to enable persons to perform the simple daily tasks necessary to earn incomes in a commercial culture. The functional literacy taught in Africa was highly concentrated in cities because peasant households practicing subsistence agriculture had minimal use for literacy.

Educational literacy is knowledge acquiring literacy. It was taught to the children of households that were permanent city residents who were in daily contact with the complexities of urban culture, monetized commerce, and government. Knowledge acquiring education was necessary to prepare students to attend secondary schools and universities where they could learn the skills needed to participate in national and global commerce and politics, and understand how they operated. Knowledge acquiring education was what the European governing elites brought with them when they came to west Africa to trade and govern.

Where did the literate persons come from who staffed the bureaucracies of central governments and businesses?

Before the scramble for Africa began (1880), functional literacy had a firm foundation in British coastal enclaves because British enclaves were older and more firmly established than the French. A relatively high incidence of urban literacy was directly related to export businesses. Indigenous merchants enthusiastically supported teaching functional literacy and used some of their wealth to support and extend it. Indigenous merchants who assembled commodities for export needed literate clerks. Indigenous teachers taught literacy and it was taught in english because this was the language of commerce.

Most teachers were Christian. Before evangelical Christianity entered British west Africa in substantial numbers (after 1860) there was already a close identification between Christianity, literacy, and commerce; and this relationship was of indigenous origin. When imperial expansion accelerated after 1880, this group welcomed imperial peace. By 1920, primary education for Africans was firmly established in coastal regions. Groups of primary schools were usually managed and partially funded by missionaries, but not always. There were many private primary schools of highly variable quality.

More often than not, children enrolled in these schools were the children of Christian converts. Functional literacy was a highly desirable skill for the children of ambitious families with a low social status. Literacy would make them employable as messengers, interpreters, foremen, police, and storekeepers. Literacy was an opportunity for upward mobility outside the status structure of the subsistence social order.

The existence of primary schools established by missionaries allowed British colonial governors to minimize funding of primary schools that taught functional literacy. Most of the funding was grants-in-aid to existing schools, provided they met minimum standards of competency. Many pupils in these schools were the children of indigenous merchants who were already literate. They wanted their children taught in schools with knowledge acquiring curriculums in order to qualify them for joining the European commercial and governing elites. They wanted curriculums that were comparable to those that had educated resident Europeans elites so that their children would be competitive candidates for secondary education.

In 1903 the French established a colonial education system. It was specifically designed to assist the political administration of their colonies by teaching functional literacy. Education was free for Africans who qualified and it was secular because a high percentage of the population was Muslim. The language of instruction was french because french was the only common language, and it was a language that prepared graduates to learn new skills, particularly technical skills.

As the colonial education system evolved, it excluded most Africans from city schools that had knowledge acquiring curriculums. Entry of Africans to these schools was restricted to the few who could be employed as assistant administrators in departments of the central government. Few slots were allocated to them.

By 1920, the few Africans with secondary education in both British and French colonies were highly critical of the restricted education opportunities that precluded entry into governing elites. The aspiration of educated Africans was to share the power exercised by the European governing elites. African merchants who lived in coastal cities were especially anxious for their children to attend schools with knowledge acquiring curriculums because they considered themselves to be adjunct members of the European commercial and governing elites.

Educated Africans, whatever their origins, wanted to end indirect rule and replace illiterate tribal chiefs and feudal rulers with educated Africans like themselves. They strongly supported bureaucratized central governments with more Africans being trained and appointed to offices that made them part of the governing elite. They also wanted greater opportunities to acquire university educations in Europe in order to replace many of the Europeans who were district officers and resident advisors.

Both British and French governors had strong doubts about the ability of Africans with secondary education or university training to manage economic development. They would have to enforce policies that induced peasants to increase the production of export crops, and this was not part of their experience or training. Nor did they have the cultural comprehension (political commitment) to maintain the operation of the physical infrastructure that was essential for increasing per capita production of commercial wealth.

They feared that the principal interest of educated Africans was enjoyment of the perquisites of governance instead of dealing with continual peasant resistance to paying money taxes, and the equally difficult job of mobilizing peasant labor to build infrastructure projects. Many senior colonial administrators believed that most educated African would use the political power of their offices to become rich rather than induce the production of new wealth.

This posed a serious dilemma for imperial policy makers during the 1930s. Many persons in the imperial infrastructure were coming to the conclusion that preserving indirect rule was incompatible with economic development because it was increasingly obvious that most indirect rulers were indifferent or hostile to economic development. Bureaucratizing more functions of the central government, with increased African participation in non-policy making positions, could accelerate economic development. This did not happen because of the drastic decline in commodity prices during the Great Depression (1931-1937) and the exigencies of World War II (1939-1945). These events froze the process of economic development and the social changes that accompany imperial commerce and governance.

WWII exposed the fragility of imperial governance. Educated Africans recognized its weakness and this made independence inevitable. With the return of peace (and the weakened economies of England and France), they could use the intellectual skills they learned in secondary schools and universities to mobilize discontent with alien rule. Neither Britain nor France had sufficient revenues to pay for using force to preserve imperial governance; and increasing numbers of Africans were willing to use violence to install an indigenous governing elite. The British colonial secretary, like his French counterpart, knew that decolonization would come sooner than later.

At the same time that British and French authorities promised independence, they realized they had to train new governing elites; therefore, they acceded to African desires for urban schools that had similar curriculums with urban schools in Britain and France. They rapidly increased budgets for secondary and university education. Enrollments in newly established African secondary schools and universities rapidly increased. The new secondary schools and universities were often affiliated with comparable secondary schools and universities in Britain and France. The purpose of affiliation was to transfer knowledge acquiring curriculums and insure that the grading of examinations was comparable to British and French secondary schools and universities. Africans who were leading independence movements insisted that diplomas or degrees earned by Africans were an accurate measure of intellectual competence. To a considerable extent, curriculum parity and testing equivalency was achieved by the mid-1960s for students who had qualified for admittance to secondary schools and universities.

The structure of post-colonial education was strongly elitist. Like their imperial predecessors, the diplomas and degrees earned in African schools were essential qualifications for membership in governing elites. But what kind of an elite? Would post-colonial governing elites use the coercive power of governance to induce per capita increases in commercial wealth? Or would they use the power of governance to preserve the subsistence statusquo and use funds that were formerly used to build and maintain infrastructure projects to enrich themselves? In 1960, this was an unknown factor when west African colonies became west African nations.

INTERPRETATIONS

Independence: Independence has three different usages by contemporary scholars who describe and analyze the dissolution of European commercial empires. They are: 1) apologize for the violent conduct of feudal principalities and tribal rulers before imperial governance imposed peace; 2) defend village autonomy that is essential for preserving subsistence agriculture; 3) describe the creation of post-colonial sovereign nations. Only the third usage is valid.

During the nineteenth century most districts in west Africa had low population densities because of endemic warfare. The authors of *The Making of Modern Africa: The Nineteenth Century* provide an excellent example of the first use of the word independence. They evaluate the impact of imperial governance on the tribes and feudal principalities that were engaged in continuous internecine warfare. It is negative. "The wars created the opportunity for British intervention. . . .While appearing to be bringing peace to the Yoruba people the British actually deprived them of their independence." [10] This statement is politically correct. It is anti-colonial. It also indicates a vacuum of critical analysis.

Independence is a weasel word. As used by the authors of *The Making of Modern Africa* it meant preserving indigenous forms of government whether tribal or feudal. During the nineteenth century, the independence of feudal principalities meant irresponsible power to wage war in order to expand borders and capture and enslave peasants so that warrior households could transfer all varieties of subsistence labor to them. The principal use of slaves was as agricultural laborers. Warriors performed minimal agricultural labor; therefore, warfare had a high social value and agricultural and other subsistence labor had a low social value. Slaves that were not needed to grow the food that fed warrior households were sold to merchants who took them to the coast where they were exchanged for guns and other products manufactured in Europe. Slaves were the principal export commodity of warrior households. As used by the authors of *The Making of Modern Africa*, independence apologizes for warfare that had a principal purpose of preserving societies based on slave labor that hugely limited the creation of commercial wealth.

Many other scholars, like the authors of *The Making of Modern Africa*, use the word independence to explicitly condemn the armed intrusion of imperial governance into subsistence cultures. They assume that the governing elites of feudal principalities wanted to participate in global commerce, but on their own terms. In fact, the principal interest of these rulers was preserving the subsistence statusquo and their status as governing elites. These scholars excuse the depopulating warfare, endemic hunger, and frequent brutality that were the results of slave raiding and other forms of internecine warfare because the rulers were indigenous; therefore, these principalities should have retained their independence.

The second misuse of independence is by scholars who analyze the economic performance of post-colonial nations. Most of them apologize for the failure of these governments to increase per capita food production and, thereby, alleviate endemic hunger. This failure is disguised by using the word independence to describe village autonomy. Village autonomy is assumed to be good; therefore, the positive word independence is used to describe it. These scholars, however, do not understand that autonomous (independent) peasant villages preserve subsistence labor norms, especially in food production. Nor do they understand that subsistence labor norms perpetuate seasonal hunger in poor crop years and famine conditions in consecutive poor crop years.

Autonomy allows village councils to enforce customary laws mandating subsistence land use and harvest sharing in poor crop years by prohibiting energetic households from converting their land to cultivating crops for sale on anonymous markets. The ethic of subsistence sharing dictates that food surpluses produced by energetic households cannot be sold for their benefit. Their surplus must be shared among hungry households in poor crop years. Village autonomy preserves subsistence labor norms and prevents energetic households from enjoying the fruits of their labor; therefore, energetic households do not produce assured food surpluses. Village autonomy (independence) is a principal restraint on economic development.

The correct use of independence is to describe the transition from colonies to independent nations that exercise sovereign power within their borders. Sovereignty was an unknown (and unknowable) concept to warrior/rulers of feudal principalities and tribal chiefs in Africa and elsewhere. Feudal principalities had fluid borders, were governed by elites who were ignorant of the rest of the world, had few restraints on their personal conduct, rejected the creation of new forms of commercial wealth they could not control, and lived in symbiosis with peasants (free or enslaved). There is a revolutionary difference between the conduct of warrior/rulers of feudal principalities and the powers that post-colonial nations exercise within their borders. The survival of post-colonial nations depends on stable borders and peaceful participation in global commerce, not by capturing and enslaving peasants to perform subsistence labor.

Yet, many of the scholars who examine the decolonization process during the 1950s and 1960s, and its 50 year aftermath, make no distinction in the use of the word independence. For these scholars, the continuous warfare of feudal principalities before the imposition of imperial governance, the autonomy of peasant villages that preserves subsistence privation, and the creation of sovereign nations by decolonization were positive events. The best way for them to convey to their readers a politically correct (anti-colonial) interpretation of the past is to use the positive word independence to summarize the perceived virtues of subsistence cultures.

If the analysis of these scholars is accurate, then both pre and post-colonial subsistence cultures and their supporting institutions were beneficial to all participants. This assumption ignores a huge amount of contrary evidence. Imperial governance introduced revolutionary social changes. The two most important were the imposition of peace and the creation of central governments that could enforce political unity and undertake economic development. These changes are the foundation of post-colonial nations. European commercial imperialism created the conditions for post-colonial nations to exist. It is extremely unlikely that India, Pakistan, Indonesia, Malaysia, Singapore, and all of the nations of sub-Saharan Africa could have come into existence without the unification imposed on subsistence cultures by the intrusion of European commercial imperialism.

If readers accept the obvious generalization, that most post-colonial nations would not exist without the political unification molded by European commercial imperialism, I think it is accurate to claim that European commercial imperialism was a positive event. If readers accept this assessment, the word independence should be restricted to describing the sovereignty of post-colonial nations. In the interests of accurate analysis, scholars should reject using independence to describe the predatory conduct of ephemeral feudal principalities. Internecine warfare is the correct term to describe the conduct of precolonial slave raiding feudalities. Nor is it accurate to use independence to describe the social organization of food and commodity production in autonomous peasant villages. Subsistence is the word that accurately describes why peasants produce limited amounts of food and commodities when land and labor is available to produce more.

Exploitation: Exploitation is another weasel word. A high percentage of scholars use it as a pejorative term to describe the economic impact of imperial commerce and imperial governance on subsistence cultures. This is a politically correct usage because it is anti-colonial. This use also indicates a vacuum of critical analysis. This is glaringly evident when historians, anthropologists, and economists apologize for the persistence of hunger in post-colonial nations when they assert that European commercial imperialism had a negative impact on subsistence cultures. "The colonial system, primarily through taxation, forced (peasants) to concentrate on export crops to the detriment of his subsistence crops."[11] According to Crowder, monetary taxation exploits peasants by forcing them to grow exchange commodity crops in order to acquire money to pay taxes. Put another way, the necessity of acquiring money forced peasants to reduce per capita cultivation of food crops in order to grow commodity crops that could be sold for money. The result was endemic hunger.

What is the evidence for asserting that money taxation was the principal cause of endemic hunger in the colonies of European nations? There is none. Endemic hunger was present in pre-colonial peasant societies, persisted during the colonial era, and continues to be the most important long-term problem of peasant nations in Africa and elsewhere. It persists after the governing elites of post-colonial governments abolished poll and hut taxes and ended all overt attempts to coerce increased production of export commodities.

What, then, is the connection between endemic hunger before, during, and after the intrusion of imperial commerce into subsistence cultures? There is one cause. It is subsistence labor norms embodied in the subsistence compromise. Peasants could grow both more food and commodity crops if they expended the labor but they reject performing commercial labor norms if they have a choice. Village autonomy gives them this choice because the community (communal tenure) controls land use. Increased production is possible in all peasant societies but only a minority of village households are receptive to expending the necessary labor to grow more food or commodity crops for sale on anonymous markets. The vast majority of village households vigorously support the subsistence compromise as long as village councils equalize the allocation of cultivation units and enforce harvest sharing in poor crop years.

Is money taxation of peasants exploitation? Emphatically not! It is wholly accurate to define money taxation of peasants as the essential policy for economic development. In peasant nations, where peasants are the highest percentage of the population, they must be taxed in order to accumulate capital required to build infrastructure projects because there are few other sources of revenue. Money taxation is the best way to induce peasants to expend more labor in order to grow commodity and food crops for sale in anonymous markets.

Victimization: Catherine Coquery-Vidrovitch describes sporadic peasant resistance (1895-1905) when French imperial governance was being established in west Africa. "Taxation was the cause of the most enduring resistance. Everywhere the people reacted against it by passive resistance or emigration. It was a normal consequence of any repressive operation, that the village concerned melted into the forest and never returned." These revolts "incontrovertibly represented a response and a challenge to those responsible for the overturning of traditional values." [12] In other words, the expansion of imperial governance and commerce was a process of victimization. This analysis is politically correct because it is anti-colonial. It also indicates a vacuum of critical analysis.

Let us examine in detail her assertion that victimization resulted from levying monetized taxes. The inhabitants of the peasant villages she describes were able to melt into the forest because they practiced shifting cultivation. In shifting cultivation secondary vegetation is allowed to grow until it is 2 to 10 meters tall. The shade of these plants kills grass (a sunlight loving plant) that is the principal competitor of food crops. The secondary vegetation is cut and burned and seeds of food plants dibbled into the ground. One or two crops are harvested before the land reverts to secondary vegetation. Peasants then cut and burn another patch of secondary vegetation and plant crops. Shifting cultivation is an agricultural technique that requires no ground preparation and is, therefore, the cultivation technique that requires the least expenditure of labor. In contemporary peasant societies, shifting cultivation is practiced wherever there is an abundance of land and few people.

Villages of shifting cultivators frequently move when uncontrolled fires create grasslands. Cultivation of grasslands requires much greater labor inputs because the grass and weed competitors of food crops must be suppressed by turning the soil with spades, hoes, or plows. The reciprocal of better ground preparation (by turning the soil) is larger per capita harvests; but as long as secondary forest is available for cutting and burning, peasants move to them in order to minimize the labor of cultivation.

The payment of money taxes by shifting cultivators required them to perform paid labor or produce exchange commodities. During the initial stage of establishing imperial governance, they resisted performing this labor by abandoning village sites and establishing new ones at isolated locations. These peasants had been moving village sites for many years prior to the advent of European imperialism in order to escape slave raids made by warrior bands of Muslim sultanates. The dispersed villages of politically fragmented animist tribes in the forest were easy prey to slave raiders—if the villages could be found. Dispersal gave some protection from these raids, so that they could practice their most important social value: minimal expenditures of agricultural labor. The ability of imperial governors to impose monetized taxation was in direct proportion to ending internecine warfare, ending slave raiding, enforcing emancipation, and building vehicle tracks into villages.

Coquery-Vidrovitch, like other politically correct historians, censures the French government for refusing "to inject technicians and capital in large quantities, in order to develop the country in real terms without making a sparse and over-exploited population bear the burden of an archaic system of pillage." [13] If she believes that the intrusion of imperial commerce into subsistence cultures was pillage, what was slave raiding? She describes slave raiding but does not use the uncompromising language of censure that she applies to the economic development policies that levied money taxes and mobilized paid corvee labor.

Her analysis seems to tell readers that the purpose of imperial governance was to preserve the subsistence labor norms of peasants who rejected growing exchange commodity crops or performing paid labor to acquire money to pay poll and hut taxes. Peasants are absolved from contributing their labor to economic development because coercion was required to mobilize their labor; and the labor required to initiate the process of economic development was not essential to their subsistence. While she believes that economic development was desirable, she also believes that frenchmen should have done this labor because economic development was a concept that was incomprehensible to peasants who fled into the forest to escape paid labor. This analysis shows no understanding that the intrusion of imperial commerce and economic development were identical policies.

Most scholars who describe and analyze subsistence cultures fail to understand that peasants do not have the same social values as themselves. Peasants measure their social security by control of land use that is guaranteed by village autonomy (independence), not by money incomes. Colonial administrators understood this reality. They understood that some variety of coercion was usually necessary to induce peasants to accept monetization, and the most efficient way to intrude monetization into peasant villages was money taxation. After monetization, households had to be further induced to produce small per capita amounts of exchange commodities in order to pay poll and hut taxes. Within a few years peasant households learned to take advantage of favorable terms of trade for the exchange commodities they produced because the money they acquired could be used to purchase manufactured products of superior utility that storekeepers brought to their villages over access roads they had been coerced to build.

NOTES

1. Paul Bairoch, "European Trade Policy, 1815-1914," in Peter Mathias, Sidney Pollard, eds. *Cambridge Economic History of Europe: The Industrial Economies,* Vol. 8, 103.
2. In the second half of the nineteenth century the British parliament charterer four monopoly corporations with governing power for specific geographic regions: Royal Niger Company; Imperial British East African Company; British South African Company; British North Borneo Company. The French, Belgian, and Portuguese governments did the same in order to transfer as much of the cost of governance as possible to private agencies to minimize subsidies from national treasuries.
3. Michael Crowder, *West Africa under Colonial Rule,* 183-185. Martin A. Klein, "Slavery and Emancipation in French West Africa," in Martin A. Klein, ed. *Breaking the Chains,* 171-173, 187-190
4. David K. Fieldhouse, *Economics and Empire,* 340.
5. D. E. Schremmer, "Taxation and Public Finance: Britain, France, and Germany," in Peter Mathias, Sidney Pollard, eds. *Cambridge Economic History of Europe: The Industrial Economies,* Vol. 8, 366-369, Table 47.
6. Catherine Coquery-Vidrovitch, "Western Equatorial Africa," in Roland A. Oliver, G. N. Sanderson, eds. *Cambridge History of Africa,* Vol. 6, 303.
7. Ronald E. Seavoy, *Famine in Peasant Societies,* 22.
8. Ronald E. Seavoy, *Subsistence and Economic Development,* 76.
9. Ronald E. Seavoy, *Subsistence and Economic Development,* 66.
10. Adiele E. Afigbo, Emanuel A. Ayandele, R. J. Gavin, John D. Omer-Cooper, Robin Palmer, *The Making of Modern Africa: The Nineteenth Century,* 102. Ronald E. Seavoy, *Subsistence and Economic Development,* 176-178.
11. Michael Crowder, *West Africa under Colonial Rule,* 274, 316. Michael F. Lofchie, "Political and Economic Origins of African Hunger," *Journal of Modern African Studies,* Vol. 13, 558, 563. Ronald E. Seavoy, *Subsistence and Economic Development,* 118-145.
12. Catherine Coquery-Vidrovitch, "Western Equatorial Africa," in Roland A. Oliver, G. N. Sanderson, eds. *Cambridge History of Africa,* Vol. 6, 312, 314.

13. Catherine Coquery-Vidrovitch, "Western Equatorial Africa," in Roland A. Oliver, G. N. Sanderson, eds. *Cambridge History of Africa*, Vol. 6, 315. Ronald E. Seavoy, *Subsistence and Economic Development*, 109-111.

REFERENCES

Afigbo, Adiele E., Emanuel A. Ayandele, R. J. Gavin, John D. Omer-Cooper, Robin Palmer. *The Making of Modern Africa: The Nineteenth Century*, London, Longman, 1986 (chapters 1, 2, 3, 4)

Ashby, Eric. *African Universities and Western Tradition*, Cambridge, Harvard University Press, 1964

Bairoch, Paul. "European Trade Policy, 1815-1914," in Peter Mathias, Sidney Pollard, eds. *Cambridge Economic History of Europe, The Industrial Economies: The Development of Economic and Social Policies*, Vol. 8, Cambridge, Cambridge University Press, 1989 (sections 7, 8)

Blakemore, Priscilla. "Assimilation and Association in French Educational Policy and Practice: Senegal, 1903-1939," in Vincent M. Battle, Charles H. Lyons, eds. *Essays in the History of African Education*, New York, Teachers College Press of Columbia University, 1970

Cell, John W. "Colonial Rule," in Judith M. Brown, William R. Louis, eds. *Oxford History of the British Empire: The Twentieth Century*, Vol. 4, Oxford, Oxford University Press, 1999

Cipolla, Carlo M., ed. *The Emergence of Industrial Societies*, Part 1, Glasgow, Fontana-Collins, 1973 (chapters 1, 2, 3)

Cipolla, Carlo M., ed. *The Industrial Revolution, 1700-1914*, London, Harvester Press/Barnes and Noble, 1976

Coquery-Vidrovitch, Catherine. "Western Equatorial Africa," in Roland A. Oliver, G. N. Sanderson, eds. *Cambridge History of Africa: From 1870 to 1905*, Vol. 6, Cambridge, Cambridge University Press, 1985

Crowder, Michael. *West Africa Under Colonial Rule*, London, Hutchinson, 1968 (parts 3, 5, 6)

Crowder, Michael. "The White Chiefs of Tropical Africa," in Lewis H. Gann, Peter Duignan, eds. *Colonialism in Africa, 1870-1960: The History and Politics of Colonialism, 1914-1960*, Vol. 2, Cambridge, Cambridge University Press, 1970

Davis, Clarence B., Kenneth E. Wilburn, eds. *Railway Imperialism*, New York, Greenwood Press, 1991 (chapters, 3, 6, 8, 9)

Deane, Phyllis, "The Industrial Revolution in Great Britain," in Carlo M. Cipolla, ed. *Fontana Economic History of Europe: The Emergence of Industrial Societies*, Vol. 4, Glasgow, Fontana/Collins, 1973

Falola, Toyin A., A. D. Roberts, "West Africa," in Judith M. Brown, William R. Louis, eds. *Oxford History of the British Empire: The Twentieth Century*, Vol. 4, Oxford, Oxford University Press, 1999

Fieldhouse, David K. *Economics and Empire, 1830-1914*, Ithaca, Cornell University Press, 1973 (chapters 1, 2, 6, 7, 10, maps)

Fieldhouse, David K. *Colonialism, 1870-1945: An Introduction*, New York, St Martins Press, 1981

Fohlen, Claude. "The Industrial Revolution in France, 1700-1914," in Carlo M. Cipolla, ed. *Fontana Economic History of Europe: The Emergence of Industrial Societies*, Vol. 4, Glasgow, Fontana/Collins, 1973

Gifford, Prosser, Timothy C. Weiskel. "African Education in a Colonial Context: French and British Styles," in Prosser Gifford, William R. Louis, eds. *France and Britain in Africa: Imperial Rivalry and Colonial Rule*, New Haven, Yale University Press, 1971

Gutteridge, William F. "Military and Police Forces in Colonial Africa," in Lewis H. Gann, Peter Duignan, eds. *Colonialism in Africa, 1870-1960: The History and Politics of Colonialism, 1914-1960*, Vol. 2, Cambridge, Cambridge University Press, 1970

Hargreaves, John D. "British and French Imperialism in West Africa," in Prosser Gifford, William R. Louis, eds. *France and Britain in Africa: Imperial Rivalry and Colonial Rule*, New Haven, Yale University Press, 1971

Hargreaves, John D. "Western Africa, 1886-1905," in Roland A. Oliver, G. N. Sanderson, eds. *Cambridge History of Africa: From 1876 to 1905*, Vol. 6, Cambridge, Cambridge University Press, 1985

Headrick, Daniel R. *The Tools of Empire: Technology and European Imperialism in the Nineteenth Century*, New York, Oxford University Press, 1981

Jeffries, Charles J. *The Colonial Empire and Its Civil Service*, Cambridge, Cambridge University Press, 1938 (chapters 8, 10, 11, 13, 14, 15)

Kilson, Martin. "The Emergent Elites of Black Africa, 1900-1960." In Lewis H. Gann, Peter Duignan, eds. *Colonialism in Africa, 1870-1960: The History and Politics of Colonialism, 1914-1960*, Vol. 2, Cambridge, Cambridge University Press, 1970

Kirk-Greene, Anthony. *On Crown Service: A History of HM Colonial and Overseas Civil Service, 1837-1997*, London, Tauris Publishers, 1999 (chapters 1, 2)

Kitchen, Helen, ed. *The Educated African: A Country-by-Country Survey of Educational Development in Africa*, New York, Praeger, 1962

Klein, Martin A. "Slavery and Emancipation in French West Africa," in Martin A. Klein, ed. *Breaking the Chains: Bondage and Emancipation in Modern Africa and Asia*, Madison, University of Wisconsin Press, 1993

Kranzberg, Melvin, Carroll W. Pursell, eds. *Technology in Western Civilization: The Emergence of Modern Industrial Society, Earliest Times to 1900*, New York, Oxford University Press, 1967 (chapters 7-17)

Landes, David S. *The Unbound Prometheus: Technical Change and Industrial Development in Western Europe from 1750 to the Present*, Cambridge, Cambridge University Press, 1969 (chapters 2, 3, 4)

Lilley, Samuel. "Technological Progress and the Industrial Revolution, 1700-1914," in Carlo M. Cipolla, ed. *Fontana Economic History of Europe: The Industrial Revolution, 1700-1914*, Vol. 3, London, Harvester Press/Barnes and Noble, 1976

Lofchie, Michael F. "Political and Economic Origins of African Hunger," *Journal of Modern African Studies*, Vol. 13, 1975

Miers, Suzanne, Igor Kopytoff, eds. *Slavery in Africa: Historical and Anthropological Perspectives*, Madison, University of Wisconsin Press, 1977

Miers, Suzanne, Martin Klein, eds. *Slavery and Colonial Rule in Africa*, London, Frank Cass, 1999

Nwauwa, Apollos O. *Imperialism, Academe and Nationalism: Britain and University Education for Africans, 1860-1960*, London, Frank Cass, 1997 (epilogue)

Pakenham, Thomas. *The Scramble for Africa: White Man's Conquest of the Dark Continent from 1876 to 1912*, New York, Avon Books, 1992 (chapters 9, 10, 11)

Rosenberg, Nathan, L. E. Birdzell. "Science, Technology and the Western Miracle," *Scientific American*, Vol. 263, November 1990

Schremmer, D.E. "Taxation and Public Finance: Britain, France, and Germany," in Peter Mathias, Sidney Pollard, eds. *Cambridge Economic History of Europe: The Industrial Economies: The Development of Economic and Social Policies*, Vol. 8, Cambridge, Cambridge University Press, 1989

Seavoy, Ronald E. "The Shading Cycle in Shifting Cultivation," *Annals of the Association of American Geographers*, Vol. 63, 1973

Seavoy, Ronald E. "The Origin of Tropical Grasslands in Kalimantan, Indonesia," *Journal of Tropical Geography*, Vol. 40, 1975

Seavoy, Ronald E. "Social Restraints on Food Production in Indonesia Subsistence Culture," *Journal of Southeast Asian Studies*, Vol. 8, 1977

Seavoy, Ronald E. *Famine in Peasant Societies*, Westport, Greenwood Press, 1986 (chapters 1, 3)

Seavoy, Ronald E. "Hoe Shifting Cultivation in East African Subsistence Culture," *Singapore Journal of Tropical Geography*, Vol. 8, 1987

Seavoy, Ronald E. *Famine in East Africa: Food Production and Food Policies*, Westport, Greenwood Press, 1989

Seavoy, Ronald E. *Subsistence and Economic Development*, Westport, Praeger, 2000

IMPERIAL GOVERNANCE
AS REVOLUTION

REVOLUTION DEFINED

The revolution was the forcible intrusion of imperial commerce and governance into subsistence cultures. After imperial governance was established, the commercial sector was gradually enlarged by a combination of rewards, inducements, threats, and force. The imperialism that operated in west Africa in the second half of the nineteenth century was similar to the imperialism that operated in India and the Indies in the eighteenth century, except that the military force available to European nations was vastly larger.

In both instances military force created the political conditions necessary to institutionalize a commercial sector. Thereafter, indigenous persons were trained to participate in imperial commerce and governance. These persons included bureaucrats, teachers, clerks, soldiers, policemen, village storekeepers, and merchants in many kinds of small business. All of these persons improved their status under the protection of imperial governance.

Both imperial commerce and governance were sustained by the performance of commercial labor norms by full-time paid laborers who earned money in the form of wages, salaries, and entrepreneurial profits. Currently, commercial labor norms operate only in the cities and along transportation arteries that are tenuous urban extensions into the hinterlands. The commercial sectors of post-colonial nations in west Africa are small and fragile because agriculture remains almost totally subsistent and economic development is a low priority for most governing elites. Since independence in the 1960s, non-oil exports in most post-colonial nations have stagnated or declined.

IMPERIAL LEGACIES

In the following discussion I focus on five imperial legacies in order to help readers understand how imperial governance created commercial sectors in the colonies of west Africa. The five legacies are: 1) central governments; 2) infrastructure institutions; 3) anonymous markets; 4) tropical medicine; 5) export commodities.

Central Governments: After peace was effectively enforced, governance was lodged in central governments that were hierarchical and bureaucratic. Unlike feudal and tribal rule, laws defined the missions of the several departments that constituted central governments. These laws defined the functions of departments and authorized them to act on a continuing basis (official duties). Annual appropriations funded their activities. Bureaucracies are hierarchical in order to enforce disciplined conduct on staff members. Personnel are paid salaries and it is assumed that their jobs constitute a lifetime career. Ideally, administration is uniform and impersonal.

Uniformity of performance requires personnel who are technically qualified and will exercise discretionary authority within limits defined by written rules. Written rules authorize heads of departments to act in particular cases, and prohibit them from acting in other cases. Bureaucracies are essential for coordinating the continuing operation of technologies. Stated another way, bureaucracies are necessary to rationalize the use of the limited amounts of money, labor, and other material resources that can be allocated to a single function. Railroads are the most obvious colonial technology that had to operate on a continuing basis, but bureaucracies to collect taxes and adminis-

ter native affairs were equally important functions of the central governments of west African colonies.

Infrastructure Institutions: Why were infrastructure facilities
so limited when post-colonial governing elites assumed power? This
is the wrong question. The correct question is why they existed to
the extent they did. They were built in spite of:

the deliberate preservation of indigenous social and economic forms by colonial
governments. Outside Africa no advanced economy preserved precapitalist social
patterns, and to the extent that these were artificially protected in colonial Africa
by Britain and France, they obstructed economic development. [1]

Imperial governors had to accept peasant resistance to economic
development or risk rebellions. They were the first persons to compre-
hend the limitations of imperial governance because of the smallness of
tax revenues and the extreme scarcity of human skills. The greatest
shortage of human skills was functional literacy; the second obstacle to
economic development was an unpredictable food supply from subsistence agriculture; and the third was the impossibility of generating sufficient tax revenues because of the extreme reluctance of peasants to
increase per capita production of export commodities or to perform
paid labor as long as they controlled land use.

The best measure of the weakness of imperial governance was lack
of traffic on the skeletal networks of railroads. Sally H. Frankel quotes
the 1934 report of the manager of Nigerian railways that summarizes
how this weakness restrained the process of commercialization.

The whole Colony has greatly benefited from the transportation facilities which
have been provided from the resources of the State. The present recurring deficit
is due to heavy interest charges and insufficient receipts to meet them. . . . The
main direction in which the annual capital charges could be met year by years
from railway earnings must be the carriage by it of a very large volume of
agricultural products. . . . A sufficient volume of export products does not now
exist. [2]

Most of Nigeria's railroads were built ahead of demand in anticipation that commercializing policies enforced by imperial governors
would induce peasants along rights-of-ways to cultivate commodity
crops. This did not happen to the extent anticipated, and the sharp
decline in commodity prices during the Great Depression restricted

the ability of district officers to induce peasants to increase plantings. Frankel goes on to generalize about all of the railroads built in sub-Saharan Africa. They could pay their construction costs and earn profits only if they served commercial enclaves like the diamond mine at Kimberley, the gold mines of the Witwatersrand, and the copperbelt mines of Northern Rhodesia (Zambia) and the Belgian Congo (Congo Republic).

Railroads built in anticipation of inducing/coercing peasants to produce exchange commodities in excess of subsistence needs were risky investments. Insufficient revenues meant that construction costs were a heavy burden on limited colonial revenues; therefore, their construction had to be justified by administrative necessity. Frankel again summarizes how railroads in particular, and transportation in general, had failed (up to 1938) to achieve sufficient revenues to justify construction. "In general, African railways have been constructed on the basis of a too optimistic view of the rate of economic development in the territories they serve, and many of them have been built in areas where little economic progress can be expected." [3]

Given continuous revenue deficits and the necessary caution of imperial governors in trying to induce peasants to produce increased quantities of export commodities, the accomplishments of imperial governance in building infrastructure facilities were impressive.

The positive achievements of Britain and France in creating the basis for a Western economy in Africa was to a large extent paid for by African labor and resources. In this, the experience of British and French in colonial Africa was identical with that of all relatively underdeveloped countries in other parts of the world, whether sovereign states or colonial dependencies. [4]

Construction of most infrastructure projects began from a near zero base of tax revenues and human skills; and the speed and quality of construction was always retarded by the reluctance of peasants to perform paid labor. Only the skill of colonial governors enabled central governments to nibble at the edges of subsistence inertia. Put another way, a principal impediment to economic development was the shortness of the era of imperial governance. Given these realities the infrastructure facilities inherited by post-colonial governing elites were limited. It could not have been otherwise.

What were the infrastructure institutions that imperial governance intruded into the subsistence cultures? There are three categories: invisible, visible to knowledgeable observers, and highly visible to casual observers.

Some of the invisible institutions were domestic peace, monetization, money taxation, production of export commodities for sale on the global market, the introduction of freehold tenure (for urban land only), rule of law in both civil and criminal jurisdictions, contract law to govern commercial relationships, public health services like potable water and sewers in cities, and vaccinations.

Knowledgeable observers know that national identity is an imperial legacy. Colonial boundaries became national boundaries and the concept of national identity that exists in the minds of African governing elites was molded by imperial governance. Knowledgeable observers are also aware that the fragile sense of nationality is concentrated in governing elites and city residents, and that it barely exists elsewhere.

Monetization is so pervasive that most persons assume it always operated. The availability of people who will perform full-time paid labor is assumed to be universal but knowledgeable observers know that most peasants and displaced peasants reject becoming full-time paid laborers as long as other sources of subsistence are available. Knowledgeable observers also know that increased functional literacy taught in school systems is an imperial legacy that was established to prepare persons to staff government bureaucracies or become full-time paid laborers in the commercial sector. Literacy in the commercial sector is readily observed in signs on city shops. It is less easily observed in the departments of central governments and the number of salaried employees who staff businesses.

The most visible imperial institutions bequeathed to post-colonial governing elites are: 1) central governments that are readily visible in monumental buildings of Victorian style architecture; 2) bureaucracies; 3) commercial cities; 4) using European languages to conduct government and business; 5) varieties of Christianity introduced from Europe that help communicants accommodate to social change; 6) complex technologies managed by bureaucracies. Other highly visible institutions are post offices, institutional credit from banks (often observed in monumental buildings); health care (visible in monumental hospitals); secondary schools and universities (in monumental buildings); and professional police and soldiers who are paid salaries.

During the era of imperial governance there was a continuous introduction of technology, mostly in skeletal amounts. Some of them were railroads, all weather roads, airports, deep water ports, telephones, radios, and generation of electricity. Learning how to install, operate, and maintain these technologies required learning a European language. Likewise, there had to be a common language to conduct government and business because no local language was widely enough spoken; and the designation of a local language as the language of government could have provoked ethnic unrest. Furthermore, local languages lacked technical vocabularies.

Anonymous Markets: Anonymous markets are usually distant markets where sellers do not know consumers. Money is essential for conducting this trade. Anonymous markets did not exist in most peasant villages in west Africa, or they existed for one or two commodities like salt and iron bars that village blacksmiths shaped into weapons or agricultural implements. The imposition of peace, pervasive monetization, and improved transportation were prerequisites for inducing peasants to increase production of exchange commodities for sale on anonymous markets. This was particularly true for export commodities but it was also true for food grains needed to feed city residents. In both instances agricultural surpluses were produced to acquire target sums of money. The subsistence strategy of acquiring target sums of money is most visible in the production of commodities like cocoa beans or the fruit of oil palms. Harvests from two or three trees satisfied household needs but selling the harvests from 15 or 20 trees acquired target sums of money.

Peasant villages have two distinct markets—village markets and storekeeper markets—and there is little overlap. Village markets are means of subsistence sharing. They are monetized barter; and money is the means of fair exchange. Household survival does not depend on this trade because every household in a village could grow or produce a similar array of food or handicraft items for its own consumption. . . . These are not anonymous markets because all buyers and sellers know each other; and profit is not the principal motivation for holding them or for sellers who participate in them. [5]

Storekeeper markets are where peasants sell exchange commodities in order to purchase a limited variety of manufactured items that have greater utility than handicraft items. Storekeepers are essential intermediaries between the subsistence sector that produces exchange commodities and the commercial sector that supplies manufactured items. Storekeepers assemble small amounts of exchange commodities produced from many households and transport them to cities where they are aggregated and exported; or they aggregate food crops for consumption in cities. Export commodities and food consumed in cities constitute an anonymous market. Anonymous markets could not exist without storekeepers and the willingness of most peasant households to produce limited quantities of exchange commodities that have an instant sale.

Village storekeepers had to be functionally literate because transactions with illiterate peasants had to be conducted with money of account recorded in books. They had to be literate in order to purchase an inventory of manufactured products that peasants wanted to buy; and to sell the exchange commodities they assembled. The commercial sector could not have been created and institutionalized without local agents of imperial commerce. In west Africa a high percentage of the traveling merchants and storekeepers during the era of imperial governance were strangers. They came from Lebanon and Syria and were welcomed by imperial governors.

Tropical Medicine: This discussion of tropical medicine is surrogate for discussing the introduction of all technical skills. Research in tropical medicine was a necessity when European governing elites became permanent residents in the tropics. The most important part of the elite was the army because the creation of commercial sectors ultimately depended on the presence of European soldiers to perform much of the initial warfare. Thereafter, indigenous troops fought most, but not all, of the battles. Soldiers had to be healthy, especially European soldiers, because of the skills they possessed, and because there were so few of them.

Between 1850 and 1860 there was a substantial drop in mortality rates from infectious diseases among British troops stationed in the tropics and, thereafter, the decline continued at a slower rate. Between 1830 and the beginning of WWI in 1914 the incidence of fatal diseases for European soldiers was reduced by 85 to 95 percent. Civilian personnel also experienced a similar decline in mortalities. The decline began long before the discovery of modern medicines.

What were the causes of mortality decline? The principal cause was public health measures. Nineteenth century research discovered few cures for diseases, either temperate or tropical, but the research of Louis Pasteur clearly identified the relationship between germs and disease, and this was the incentive for medical doctors to focus on preventing the transmission of diseases caused by bacteria. Sanitation was the principal cause of declining mortalities, although, vaccination against smallpox (and typhoid after 1910), were more dramatic public health measures. The principal improvements in sanitation were: 1) filtration to produce potable water; 2) drainage of living sites; 3) sewage deposal; 4) sanitary food preparation; 5) ventilation; 6) use of soap to keep bodies clean; 7) regular changes of clothing.

The principal means of reducing the incidence of highly infectious diseases like cholera was filtration of potable water that supplied commercial cities and military cantonments. Sewer systems that drained living sites reduced the contamination of surface water and thereby reduced the incidence of diarrhea, dysentery, and typhoid, as well as reducing breeding sites for mosquitoes. Good ventilation and less crowding in rooms reduced the incidence of tuberculosis; and doors, screens, netting over beds, and building floors off of the ground reduced the incidence of insect transmitted diseases like malaria. Improved nutrition was another factor. It increased African resistance to infectious diseases because malnutrition (and related diseases) was the principal cause for rejecting African recruits for the police and army. There is less direct evidence between nutrition and reduced mortalities for European soldiers because European soldiers and civilians always had adequate diets. Nutrition improvements for soldiers centered on sanitary food storage and better preparation, especially when soldiers were on the march.

African soldiers were the most obvious beneficiaries of sanitation facilities because their labor built public health facilities in their can-

tonments. Africans working in the commercial sectors were also beneficiaries of European sanitation facilities because they lived in cities, performed commercial labor norms, and had money to purchase medicines
when medicines became available. Another place where Africans shared
the benefits of public health facilities was mining. Only healthy Africans
were recruited as miners and they, like soldiers, lived in compounds and
performed paid labor every day. They always had adequate diets because most underground labor was strenuous, but only after 1900 was it
recognized that their health had to be safeguarded in order to ensure a
continuing supply of recruits. By about 1920, the mortality rates of African miners were similar to the mortality rates of African soldiers because
both had adequate nutrition and both lived in communities where sanitation rules were enforced.

In the 1890s two schools of hygiene and tropical medicine were
founded in England (at London and Liverpool) and a similar school
was founded in France. By the mid-1890s doctors in these schools
had published several manuals of hygiene that applied to specific tropical localities, and they were periodically updated so that the results of
new research would reach doctors in the field. Sanitation facilities
are the most important medical legacy of the imperial era. "The tri-
umph of nineteenth-century medicine was prevention, not cure; and
the key was the provision of clean water. A better water supply had
been the most important single cause of the great mortality improvements over the mid-century." [6]

During the colonial era improved sanitation was possible in all
peasant villages that mobilized the labor to dig wells and drainage
ditches to reduce sources of water contamination. Other instantly
available practices were better personal hygiene, building dwellings
with floors off of the ground (no earth floors), building chimneys to
ventilate smoke from cooking fires, and digging pits where villagers
could defecate. Few peasant villages or households availed themselves of these benefits, and most peasant villages in the twenty-first
century are equally unwilling to expend the labor necessary to improve village and household sanitation.

Besides training medical doctors to diagnose and treat tropical
diseases, the staffs of the schools of tropical medicine conducted re-

search to find cures. Two of the earliest cures were quinine for malaria and potassium-antimony-tartrate for bilharzias (schistosomiasis). Peasants did not share these cures because medicine cost money, and the target sums they acquired were not large enough to purchase medicines when they became available.

The five principal medical legacies from imperial governance are: 1) public health policies that dramatically reduced mortalities in commercial cities; 2) most tropical diseases could be accurately diagnosed; 3) discovery of insect vectors that transmitted most tropical diseases; 4) discovery of medicines to cure many tropical diseases; 5) availability of medicines to persons with money to purchase them.

Export Commodities: Imperial governance introduced many changes in the peasantry's subsistence strategy. Some of them were: 1) monetization; 2) money taxation; 3). cultivation of export commodity crops to acquire target sums of money; 4) relatively safe long distance transportation that allowed peasants to migrate to where they could perform paid labor in order to acquire target sums of money.

At the time of annexation, subsistence agriculture began at the boundaries of the overgrown villages where tribal chiefs and feudal rulers lived in symbiosis with the peasantry. At independence, subsistence agriculture began at the boundaries of the small commercial cities that replaced these villages; and 40 years later this is unchanged. Peasants continue to perform subsistence labor norms that produce subsistence amounts of food, and seasonal hunger is as frequent as in the past, with one significant difference. Hunger is now alleviated by food imports from industrial nations instead of being endured. The money to purchase the food comes from the sale of export commodities. Instead of being used to acquire manufactured products, it is used to purchase food. During seasons of hunger young children and older persons might die of malnutrition and related diseases but a higher percentage of adults survive.

Colonial governors were fully aware of the frequency of local and regional famines in the immediate past. Some of the persons involved in imperial expansion had observed them and famines were frequently mentioned in the accounts of European travelers; and folk memory remembered the worst ones. In any case, seasons of hunger could be observed in all years, in various districts in all colonies if Europeans made the effort to visit the affected districts. [7]

Post-colonial governing elites have not enforced policies to induce peasants to increase per capita production of export commodities or food crops in order to alleviate seasonal hunger. They have been less willing to disturb the subsistence social order than the imperial governors who preceded them. Like the feudal rulers of the pre-colonial era, they live in symbiosis with the peasantry.

AGENDA OF INDEPENDENCE

The post-colonial governing elites of west African nations inherited commercial sectors with solid institutional foundations that could be used to continue the process of economic development. Independence was the opportunity for governing elites to expand the commercial sectors they inherited by vigorously inducing the commercialization of agriculture (particularly commodity crops for export), and enlarging infrastructure facilities. Independence was also the opportunity for more persons to acquire literacy, learn new skills, and perform full-time paid labor so they could improve their health, increase their longevity, and enjoy a higher standard of material welfare.

Post-colonial governing elites, however, had a different agenda. Their first priority was retaining power. The second was dampening tribal, religious, and regional rivalries in order to prevent communal conflicts. The third was dampening urban unrest that could produce destabilizing riots. The fourth was attracting investments to build showcase industrial projects that were easily taxed, with patronage being a principal use of this revenue.

Retaining Power: The best way to retain power was to claim that a single political party was necessary to implement economic development. One party government was an imperial legacy because imperial governance had been one party government. Almost all post-colonial governing elites claimed that governance by a single party would be more efficient than imperial governance at enlarging infrastructure facilities and building an industrial base.

After post-colonial governing elites consolidated their power they established departments of central planning. This was to ensure that enlarged infrastructure facilities were designed to meet the aspirations of Africans instead of the needs of imperial commerce. The proposed plans had varying durations (5 years, 7 years, 10 years). By 1965 (eight years after the independence of Ghana and five years after the independence of Nigeria), it was apparent to knowledgeable observers that the economic planning policies initiated by post-colonial governing elites were failures because they were not guided by experience.

The new political leaders did not adequately understand the policies that had guided imperial investments in infrastructure facilities. As a result, planning did not follow the obvious path of making incremental increases in investments in inherited infrastructure facilities that could induce greater peasant participation in the commercial sector. This is where investments would generate the greatest long term results. Experience is the only reliable guide for making the most profitable investments, and this required field investigations. These investigations were not made. Instead, planning was done without "an economist who understands how the economy really works in the African context and what broad institutional forces affect it. Unfortunately, in today's scientific environment, governments too often believe that an economist-mathematician, if suffiently incomprehensible, is the best planner." [8]

An integral part of development planning was a policy of import substitution. It meant subsidizing factories to manufacture products that had large domestic markets. In Nigeria factories were built to weave cotton textiles but they were dependent on imported thread. Several breweries were also subsidized but all of the ingredients except water had to be imported. In both cases, cotton to manufacture thread and food grains for malting into beer could have been grown in Nigeria. They were not. In the 1990s, "judged by the gap which today still exists between these grandiose, vague, and idealistic objectives and actual levels of development attained, the plans must be written off as having completely failed, not only in Nigeria and Ghana, but throughout West Africa."[9] In other words, the post-colonial governing elites of west African nations, particularly in Nigeria, have preserved the subsistence social order more effectively than imperial governors.

After centralized planning of economic development failed, planning policies faded into the background but the bureaucracies created to implement them remained. These bureaucracies became sources of patronage. Department administrators became feudal barons. Their motives were similar to medieval feudal barons in Europe except they controlled bureaucracies, not arable land. Their budgets were used to pay the salaries of clerks who were their retainers. Single party government was something very different from the bureaucratic cadres of imperial governments. Its principal purpose was to enjoy the perquisites of power. More accurately, post-colonial office holding was an opportunity to become rich.

In 1985, in the small nation of Benin, bureaucratic personnel consumed 65 percent of the national revenue; in the Ivory Coast it was 58 percent, and in Senegal it was 47 percent. The job of retainers was to maintain the political statusquo in order to preserve governing elites in power until replaced by military leaders who claimed they would end the worst forms of corruption. The usual result of military intervention was generals enriching themselves.

Preventing Communal Violence: This is the most difficult problem that post-colonial governing elites have had to manage. The threat of communal violence is never far below the surface of the political landscape; therefore, averting it takes up disproportionately large amounts of their time. The boundaries of west African colonies were made with little regard for the boundaries of ethnic groups. As a result, the populations of most west African nations are composed of heterogeneous peasant societies speaking different languages, practicing different religions, and adhering to widely different customs. The impact of imperial governance on these societies has been highly diverse; and their participation in the commercial sector has been equally diverse. This reality makes the art of governance a continual juggling act.

Most post-colonial political leaders have been reasonably successful at balancing ethnic rivalries in order to maintain political unity. But not always! They failed in Rwanda, Burundi, Congo, and Sierra Leone where fragile central governments dissolved or had their authority restricted to capital cities and environs. Whenever this happened the seas of subsistence that surround commercial cities became seas of anarchy.

What resources do governing elites have at their disposal to maintain the national unity that is essential for preserving the commercial sector? Patronage is the principal glue that preserves political unity. Patronage means the distribution of bureaucratic jobs to regional, religious, and language brokers. A high proportion of the money to pay their salaries comes from taxing showcase industrial projects that produce raw materials for export, or from taxing the peasantry's exchange commodities destined for export, or from foreign aid supplied by the International Monetary Fund, World Bank, or industrialized nations. This strategy of governance depends on using revenue and foreign aid for patronage rather than making investments designed to increase taxable wealth. In nations without oil revenues, day to day problems are met by political expediency to the full extent of the revenues available for distribution. The usual destiny of the commercial sectors of these nations is a slow slide to extinction. Before this happens external credit is usually forthcoming to avert economic and political collapse.

Preventing Urban Riots: The most obvious post-colonial bureaucratic baronies are parastatal marketing boards. Parastatal marketing boards are monopolies that are wholly owned by central governments. Many were created during the colonial era. They purchased export commodity crops from peasants at below domestic market prices in order to sell at world market prices. The differential was a capital fund that was usually used to build infrastructure projects. Post-colonial governing elites seldom used funds from these boards for this purpose. Frequently, the funds have been used to build high rise, glass enclosed buildings for bureaucratic offices, or stadiums for sporting events that are also used for political rallies.

After independence, additional parastatal marketing boards were established to purchase food crops from peasants at below domestic market prices. The food was then sold to city residents at below world market prices. City residents in post-colonial nations live on cheap food. A high percentage of urban residents are displaced peasants who are attracted to cities by food that can be purchased by performing monetized subsistence tasks on a day to day basis. In other words, cheap food allows subsistence labor norms to be transferred to shantytowns surrounding cities. The purpose of cheap food for city residents is to dampen urban unrest that could explode into politically destabilizing riots.

Shantytowns are attractive to peasants because they provide a much more varied social life than villages, but peasant migration to shantytowns has seriously reduced marketed food supplies. Peasants who remain in villages continue to produce food in subsistence amounts and market a small percentage of harvests as their exchange commodity. In the total population, however, there is a smaller percentage of peasants actually producing food and a higher percentage living in cities than in the colonial era. In the meantime, migration increases the percentage of urban residents in the total population and peasant households remaining in villages do not market enough food to feed shantytown residents.

Where does the food come from? There is only one source. It is from commercial agriculture in industrial nations, and a high percentage comes as gifts. Only nations with substantial oil revenues or revenues from other export commodities can pay for it. For nations without oil revenues, the International Development Association is the principal supplier. It is an agency of the World Bank. According to Afigbo, by the 1990s:

The point has now been reached at which few West African countries can feed themselves, not even so-called rich Nigeria which now spends huge proportions of her external reserves importing rice, frozen fish, and meat and—what is more humiliating—palm oil. The food crisis in West Africa has reached a point where . . . in 1972 Ghana was forced to launch Operation Feed Yourself (OFY). Nigeria followed in 1976 with an Operation Feed The Nation (OFN). [10]

Showcase Projects: The most important showcase projects are oil production (Nigeria, Angola), bauxite mining (Guinea), gold (Ghana), diamonds (Tanzania), chromite (Zimbabwe), diamonds and uranium (Namibia), and copper mining (Zambia, Congo Republic). They provide most of the tax revenues for distribution to political supporters. Other showcase projects are hydroelectric dams built with foreign aid to supply electricity for industries that were never built, and monumental government buildings in capital cities to house unneeded bureaucracies. These edifices have great political visibility but consume funds that should have been allocated to less visible but more productive projects of economic development.

INTERPRETATION

In the perspective of 40 years of independence (1960-2000), the post-colonial governing elites of west African nations have failed to adequately nurture the commercial institutions they inherited because it is very doubtful if any leaders had an accurate understanding of the economic problems of being independent. After independence, there was a pause while governing elites consolidated power. In most post-colonial nations it has been a very long pause because the new governing elites had little understanding of the enormous amount of inertia that is inherent in populations that are 70 to 90 percent peasants.

The only way to overcome this inertia is a commitment to govern with austerity and purpose, like the imperial governments that preceded them. To do this, post-colonial governing elites had to follow directly in the footsteps of imperial governing elites. They had to form an interlocking partnership with the police and army to enforce policies of political economy that could induce economic development similar to the policies that guided the industrialization of Japan, the Soviet Union, South Korea, and Taiwan. These were one party governments that had a vision and they acted with purpose.

The most common vision guiding the actions of leaders of post-colonial governing elites was Marxist ideology. It was usually learned at European universities as part of the process of learning how to use European intellectual thought to justify independence. The theoretical concepts of class struggle and revolution of the proletariat served that purpose; however, these ideological abstractions immunized them from

understanding the significance of imperial commercial expansion in
the nineteenth century that incorporated African subsistence culture
into the global economy. Marxist ideology distracted them from understanding that the commercial sectors they inherited could serve
as a foundation for future national prosperity if policies of economic
development were more vigorously enforced than under imperial governance. The governing elites of most post-colonial nations discarded
this option when confronted with its political risks. Instead, they
opted for patronage to preserve the subsistence statusquo and their
place in it.

Economic development policies have largely lapsed, as has imperial peace. During imperial governance the possibility of peasant
rebellions and communal conflict bubbled just below the surface and
this was a very large restraint on vigorous enforcement of commercializing policies. Most post-colonial governing elites have been less
effective in dealing with this reality than imperial governors. Ethnic
conflicts and civil wars are frequent events. In the global economy
these wars are peripheral events and will remain peripheral as long
as subsistence institutions dominate the social structures of these nations.

By comparing the accomplishments of colonial governing elites to
the accomplishments of post-colonial governing elites (in an equal
period of time), the accomplishments of colonial governance are impressive. During the 40 years between 1920 and 1960 when imperial governance was one party government, imperial governors created central governments and commercial sectors. The central governments had treasuries that were used, when revenues allowed, to
accelerate the production of commercial wealth. Although the treasuries were small, by the time of decolonization government and commercial institutions were operating on a solid fiscal and technical basis. In most sub-Saharan African nations, smoothly operating central governments were transferred to post-colonial governing elites.
Departing imperial governors hoped that new governing elites would
continue the process of economic development by more efficiently
enforcing policies they had put in place; and that had created commercial wealth where little had previously existed.

During more than 40 years of independence, from 1960 onward, improvements in infrastructure facilities have been less than impressive. In most post-colonial nations without oil revenues, economic development has stagnated or there have been only marginal improvements. In nations with marginally improved infrastructures, a high percentage of them have been funded by foreign aid or by defaulted loans made by the World Bank and other international lending agencies. Furthermore, after construction was completed there have been minimal provisions for maintenance. I think it is accurate to conclude that most of the post-colonial governing elites of west African nations have hugely neglected the infrastructure institutions they inherited from imperial governments.

SUMMARY

This chapter has investigated the creation of commercial sectors during the colonial era in west Africa and how they operate in post-colonial nations. West Africa was investigated because the creation of commercial sectors began at a late date in a region that had a near vacuum of political, economic, and social institutions that imperial governance could mold to fit the needs of a commercial sector. Because of the lack of these institutions, they had to be introduced from Europe. This was a difficult process that was barely complete when indigenous political leaders claimed the right to govern independent nations.

West African nations are, therefore, a good test of the power of the global economy to impel governing elites of peasant nations to continue the policies of economic development they inherited from imperial governance. For the most part, post-colonial governing elites have failed to overcome peasant resistance to performing commercial labor norms in food and commodity production. The failure of governing elites to enforce policies to commercialize the subsistence cultures they govern strongly contributed to the disintegration of central governments in the 1990s in Sierra Leone, Congo Republic, Angola, Mozambique, Rwanda, and Burundi.

I have not discussed the incorporation of South American nations into the global economy because they participated in it from the moment indigenous cultures were conquered and European settlers arrived. There were always sufficient numbers of commercially motivated settlers in the Spanish and Portuguese colonies to create and maintain institutions that could continuously enlarge the commercial sector. Some governing elites were more efficient than others, but there was never any question that the economic development of post-colonial nations in Central and South America depended on enlarging the commercial sector in order to enlarge participation in the global economy. Put another way, economic development in these nations in the nineteenth and twentieth centuries was export driven. Most commodities produced for export were produced by persons performing commercial labor norms.

Why was decolonization in west Africa a peaceful transfer of power? The short answer is that imperial governance dissolved because it had outlived its usefulness. There are several strands to this generalization. During WWII the weakness of imperial governance became obvious. Following the war, there were many politically ambitious Africans who had attended European universities and developed skills that could unite the diverse ethnic groups in their colonies for the single purpose of ending alien rule. Their ability to mobilize discontent was coupled with public opinion in Britain and France that was unwilling to approve spending money to forcibly retain imperial possessions. Nor was public opinion willing to approve major capital investments to enlarge infrastructures when huge capital investments were needed to reindustrialize western Europe. Decolonization in sub-Saheran Africa and elsewhere was a nonissue, and it had the tangible advantage of transferring the costs of governance and economic development to indigenous taxpayers.

Finally, and probably the most important reason for consenting to the dissolution of empires, was the availability of raw materials from within the borders of industrial nations or from other nations that produced and sold them on the global market. The known inventory of raw materials (oil fields, metal mines, and tropical agricultural commodities, or temperate climate substitutes) was adequate to restore prosperity to the industrial nations of western Europe and supply them with raw materials for the foreseeable future. In effect, tropical Africa, India, and Indonesia could disappear from the commercial map and industrialized nations would continue their prosperity with only minor adjustments in their trade patterns. For example, as copper production declined in the nationalized mines of the African copperbelt in Zambia and Congo Republic, production increased in Chile and elsewhere to supply the deficit.

The nations of the periphery have rarely assumed the importance ascribed to them as markets or investment outlets, or even as sources of raw materials. This was true during the era of the so-called new imperialism of the late nineteenth century; it is equally true during the modern era of decolonization and the multinational corporation. [11]

In many ways the dissolution of the British and French empires followed nineteenth century commercial policies. A large part of the diplomatic relations between industrialized nations during the nineteenth century was concerned with avoiding war and expanding international commerce. England's policy of free trade was designed to further these goals by: 1) attracting cheap raw materials to Britain; 2) expanding the global market for products manufactured in Britain, particularly to the post-colonial nations of South America; 3) dampening international commercial rivalries by allocating colonies to other European nations and Japan in order to provide them with raw materials they considered desirable for continued industrial growth. Acquisition of colonies by industrial nations in western Europe dampened commercial rivalry by sharing long range opportunities for increasing commerce in regions where little international commerce existed. The acquisition of territorial empires composed of ethnically and culturally diverse people was an unavoidable byproduct of the perceived need to seek assured supplies of some raw materials that were thought to be scarce, and to secure long term markets for manufactured products.

William Roger Louis and Ronald Robinson accurately summarize the purpose and evolution of territorial empires of the nineteenth century, and decolonization after 1945. "The formal Empire contracted in the post-war years as it had once expanded, as a variable function of integrating countries into the international capitalist economy." [12]

Put another way, the territorial imperialism in sub-Saharan Africa in the late nineteenth century was the last link in incorporating all subsistence cultures into the global economy, a process that began when da Gama sailed to India and Columbus to the Americas. Decolonization was the means of preserving their participation in the global market with minimal expense incurred by the principal industrial nations.

The central governments of peasant nations exert considerable control over internal commerce but have little power to influence participation in the global market because global commercial policies are controlled by the principal industrial nations. This will not change for the foreseeable future. Two terms, neocolonialism and informal empire, accurately describe the relationship of most post-colonial nations to the principal industrial nations. The colonial relationship, however, is no longer with one industrial nation. It is between all peasant nations and the International Monetary Fund, World Trade Organization, and World Bank. These institutions were created by the principal industrial nations to manage the global economy.

In the next two chapters I will identify, describe, and analyze the policies and institutions that have been responsible for guiding the evolution of the global economy during the second half of the twentieth century. The spectrum of national participation goes from the subsistence restraints on producing new wealth that dominates the social structures of peasant nations to the highly educated, highly disciplined, highly paid, and highly productive work forces of the principal industrial nations. The parochial events of decolonization will be invisible because the production of new wealth is concentrated in industrial nations. Likewise, the necessity for maintaining global peace, that is essential for producing new wealth, is wholly in the hands of the principal industrial nations.

NOTES

1. David K. Fieldhouse, "The Economic Exploitation of Africa," in Prosser Gifford, William Roger Louis, eds. *France and Britain in Africa*, 640-641.
2. Sally Herbert Frankel, *Capital Investment in Africa*, 390-391.
3. Sally Herbert Frankel, *Capital Investment in Africa*, 418.

4. David K. Fieldhouse, "The Economic Exploitation of Africa" in Prosser Gifford, William R. Louis, eds.*France and Britain in Africa*, 640.
5. Ronald E. Seavoy, *Subsistence and Economic Development*, 16.
6. Philip D. Curtin, *Death by Migration*, 111. See also p 159.
7. Michael J. Watts, *Silent Violence*, 100-104. Ronald E. Seavoy, *Subsistence and Economic Development*, 117-145. Ronald E. Seavoy, *Famine in East Africa*, 132-143.
8. Andrew M. Kamarck, *The Economics of African Development*, 213.
9. Adiele E. Afigbo, Emanuel A. Ayandele, R. J. Gavin, John D. Omer-Cooper, Robin Palmer, *The Making of Modern Africa: The Twentieth Century*, 67.
10. Adiele E. Afigbo, Emanuel A. Ayandele, R. J. Gavin, John D. Omer-Copper, Robin Palmer, *The Making of Modern Africa: The Twentieth Century*, 69. See also, Ronald E. Seavoy, *Subsistence and Economic Development*, 85-87, 119.
11. Benjamin J. Cohen, *Crossing Frontiers*, 300.
12. William R. Louis, Ronald Robinson, "The Imperialism of Decolonization," *Journal of Imperial and Commonwealth History*, Vol. 22, 1994, 495

REFERENCES

Abernethy, David B. "Nigeria," in David G. Scanlon, ed. *Church, State, and Education in Africa*, New York, Teachers College Press, Columbia University, 1966

Afigbo, Adiele E., Emanuel A. Ayandele, R. J. Gavin, John D. Omer-Cooper, Robin Palmer. *The Making of Modern Africa: The Twentieth Century*, London, Longman, 1986 (chapter 3)

Berg, Elliott J. "The Development of a Labour Force in Sub-Saharan Africa," *Economic Development and Cultural Change*, Vol. 13, 1965

Blau, Peter M. *Bureaucracy in Modern Society,* New York, Random House, 1956 (chapters 1, 2)

Cohen, Benjamin J. *Crossing Frontiers: Explorations in International Political Economy*, Boulder, Westview Press, 1991

Curtin, Philip D. *Death by Migration: Europe's Encounter with the Tropical World in the Nineteenth Century*, Cambridge, Cambridge University Press, 1989

Farley, John. "Bilharzia: A Problem of Native Health, 1900-1950," in David Arnold, ed. *Imperial Medicine and Indigenous Societies*, Manchester, Manchester University Press, 1988

Farley, John. *Bilharzia: A History of Imperial Tropical Medicine*, Cambridge, Cambridge University Press, 1991 (chapters 1, 2, 8)

Fieldhouse, David K. "The Economic Exploitation of Africa: Some British and French Comparisons," in Prosser Gifford, William R. Louis, eds. *France and Britain in Africa: Imperial Rivalry and Colonial Rule*, New Haven, Yale University Press, 1971

Frankel, Sally H. *Capital Investment in Africa: Its Course and Effects*, London, Oxford University Press, 1938 (chapter 5)

Hogendorn, Jan S. "The Origins of the Groundnut Trade in Northern Nigeria," in Carl K.Eicher, Carl Liedholm, eds. *Growth and Development of the Nigerian Economy*, East Lansing, Michigan State University Press, 1970

Jackson, Robert H. *Quasi-States: Sovereignty, International Relations, and the Third World*, Cambridge, Cambridge University Press, 1990 (pp 21-26, chapters 4, 5)

Kamarck, Andrew M. *The Economics of African Development*, New York, Praeger, 1967 (chapter 10)

Kingsley, J. Donald. "Bureaucracy and Political Development, with Particular Reference to Nigeria," in Joseph LaPalombara, ed. *Bureaucracy and Political Development*, Princeton, Princeton University Press, 1963

Lofchie, Michael F. "The Decline of African Agriculture: An Internalist Perspective," in Michael H. Glanz, ed. *Drought and Hunger in Africa*, Cambridge, Cambridge University Press, 1987

Louis, William R., Ronald Robinson. "The Imperialism of Decolonization," *Journal of Imperial and Commonwealth History*, Vol. 22, 1994

McIntyre, William D. *British Decolonization, 1947-1997: When, Why and How Did the British Empire Fall?* New York, St Martins Press, 1998

MacLeod, Roy, Milton Lewis, eds. *Disease, Medicine, and Empire: Perspectives on Western Medicine and the Experience of European Expansion*, London, Routledge, 1988 (chapters 12, 12, 13, 14)

McPhee, Allan. *The Economic Revolution in British West Africa*, London, Frank Cass, 1971 (reprint of 1926 edition) (chapters 6, 7, 8)

Nixon, Charles R. "The Role of the Marketing Boards in the Political Evolution of Nigeria," in Carl K. Eicher, Carl Liedholm, eds. *Growth and Development of the Nigerian Economy*, East Lansing, Michigan State University Press, 1970

Seavoy, Ronald E. *Famine in East Africa: Food Production and Food Policies*, Westport, Greenwood Press, 1989

Seavoy, Ronald E. *Subsistence and Economic Development*, Westport, Praeger, 2000

Watts, Michael J. *Silent Violence: Food, Famine and Peasantry in Northern Nigeria*, Berkeley, University of California Press, 1983 (chapters 6, 7)

IMPERIAL COMMERCE BECOMES GLOBAL COMMERCE

NEW FOUNDATION OF GLOBAL COMMERCE

Industrialization is the new foundation of the global market. It rests on the old foundation of rival commercial empires created by western European nations in the sixteenth, seventeenth, and eighteenth centuries. The fundamental propellant of the old imperial commerce was the search for profits. Merchants from western European nations began the search about 1450 and by 1500 the search was global. The search for profits could not have been sustained without the support of central governments. Central governments encouraged and protected imperial commerce because it increased tax revenues that were not dependent on feudal obligations. Revenues from external commerce went directly to the crown (central government) and could be used for purposes deemed essential for imperial or dynastic aspirations.

Industrialization, however, changed the scale of imperial rivalries. It made possible a quantum leap in military and naval power; and the ability to project this power anywhere in the world. In the second half of the nineteenth century, the imperial rivals of Britain had to catch up with the British lead in industrialization. Industrialization also created new imperial rivalries, especially with Germany. When industrial output in Germany equaled and then surpassed Britain, an increasing amount of German industrial capacity was devoted to military and naval construction to project Germany's imperial ambitions in Europe and elsewhere. German militarism terminated in the disaster of WWI, followed by the equally great disaster of WWII. [1]

After WWII, preventing future wars among the principal industrial nations was the guiding vision of western European and North American political leaders. The search for profits was unchanged but there had to be a different rationale than imperial rivalries. Only cooperative policies of political economy among industrial nations would maximize the production of new wealth. The reciprocal of producing new wealth was taxing it in order pay for social services for the working populations of industrial nations. Seen from a different perspective, imperial commercial rivalries among the principal industrial nations would be replaced with competition between global and multinational corporations. The new commercial rivalry would be on a corporate scale that crossed all national boundaries. This would reduce commercial rivalries among industrial nations to manageable proportions.

The principal cooperative policies that have evolved after WWII to guide the new global economy are: 1) encouraging freer trade among industrial nations in order to end old imperial rivalries; 2) creating organizations to manage the expansion of global commerce with minimal dislocations within industrial nations; 3) regional free trade associations as intermediaries to global free trade, especially among industrialized nations; 4) encouraging peasant nations to accept investments by global and multinational corporations in order to increase taxable wealth; 5) sharing raw materials on the basis of an ability to purchase them at free market prices. Leaders of the Soviet Union had their own vision of how global commerce should be managed. It was the pre-WWII commercial imperialism of economic self-sufficiency that was disguised by the Soviet version of the Marxist religion.

From its inception the purpose of the new global economy was to equalize opportunities for all nations to create new wealth on the basis of comparative advantages in terms of trade that they possessed or could develop. Production of new wealth was the first priority because improvements in the social welfare of employed persons depended on increasing the tax revenues of central governments.

Many people are critical of the impact of the new global economy on peasant nations because of the social dislocations that accompany the commercialization of subsistence cultures. Critics of globalization claim that the investments made by global corporations in peasant nations blind industrial nations to the imperative of social justice. Alternatively, policies that maximize the production of new wealth by global corporations pose a threat to human rights. Social justice and human rights are ambiguous concepts because they have no generally accepted definitions; therefore, they mean what these critics want them to mean. This allows them to use these concepts to serve their agendas.

Their agendas usually oppose investments by global and multinational corporations in peasant nations because they claim that the new wealth is not equitably shared or, alternatively, it perpetuates the absolute poverty of neocolonial dependency. They believe that peasant nations can industrialize using their own resources; therefore, investments by global and multinational corporations thwart democratic socialist governments because they are a powerful interest that excludes peasants from political power. Cheryl Payer summarizes why these critics oppose the new global market.

The World Bank is perhaps the most important instrument of the developed capitalist countries for prying state control of its Third World member countries out of the hands of nationalists and socialists who would regulate international capital's inroads, and turning that power to the service of international capital. [2]

"Capitalist economic development makes people poor by depriving them of their share of the world's natural resources and of access to political power. . . . These people (are) the victims of development." [3] These criticisms assume that peasants want full time employment and that there is a finite amount of natural resources in the world. Both assumptions are wrong. These critics are conspicuous in ignoring the refusal of peasants to perform commercial labor norms in agriculture that can produce assured food surpluses (without Green

Revolution inputs), as occurred in seventeenth century England. They equally ignore high birthrates, transfer of agricultural labor to women and children, deforestation, and erosion that are the highly visible measures of subsistence labor norms.

The post-WWII policies of political economy that transformed South Korea and Taiwan from peasant nations into industrial nations are invisible to them. The rapid increase in wealth in these nations was due to the mobilization of domestic and imported capital in order to increase the production of products for sale on the global market. Critics of the global economy who defend the political and economic isolation of peasant nations are blind to the possibility that any peasant nation can industrialize if governing elites adopt policies that induce its citizens to perform commercial labor norms, acquire literacy, and learn new skills. Put in another perspective, these critics of the new global economy do not blame the subsistence statusquo of peasant nations on governing elites. The blame is always elsewhere.

The micro-vision of these critics is diametrically opposed to the assumptions of the political and business leaders who are building the global economy. These leaders share a vision that the creation of new wealth has no limits; and the production of new wealth must take priority over policies to redistribute existing wealth. They believe that there is an infinite amount of human and natural resources waiting to be mobilized to produce new wealth, and the best way to maximize the production of new wealth is to remove as many barriers as possible to global commerce. The purpose of maximizing the creation of new wealth is the enjoyment of consumer cultures for persons who perform the commercial labor norms that produce consumer products and services.

THE GLOBAL VISION

In 1945, U.S. political leaders were determined that there would not be a repetition of the settlement at the end of WWI (1918) that preserved the commercial rivalries of industrial nations. After WWI, the governing elites of European nations and Japan were intent on making their economies as self-sufficient as possible in raw materials and industrial skills. The Great Depression that began in 1930 and persisted to 1937 intensified rivalries among the principal industrial nations because they used every restrictive device available to channel trade to nations in their spheres of influence or to protect domestic industries. The purpose of these policies was industrial self-sufficiency. When one industrial nation began directing its trade for protectionist or strategic reasons, it generated retaliatory action by affected nations. During the interwar years (1918-1938), the pre-WWI commercial rivalries among the principal industrial nations intensified.

Before WWII ended, political leaders in the United States, with strong support from England, Canada, and Australia, were determined to prevent a recurrence of the imperial commercial rivalries that had contributed to igniting the war. After the war most postwar political leaders of western European nations had a similar vision. The old system had to be replaced. Prosperity was the essential foundation for sustaining peace among the principal industrial nations that were capable of waging global war. Postwar leaders clearly understood the advantages of reestablishing international trade in manufactured products as soon as possible because the political stability and the commercial prosperity of western European nations depended on full employment. The quickest way to achieve full employment was to increase global commerce.

During the four years following the surrender of Germany (May 1945) and Japan (August 1945) the western allies faced four problems: 1) how to protect western Europe and Japan from possible Soviet aggression after the Soviet Union isolated itself from participation in global commerce; 2) how to incorporate Germany and Japan into a new political and economic system without creating long term military threats to their neighbors; 3) how to reindustrialize western Europe and Japan; 4) how to revive international trade without reviving imperial commercial rivalries. The United States was in a preeminent position to define policies that sought solutions to these problems because it was the preeminent industrial nation.

Most postwar political leaders of western European nations knew that the end of war was a one-time window of opportunity to lay the foundation for a new global system of trade that fairly balanced benefits among industrial nations. United States political leaders insisted on policies where the competition would be among business corporations, not between rival commercial empires. This meant dissolution of the colonial empires assembled in the nineteenth and twentieth centuries.

The vision of non-Soviet political leaders in 1945 was a future that had as few barriers to international commerce as was politically possible. Removal of tariffs and other impediments to commerce would be huge incentives for business leaders to rationalize industrial production and related commercial services across national boundaries. Freer trade would also facilitate the transfer of capital and technologies to nations where property was safe, profits were taxed at reasonable rates, and where investments could be made on the basis of opportunities to earn profits, not for strategic purposes. In 1945, a global economy powered by global and multinational corporations was only a vision.

BRETTON WOODS AGREEMENT

The first step in fulfilling a vision of future global prosperity was the Bretton Woods Agreement that was negotiated in July 1944. Delegates from 44 nations took part in deliberations and when it went into operation in December 1946, 32 nations agreed to conduct their international financial transactions by its rules. Its purpose was to create a stable system of exchange rates for the currencies used in international trade and, eventually, to have all currencies freely convertible. It was designed to serve the needs of industrial nations because 80 percent of pre-WWII international commerce was among industrial nations. All participants agreed that stability in the value of national currencies and full convertibility would help prevent the reappearance of imperial commercial rivalries.

The heart of the Bretton Woods Agreement was fixing the exchange rates of the currencies of participating nations within a narrow range of fluctuations against the U.S. dollar. Fixed exchange rates would prevent competitive devaluations by nations that wanted to make their exports more competitive with the exports of other nations. The agreement allowed nations that accumulated dollars to exchange them on demand for gold owned by the U.S. government. At the end of WWII, the United States owned 60 percent of the world's supply of gold bars, valued at $35 an ounce. This stock of gold was six times the value of dollars in circulation worldwide; and because there was ample gold and a desperate need by the industrial nations of western Europe to use dollars to purchase raw materials and machine tools, few dollars were converted into gold. The value of the dollar in terms of gold was stable and it was the only currency that was fully convertible into all other currencies.

The U.S. dollar was also the principal source of liquidity in international trade. Its liquidity was maintained by continuous deficits in balance of payments in the 1950s and 1960s. Deficit spending was mostly for defense during the cold war. Dollars that were accumulated by the central banks of industrial nations, especially NATO nations, became a fund of overseas dollars (eurodollars). The convertibility of these dollars into all other currencies was the source of liquidity in global commerce. It also made the United States into the central banker of global commerce as well as making the dollar the principal reserve currency of the central banks of most nations outside the Soviet sphere of influence. The anchoring effect of fixed exchange rates produced price stability worldwide. This translated into low inflation and no cutthroat devaluations by the seven principal industrial nations in order to achieve short term competitive advantages in the global market. The group of seven nations (G7) were Britain, Canada, France, Germany, Italy, Japan, and the United States.

The maintenance of fixed exchange rates required a reservoir of liquidity available to nations with temporary imbalances plus a prearranged borrowing procedure. The pool of liquidity was called the International Monetary Fund (IMF). It was created by capital contributions by member nations. It became operational in March 1947 and its mission was to supervise the operation of exchange rates and mitigate financial difficulties of industrial nations when they had balance of payment problems. In order to qualify for loans, member nations had to change the policies that had created imbalances and agree to a schedule of repayments. If they failed to implement the conditions required by IMF directors, access to funds was suspended until the necessary policy changes were made.

Until 1973 most of the business of the IMF was with industrial nations. After that year it changed is mission. The new function of the IMF is covered in another section of this chapter.

Immediately after the war, full convertibility among the currencies of the G7 nations was impossible because the reindustrialization of western Europe required central governments to allocate scarce dollars to the most productive uses. Preferential allocations were to industries that were essential for restoring industrial productivity to pre-WWII levels as soon as possible; however, even with the most stringent allocation to the most important industries there were not enough dollars to accelerate productivity because too many factories had been neglected or destroyed during the war.

Negotiators at Bretton Woods knew that the postwar reindustrialization of European nations would require their industries to purchase large amounts of raw materials and machine tools. Much of these purchases would have to be made in U.S. dollars. European nations did not have them. Purchases would have to be made with credit and, in the immediate postwar years the amount of credit needed was much greater than the financial resources of all European nations. Where would the credit come from? A credit crisis never occurred because the Marshall Plan supplied the necessary raw materials and machine tools to sustain the reindustrialization of western European nations.

The Marshall Plan (officially, Economic Cooperation Act of 1948) solved the dollar shortage. Between 1948 and 1952 the Marshall Plan gave 13 billion dollars to western European nations to purchase raw material and machine tools in order to restore their productive capabilities. Increased production from rebuilt (and modernized) industries had two strategic purposes: full employment and political stability.

The Marshall Plan, however, was not a free ride for European nations. The plan required recipient nations to lower trade barriers and speed payments for products traded among themselves. The political leaders of western European nations were anxious to put these policies into operation because they clearly understood that trade barriers and delays in payment impeded full convertibility, as well as impeding the closer integration of the economies of western European nations. In order to speed payments for trade among themselves the European Payments Union (EPU) was organized in 1950. It was a multilateral clearinghouse to facilitate the economic integration of western Europe and was one of the precursor institutions to the Treaty of Rome (1957) that established the European Common Market.

During the five years the Marshall Plan operated, currency controls conserved the dollar reserves of recipient nations. As the value, volume, and efficiency of industrial production increased—and the integration of the economies of European nations proceeded—currency controls among European currencies were gradually relaxed. By 1955 most European currencies were fully convertible among themselves, but full convertibility into U.S. dollars did not occur until 1959 when the industrial productivity in western European nations reached pre-WWII levels.

In the ten years following the end of the Marshall Plan (1952-1962) industrial production in recipient nations increased an average of 39 percent, exports doubled, and these nations accumulated current account surpluses for the first time since the end of WWII. There were four principal causes for the spectacular performance of western European industry: 1) infusion of capital from the Marshall Plan; 2) removal of tariff barriers within the Common Market; 3) stable exchange rates in international trade; 4) security provided by the North Atlantic Treaty Organization (NATO) that was essential for the operation and evolution of the Common Market. The conjunction of these four policies permanently increased annual rates of industrial production among western European nations so that they were competitive among themselves, competitive with products produced in the United States, and competitive in the emerging global market that was free from past imperial rivalries.

EUROPEAN COMMON MARKET

The wartime allies were divided over how Germany was to be treated. The Soviets pillaged the industrial capacity of their zone of occupation in order to rebuild Soviet industry; and France, Britain, and the United States were undecided how their zones of occupation should be incorporated into the political and economic structure of postwar Europe. Particularly, the French feared a resurgence of German military power unless there were international restraints on German conduct.

A principal reason for forming the European Common Market was to integrate German industrial capacity into a western European market that was so interdependent that military domination by one nation would be impossible. The impossibility of one western European nation to achieve military dominance would be reinforced by an equally interdependent military alliance led by the United States. This was NATO. In a military and economic sense, the United States would be the honest broker that encouraged European economic integration.

In the immediate years after the end of the war the political leaders of western European nations were very strongly motivated to create a new political and economic order, even without encouragement from the United States. What they needed was protection from potential Soviet aggression and no veto from the United States. They got both. With 50 years of perspective, the institution building begun by political leaders of western European nations immediately after the war have been astoundingly successful in maintaining peace and producing regional prosperity on a scale that was unimaginable in 1945.

The Common Market had its origins in 1947 when the United States asked the 16 nations receiving Marshall Plan aid to organize its distribution. The Organization for European Economic Cooperation performed this function. Thereafter the political leaders of France, Germany, Italy, Netherlands, Belgium, and Luxembourg began the process of economic and political integration. The first result of their efforts was the Benelux Customs Union of 1948. It was a free trade treaty between the Netherlands, Belgium, and Luxembourg.

These two organizations created momentum for a closer economic and political integration to evolve behind the shield of NATO (organized in April 1949). In May 1950, French foreign minister Robert Schuman proposed that the production of coal and steel in western Europe become a single market in order to integrate the production of steel and steel products so closely that no European nation could wage war against its neighbors. West Germany's chancellor Konrad Adenauer and the political leaders of Italy, Belgium, Netherlands, and Luxembourg immediately endorsed it. The European Coal and Steel Community became operational in July 1952. Its success prompted political leaders in these nations to begin planning an economic union encompassing all industrial products. Negotiations proceeded, and in March 1957 the Treaty of Rome created the European Economic Community (ECC) or European Common Market. Six nations (France, Germany, Italy, Belgium, the Netherlands, Luxembourg) ratified it and multilateral negotiations began the process of lowering tariffs on all manufactured products. Agriculture was excepted.

The Treaty of Rome projected:

full economic union—the generation of a united internal market in which the national boundaries of the member states would lose their economic meaning. Not only goods but a great many other things would move freely across national boundaries. That concept required among other things that labor and capital should move freely. [4]

The treaty was possible because Adenauer was willing to make economic concessions to France and Italy in return for their political support to preserve West Germany's continued presence in Berlin in the face of continuous Soviet pressure. This support was embedded in NATO. When Dwight D. Eisenhower was elected president of the United States in 1952 the economic integration of western Europe could proceed with an assurance of security because he strongly supported strengthening NATO to counter the Soviet threat to Berlin, and just as strongly supported the economic integration of western Europe that was proceeding in Common Market nations.

Britain remained aloof from Common Market negotiations because most of her trade was elsewhere. In 1956 half of its trade was with Commonwealth nations/colonies that were in the sterling zone and only one-quarter was with continental European nations. Britain was less interested in resolving the German question by integrating its economy with the six Common Market nations because this required economic federalism that implied some form of political federation at a future date. Sovereignty had served Britain well during the war and British political leaders doubted that France and Germany could reach a sustainable agreement to integrate their economies. They believed that the best policy for Britain was to continue to preside over Commonwealth commerce during the process of decolonization; and continue to cultivate a special relationship with the United States.

Britain's response to the instant success of the Common Market was to promote the organization of a second community of European nations to reduce trade barriers. In 1960 it brokered the organization of the European Free Trade Area (EFTA). It had seven members with highly variable sized industrial sectors. The seven nations were Britain, Sweden, Portugal, Denmark, Norway, Austria, and Switzerland. About the only thing they had in common was a peripheral location to Common Market nations. Unlike the Common Market, EFTA had no plans to integrate their economic and political institutions.

From its inception EFTA was a hollow copy of the Common Market. Within a year it was moribund. In 1961 British prime minister Harold Macmillan recognized that Britain's commercial future was across the channel because its trade with the Common Market was rapidly increasing and trade with the remaining colonies and post-colonial nations was rapidly diminishing. Most post-colonial nations had stagnant economies and adopted policies that diminished commercial ties with Britain; and most of the continuing trade was in low value items. In contrast, trade with the Common Market was in higher value manufactured products because, during the 1960s, increasing industrial productivity in Common Market nations and Britain created consumer cultures.

Britain applied for membership in the Common Market in August 1961. This decision confirmed that Commonwealth commerce was not a source of economic strength because post-colonial governing elites failed to enforce policies that produced sufficient taxable wealth to pay the costs of economic development. Britain's declining trade with Commonwealth nations became the smile of the Cheshire cat: the Commonwealth remained after the commerce disappeared. The new reality was that Britain could best participate in the new global economy and best retain its special relationship with the United States by membership in the Common Market. [5]

President Charles de Gaulle of France was determined to prevent Britain's entry into the Common Market because he believed that Britain's special relationship with the United States would detract from France's influence in Common Market policies. De Gaulle believed that U.S. influence, delegated to its surrogate Britain, was not in France's best interest. De Gaulle especially wanted to limit U.S. influence in defense and agricultural policies. He believed that western Europe should have its own foreign policy (détente) with the Soviets instead of endorsing the U.S. policy of confrontation following the Cuban missile crisis (October 1962). If there was another war it would be nuclear and Europe would be the principal battlefield. In this situation European nations needed their own nuclear capability to give them some autonomy in future U.S.-Soviet crises, and France was in process of developing it. He vetoed Britain's entry into the Common Market in January 1963.

By rejecting Britain's application de Gaulle hoped to shape the commercial and military policies of the Common Market, with France defining what was best for France. Britain's presence in the Common Market would have prevented France from exercising more influence in making commercial and defense policies than its industrial capacity warranted. In effect, France would manage distancing the Common Market's commercial and military policies from U.S. hegemony.

Immediately after de Gaulle vetoed Britain's entry, Adenauer and de Gaulle solidified the French-German rapprochement by a treaty that de Gaulle thought would allow France to set the agenda for dealing with the United States and NATO. The new German chancellor, Ludwig Erhard and the bundestag (German parliament) did not approve. Most German political leaders believed that the United States, in its capacity as leader of NATO, was more important for German security than France because France was in the process of withdrawing its armed forces from NATO. This made France an unreliable ally in the defense of Germany. Britain applied for admission a second time in 1967 and again de Gaulle vetoed it. The second veto was designed to give France a predominant voice in formulating a uniform tariff policy on imports into the Common Market, especially for agricultural commodities.

Charles de Gaulle's resignation from the French presidency in April 1969 removed a roadblock to Britain's entry into the Common Market. His successor Georges Pompidou favored Britain's entry—on terms—and the conservative government elected in Britain in June 1970, led by prime minister Edward Heath, was strongly committed to entry. During the election campaign Heath presented the British electorate with an either/or picture of Britain's future as an industrial nation. He clearly linked future British prosperity to membership in the Common Market because the sterling zone was dead and increased trade with post-colonial nations never materialized. Entry into the Common Market was a bargain that Britain could not refuse.

The concessions that Britain made for entry were mostly with agriculture. Within three years, Commonwealth preference for imported food grains and other foodstuffs were to end. British citizens would pay higher food prices because more of their food would come from high cost producers in western Europe, especially from France; and Britain would have to make substantial monetary contributions to Common Market governance in Brussels. On January 1, 1973 Britain entered the Common Market with two close trading partners, Ireland and Denmark. The original six nations became nine and the precedent was set for future enlargements as political conditions allowed.

Favorable political conditions came very soon. Dictatorships ended in Portugal in April 1974; in Greece in July 1974, and in Spain in November 1975. In all three nations, democratically elected leaders succeeded to power and the new governments petitioned for entry. Membership in the Common Market would help solidify fragile democratic institutions by embedding domestic politics within the matrix of the political stability and economic prosperity of the Common Market. In other words, membership within the Common Market was the best guarantee for the orderly transfer of power in future elections in these three nations. Political leaders of Common Market nations desired their entry in order to enhance political stability, especially in southern Europe (Greece), as well as for the potential sale of more manufactured products.

All three nations, plus Turkey, applied for entry in 1977. Greece's application was approved in May 1979 and Greece entered in January 1981, with a five year transition period to bring its economy into harmony with the policies of the Common Market. Greece's membership took priority over Spain and Portugal because Greece was a member of NATO and had negotiated a customs union agreement with the Common Market in 1962. Dual membership in NATO and the Common Market tied the eastern Mediterranean much closer to western Europe in the cold war. Spain and Portugal were admitted five years later (1986) and given seven years to integrate their economies, especially agriculture, into the political economy of the Common Market. Turkey negotiated an association agreement, as did Cyprus and Malta, as a prelude to a customs union that would be a prelude for membership at an indefinite future date.

After the Common Market became operational tariffs between member nations were quickly lowered. By 1970 trade among Common Market nations was essentially free and capital transfers had minimal restraints. Business corporations could borrow and banks could lend to any corporation within the Common Market and corporate profits were freely transferable between nations. Many national corporations became multinational corporations because there were few barriers to building factories wherever they could efficiently serve the rapidly enlarging volume of consumption within the Common Market.

By 1970 there was also a common tariff on products entering the Common Market from nonmember nations. A uniform tariff meant that no Common Market nation had access to cheaper commodities or manufactured products than any other Common Market nation unless the council of ministers agreed to make exceptions for limited numbers of commodities coming from post-colonial nations. This policy was designed to achieve two results: 1) increase the bargaining power of the Common Market in negotiating trade agreements with nonmember nations and regional trade associations; 2) enhance the political cohesion of Common Market nations.

The council of ministers has not used the power inherent in a uniform tariff to shield European industry from global competition. Instead, they have used it to expand the scope of freer trade beyond the borders of the Common Market/European Union in conformity with the goal of GATT/WTO, and in conformity with the vision of post-WWII political leaders of nations with free market economies. In the process of implementing freer trade beyond the borders of the European Union, its political leaders have encouraged the politically unstable nations on the south shore of the Mediterranean Sea to implement policies that can increase the per capita production of commercial wealth. Free entry or preferentially low tariffs have been granted for many commodities produced by Morocco, Algeria, Tunisia, Egypt, Jordan, Lebanon, Syria, and Israel, as well as for 60 former British and French colonies (Lome Convention, 1975). Entry has been granted without the reciprocal that these nations preferentially purchase manufactured products from Common Market nations.

At the same time the Common Market was achieving full commercial integration (1968-1970), the U.S. dollar lost its commanding position as the strongest currency in global commerce. Continuous deficit spending for defense caused the dollar's weakness, relative to the currencies of Common Market nations and Japan. Sustained deficit spending, however, accorded with U.S. national interests. That interest was containment of Soviet power and influence outside its sphere of influence. In addition to spending disproportionately large amounts of money for mutual defense, the openness of the U.S. market to imports of manufactured products strongly contributed the prosperity of Common Market nations and Japan.

By 1970 the acute balance of payments deficits by the United States, coupled with the successful reindustrialization of Common Market nations and Japan, required a new commercial and financial relationship, but not necessarily changes in military policies. The United States insisted that Common Market nations increase its share of funding NATO and Japan increase its contributions to support U.S. military and naval units stationed in Japan. No longer could the United States disproportionately bear the costs for maintaining NATO's capability of providing security for western Europe and the nations along the eastern rim of the Pacific ocean.

United States president Richard M. Nixon acted unilaterally to shape a new commercial relationship with the Common Market and the rest of the world. In August 1971 dollars held by central banks could no longer be converted into gold, and he imposed a ten percent surcharge on all imports into the United States, except foodstuffs and raw materials. In December he urged congress to raise the price of gold to 38 dollars an ounce in order to devalue the dollar by 8.5 percent. Simultaneously, other industrial nations were pressured to revalue their currencies upward relative to the dollar. The realignment of exchange rates meant that the U.S. dollar was devalued about 12 percent. Devaluation of the dollar and revaluation of the currencies of the principal industrial nations cheapened the price of U.S. exports and made them more competitive with similar products manufactured in Common Market nations. In return for revaluing their currencies Nixon removed the ten percent surcharge on imports.

Nixon used crude coercion to force a realignment of the currencies of the principal industrial nations. His actions were incompatible with U.S. obligations to the IMF and GATT, but Common Market nations and Japan accommodated themselves to the new reality because it was in their interests. The realignment of currencies marked the end of the postwar policy of allowing preferential entry into the United States of manufactured products from Common Market nations and Japan. The years of subsidizing the industries of these nations into global competitiveness were over. In the future, commercial relations between the United States, the Common Market, and Japan would follow new rules of reciprocity.

The purpose of Nixon's unilateral action was to maintain the political and military leadership of the United States to contain Soviet imperial ambitions. Containment was Nixon's first priority because he believed it was the only way to ensure global peace (absence of nuclear war); and to achieve it he was willing to risk commercial reprisals by the Common Market and Japan, or disruption of the cohesion of the Common Market.

In February 1973 the U.S. dollar was further devalued by ten percent when the price of gold was revalued at 42 dollars an ounce. This was rapidly followed by a system of floating exchange rates for the currencies of the principal industrial nations outside the Soviet sphere of influence. Many bankers feared that this was a prelude to wildly fluctuating exchange rates that would trigger competitive currency devaluations in order to secure trade advantages. As a matter of historical record, floating exchange rates have been highly effective in promoting increased world trade but flotation killed the Bretton Woods Agreement. Floating exchange rates produced a further result: the U.S. dollar lost its status as the undisputed reserve currency. It did, however, remain the preferred currency in global commerce.

In order to remove uncertainties caused by floating exchange rates the group 10 nations (G7 nations plus Sweden, Netherlands, and Belgium) sponsored a negotiating conference. It began in Tokyo in September 1973 and continued for the next five years. New rules of reciprocity were negotiated in which the Common Market, Japan, and the United States continued to cooperate to expand the volume and value of international commerce and its increasingly visible result: consumer cultures in industrial nations.

During the 1960s and 1970s global trade in manufactured products grew faster than increases in the value of all manufactured products in industrial nations. The trend accelerated in the 1980s. The volume of global commerce increased at an annual rate of about 5.3 percent while total global production of all commodities increased at an annual rate of about 3.5 percent. Exports were an increasingly important means of achieving economic growth and its reciprocal: higher standards of living for workers in industrial nations. David Reynolds summarizes how increased global commerce helped create consumer cultures in Common Market nations and Japan. "This surge in the international trade of manufactures was at the heart of the consumer boom." [6]

From the oil crisis of 1973 to 1985, further political integration of the Common Market was on hold. The several proposed plans were ahead of the thinking of both the electorates and political leaders of

Common Market nations because they were unwilling to further compromise national sovereignty. Further reductions of trade barriers, however, had a high rate of approval among electorates. Commercial integration continued at an accelerating rate, mostly by mergers of business corporations across national boundaries.

When Jacques Delors was appointed president of the Common Market Commission in 1985 he brought with him a strategy of step-by-step commercial integration that could evolve into political integration when political opportunities presented themselves. His goal was a customs union like the freedom of interstate trade in the United States and of interprovincial trade in Canada. Delors clearly designed agenda was incorporated into the Single European Act (SEA) passed by the European parliament in January 1987. SEA committed Common Market nations to a single currency sometime in the near future as the prerequisite for a fully integrated market in western Europe.

At the same time that the Delors agenda was being implemented, unforeseen political events in central and eastern Europe were generating the opportunity for greater political integration. The Berlin wall was suddenly breached in November 1989. Shortly afterward, the East German government faltered and dissolved. The collapse of the East German government made German reunification a reality in October 1990; and one year later the Soviet Union dissolved into 15 successor nations.

French political leaders were unsure of their response to the simultaneous end of the cold war and German reunification. In many ways, the influence of U.S. president George W. Bush was decisive. He had a better grasp of how an enlarged zone of economic cooperation in Europe, with the Common Market as the core, would increase the production of new wealth that would be the foundation for establishing democratic governments in central European nations. French and British reservations were overwhelmed by Bush's unreserved support of German chancellor Helmut Kohl.

Kohl received U.S. support because he realistically appraised the opportunity. He believed that acceptance of reunification by Common Market nations was dependent on greater political integration of Common Market nations. The essential integrating measure was a common currency (euro) that would make it all but impossible for a single nation within the Common Market to wage war anywhere unless all members approved. A European currency would also continue the process of increasing European prosperity; and jeopardizing this prosperity (as measured against the rest of the world) was unthinkable. Kohl's assessment of the politics of unification accorded with the assessment of the impact of unification by Soviet general secretary Mikhail Gorbachev who could have prevented German reunification. Both the Soviets and French accepted increased political integration of western European nations in order to offset the enlarged population and increased industrial and political power of a united Germany. All parties saw the increased political integration of Common Market nations as the best guarantee of future peace in Europe.

The confluence of German, French, and Soviet interests was the impetus for transforming the Common Market into the European Union. The fruition of these negotiations was the Maastricht Treaty that was submitted to Common Market members for ratification in December 1991. It had two parts: monetary union and political union. The key measure was a common currency (euro). One of the explicit purposes of a common currency was a European alternative to the U.S. dollars as a source of liquidity in global commerce. European business corporations wanted the benefits of a currency that had global acceptance in the same way that global acceptance of the U.S. dollar benefited U.S. business corporations. As an exercise in political and economic cooperation the Maastricht Treaty equaled the Treaty of Rome (1957) that established the Common Market.

EUROPEAN UNION

Shortly after the collapse of the Soviet Union, in April 1992 the nations of the European Union committed themselves to a more perfect union when the European parliament passed the Maastricht Treaty. By December 1992, 9 of the 12 nations in the Common Market ratified it. The two immediate purposes of the Maastricht Treaty were the adoption of the euro as a common currency and a common labor policy that allowed citizens of the European Union to seek employment in all member nations. Denmark, Sweden, and Britain opted to retain their national currencies. It became operational in 1993 and the European Union (EU) came into existence.

Helmut Kohl, the German chancellor, insisted on an independent central bank because central control of credit polices was the only way to control inflation. In his opinion, and the opinion of almost all economists, central control of credit policies was also essential for guiding the investment policies of business corporations as well as for making predictable budgets by EU nations. In January 1999 all balance of payment accounts were denominated in euros, and euro coins and paper currency replaced national currencies in 2002.

The advantages of one European market, coupled with the collapse of the Soviet Union, was the opportunity for Sweden, Finland, and Austria to apply for admission to the European Union. Their principal export markets were nations within the EU and most of their commercial laws were already in harmony with laws and practices of the European Union. They were admitted in 1995. Political and business leaders in these nations clearly understood the opportunities that a politically integrated Europe would give their industries, as well as enhancing opportunities for participating in global commerce.

The disintegration of the Soviet Union in 1991 created problems as well as opportunities for the European Union. Leaders of the European Union had four principal concerns: 1) security of its eastern border; 2) preservation of the fragile democracies that succeeded communist governments; 3) control of migration from central European nations and beyond; 4) implementation of policies that would harmonize the political economies of these nations with the policies of the European Union in order to ease their entry into the EU at a future date.

In 1992 the three principal candidates for membership were Poland, Czechoslovakia, and Hungary. The number became five in 1993 when Czechoslovakia split into the Czech Republic and Slovakia and Yugoslavia disintegrated into several successor states, of which

Slovenia was the preferred candidate for entry. It was clear to EU political leaders that preparation for membership would be a slow process. Two statistics convey a generalized understanding of the dimensions of the problem. If ten nations in central and southern Europe (Bulgaria, Czech Republic, Estonia, Hungary, Latvia, Lithuania, Poland, Romania, Slovakia, Slovenia) had joined the EU in 1996, they would have increased the population 28 percent but added only 4 percent to the gross domestic product. The economic disparity of these nations with nations of the EU was most visible in agriculture, especially in Bulgaria, Latvia, Lithuania, Poland, and Romania. In the EU only 6 percent of the population is engaged in agriculture. On average, the agricultural sectors of these five nations have 22 percent of the population but they produce only 8 percent of the gross domestic product.

In 2002, these nations were poor to very poor compared to the 15 nations of the EU. Their economies varied from obsolescent to decrepit; their agricultural sectors were grossly inefficient by any measure of commercial agriculture and, although their political institutions were in transition to democracy, there was no assurance that the transition would be successful. Before these nations could enter the European Union they had to make fundamental changes in their constitutions and economic policies, and these changes could not be implemented without a large amount of social dislocations and political uncertainty. It was not clear in 1993 that these governments could manage these changes. The leaders of the European Union knew that it was in Europe's best interest to do everything possible to facilitate their entry in the shortest time. The question they faced was how the EU could guide their transition to free market economies managed by democratic governments.

Association agreements were the means of managing the transition. They allow selected commodities free entry into the European Union. Access to the EU gives the most efficient producers the opportunity to improve their competitiveness—a competitiveness that is essential for survival when these nations enter the EU. An alternative way for these nations to achieve competitiveness is to encourage global and multinational corporations to purchase domestic corporations, install new managers, invest additional capital, and train persons to use the newest technologies at optimal efficiency.

Association agreements are designed to facilitate the adoption of EU commercial laws (contracts, land tenure) that are essential for entry into the EU. They have forced ex-communist nations to create favorable marketing and investment climates for global and multinational corporations in order to increase per capita productivity. The reciprocal is forcing domestic corporations to become competitive with global and multinational corporations. No longer can they be protected by political and economic isolation that was necessary for the inefficiencies of centrally planned economies to operate.

Association agreements with ex-communist nations granted free entry of nonsensitive products to the EU; however, sensitive manufactured products paid tariffs for four to six years. In return, these nations had to open their markets within ten years to all products produced in the EU. These nations also had to adopt, within three years, the competition policy of the EU and make its intellectual property laws and domestic commercial regulations conformable to EU laws. Associate nations also had to accept direct investments from corporations operating in the EU. Nor could they impede the transfer of profits or funds to corporations within the EU. Agricultural products were a separate issue. Entry of agricultural commodities is negotiated on a concessionary basis whenever it is politically expedient; which is to say that most agricultural commodities have been excluded from association agreements.

In 50 years retrospect, the Common Market was an essential intermediate stage in the evolution of the European Union. It is also the principal model for the evolution of other regional trade associations into more economically integrated markets in the twenty-first century. By any measure, the EU has been a spectacularly successful accomplishment of political leadership. It has magnificently succeeded in creating consumer cultures in western European nations and making the economies of EU nations so interdependent that another war among them is impossible.

The EU is also the foundation for the next evolutionary change: creating a Republic of Europe. It is, however, impossible to make a timetable. In 1991, a Republic of Europe was mostly a vision. Ten years later there is a clear understanding that if the European Union evolves into the Republic of Europe, the government will be federal.

NATO

NATO had its origins in the Brussels Pact of March 1948 between Britain, France, and the Benelux nations. It was a treaty of mutual defense that committed the signatory nations to mutual support in the event of an armed attack on any one of them. It would be in effect for 50 years. It also committed these nations to "so organize and coordinate their economic activities as to produce the best possible results, by the elimination of conflict in their economic policies, the coordination of production, and the development of commercial exchanges." [7]

The Brussels Pact was designed to stop the potential expansion of the Soviet sphere of influence into western Europe but, implicitly, it could be applied to potential German expansion unless reindustrialized Germany could be integrated into an organization that could neutralize expansionist ambitions. Most political leaders in western Europe and their counterparts in the United States strongly favored defensive and commercial integration; although, U.S. leaders were not yet committed to a trans-Atlantic military alliance.

Four events forced the United States to act: 1) the forcible replacement of a democratically elected government in Czechoslovakia by a communist regime (February 1948); 2) elections in Italy (April 1948) with the communist party receiving strong encouragement from the Soviet Union; 3) a Soviet warning to Norway to remain neutral, with an unstated threat to take appropriate action; 4) the Berlin blockade that began in June 1948. These events marked the beginning of the cold war and immensely clarified political thinking in Washington. There was no longer any doubt that the reindustrialization and defense of western Europe were inseparably linked and that immediate action was imperative. Political leaders in western Europe and the United States agreed "that there could be no economic recovery without the political confidence that military security could offer and that there could be neither political confidence nor military security without guarantees of American involvement in the defense of Western Europe." [8]

The immediate and enduring mission of NATO was to provide a protective shield behind which the reindustrialization of western Europe could proceed. Its key provision was that an attack on one of the signatory nations would be an attack on all of them. NATO came into operation in July 1949 with the signatures of 11 nations: United States, Canada, Britain, France, Italy, Netherlands, Belgium, Luxembourg, Denmark, Norway, and Portugal. Its immediate purpose was to prevent Soviet military expansion into western Europe. Its corollary purpose was to provide a shield so that the political leaders of western European nations could proceed with commercial and political integration. NATO's protection was the ability of U.S. bombers operating from bases in Britain to deliver atomic bombs to most cities in European Russia.

The success of the airlift in supplying Berlin forced Stalin to end the blockade in May 1949. Although the end of the blockade was a source of relief in western Europe, the explosion of an atomic bomb by the Soviets in August 1949 renewed concern of political leaders for the safety of western Europe. During this period of recurring crises the federal republic of Germany came into existence. It was established in September 1949 and was a direct result of NATO. Without the unity and protection provided by NATO, Britain, France, and the Benelux nations would have delayed establishing the German republic.

There was also an implicit global dimension to NATO's European mission. It was to prevent a war between nations possessing nuclear weapons that would almost certainly escalate into a global conflict. Members of NATO believed that the best guarantee of global peace (or absence of war between nations possessing nuclear weapons) was peace in western Europe; and after the Soviets exploded an atomic bomb, this was obtainable only by a balance of nuclear weaponry. A balance of nuclear weaponry became the policy of peaceful coexistence.

At the same time, events on the asian side of the Pacific ocean accelerated the rearming of western Europe. In 1949 communist armies gained control of China and in February 1950 Josef Stalin and Mao Zedong signed a treaty of friendship and alliance. Four months later, in June 1950, North Korean troops invaded South Korea and were later supported by Chinese troops. The North Korean government had come into existence in the same way that East German government had come into existence. Both were part of the carve-up of territory where allied armies met after German and Japanese armies surrendered. The government of North Korea was a client of the Soviet Union and the governments of South Korea and Japan were clients of the United States. The invasion of South Korea and subsequent battles led to a truce in July 1953 that restored the post-WWII division of Korea.

After the end of the Pacific war Japan was isolated and reindustrialization depended on access to export markets. The United States controlled this access. Unlike the United States and western Europe, Japan had few natural resources within its borders. Its industries depended on imported raw materials, and it was equally dependent on export markets for its manufactured products. The great asset of Japan was literate workers and an educated middle class that was integrated into a disciplined labor force. It had little else to propel its economic recovery after it lost its commercial empire. Raw materials had to be purchased on the global market and the products of its industries had to be sold on the global market.

The start of the Korean war in June 1950 had the same energizing effect on the Japanese economy as Marshall Plan aid had on western Europe. The procurement of manufactured products from Japanese industry for use by U.S. armed forces was a huge infusion of capital at the time when Japanese industry could use it to maximum effect. The mobilization of Japanese industrial capabilities to supply U.S. armed forces in Korea made it imperative to accelerate the reindustrialization of Japan. The first step in the process was to end U.S. occupation. Thereafter, reindustrialization would be sustained by providing easy entry of manufactured products into the U.S. market. Japan regained its independence in September 1951 with the signing of a formal peace treaty. The treaty neutralized Japan, and both Japan and Taiwan were protected behind the shield of the U.S. navy.

European leaders assumed that the Korean war would divert U.S. resources from Europe. This did not happen. In the next four years mobilization of manpower and weaponry, largely funded by the United States, made NATO into an effective army that could contest a potential Soviet invasion of western Europe. An effective NATO required the participation of West German troops, and this meant rearming Germany. This was a very sensitive issue in France and Britain. How could it be managed? An acceptable commander was essential and there was only one person who could perform this function on short notice. This was Dwight D. Eisenhower. He was drafted to command NATO forces in October 1950 and supervise the building and deployment of the army.

Western European political leaders were assured of the U.S. commitment to defend western Europe when Eisenhower was elected president of the United States in 1952. After a NATO army of 100,000 men became operational, Germany was accepted into NATO (May 1955) and German army units were incorporated into it. The geopolitical term that described NATO's European mission was containment. Soviet military power would be contained within the sphere of influence it had acquired in central and southern Europe at the end of WWII, and if Soviet armies invaded western Europe, U.S. nuclear weapons would deliver massive retaliation on Soviet cities. Massive retaliation, however, was a realistic strategy only as long as the United States had a monopoly of delivery systems. In the 1950s this was long range strategic bombers.

When the Soviets produced a more effective delivery system (ballistic missiles) U.S. strategy had to change. The possession by the Soviet Union and the United States of ballistic missiles that could deliver nuclear warheads made peaceful coexistence an imperative policy for both nations. In terms of real politics, it created a balance of power that stabilized the hegemony of the Soviet Union in its sphere of influence in central and southern Europe and NATO in its sphere of influence in western Europe. The Soviet Union used its hegemony to impose client governments on central European nations; and if the communists parties in these nations selected unreliable leaders or there was popular unrest that threatened to topple these governments (as occurred in East Germany in 1953, Hungary in 1956, and Czechoslovakia in 1968), Soviet armed forces intervened.

NATO's response to Soviet possession of nuclear weapons was to extend the boundaries of containment and peaceful coexistence to the eastern end of the Mediterranean Sea. Greece and Turkey were accepted into NATO in February 1952; and a continued buildup of U.S. military power in the aftermath of the Korean war applied containment to the rest of the globe.

In western Europe, Soviet political and military ambitions were contained behind an iron curtain. The iron curtain actually existed. It was a guarded barbed wire fence constructed by the communist governments of central European nations along their western borders to keep their citizens from fleeing westward, with the consequent loss of their labor and skills. It became glaringly visible to the rest of the world in August 1961 with the building of a wall through the center of Berlin. The Berlin wall, like the iron curtain, was a hugely defensive measure. It signified that the Soviets had little interest in reducing trade barriers with Common Market nations, the United States, and Japan. Policies of industrialization in the Soviet sphere of influence would operate in self-sufficient isolation like the pre-WWII commercial empires of western European nations.

In comparison, NATO nations negotiated policies to increase trade among themselves and increase political integration as a means of mutually increasing commercial wealth. On the basis of the success of the Common Market, they became partners with the United States in molding the IMF, GATT, and the World Bank to serve the needs of a global economy. For the Soviets, containment behind the iron curtain became commercial isolation (but not political isolation), and was similar, but less extreme than the commercial isolation of North Korea behind a guarded barbed wire fence across the Korean peninsula.

The attempt of Nikita Khruschev, general secretary of the Soviet communist party, to extend the Soviet sphere of influence to the American side of the Atlantic produced the greatest crisis of the cold war. It had its origins in 1959 when Fidel Castro's guerrilla army led a popular uprising in Cuba against an unpopular and corrupt dictator. Within a year Castro announced that he was a communist who would export revolution to other Latin American nations. The United States immediately orchestrated a trade embargo against Cuba that accelerated the process of Cuba becoming a client nation of the Soviets.

In April 1961 a small group of exiles invaded Cuba in hopes of inciting a popular uprising. It was a total failure. Khruschev gambled that Castro's ability to remain in power was an opportunity to extend the Soviet sphere of influence by placing short range missiles on Cuban soil, in the same way the United States had deployed short range missiles on Turkish soil. Missiles began arriving in October 1962. The confrontation that followed was only resolved when the ships carrying missiles to Cuba made U-turns and returned to Europe. The reciprocal was withdrawal of U.S. missiles from Turkey and a pledge by the United States not to invade Cuba. During the next few years peaceful coexistence became an arms race and the cold war became frigid.

After the removal of Khruschev from power in October 1964 the Soviets devoted about 25 percent of their industrial capacity to developing ballistic missiles capable of delivering nuclear warheads anywhere in the world. By 1969 the Soviets had achieved parity with the United States in the number of intercontinental ballistic missiles (ICBM). It was apparent to the leaders of all industrial nations that it was in their interest to reduce tensions that could escalate into a suicidal nuclear war. How could tensions be resolved? How long would it take? There were no sure answers, but arms reductions had to begin with dialogue.

U.S. president Richard M. Nixon took the initiative in October 1969 by beginning negotiations with the Soviets for a strategic arms limitation treaty (SALT). This was the beginning of détente—decreasing political and military tensions between the Soviet Union and the United States, and by extension between the Soviet Union and China, and between the United States and China. The immediate objective of Nixon's diplomacy was the withdrawal of U.S. troops from Vietnam, and this required an end of hostilities. After the fighting stopped, the South Vietnamese government would have to defend its integrity without the presences of U.S. troops.

The second objective of détente was refocusing U.S. priorities on Europe in order to permanently reduce the possibilities of a nuclear war. Both the United States and the Soviet Union agreed that a realistic first step was reducing the number of ICBMs equipped with nuclear warheads—because these weapons were extremely expensive to develop and maintain in an operational condition. Parity was the only mutually acceptable agreement. There were two related issues: what types of missiles were strategic and what numbers constituted an affordable balance of power. Soviet negotiators wanted strategic to be defined as any missile that could reach Soviet territory. The United States wanted to define strategic as only ICBMs. An agreement on ICBMs was reached in May 1972 and in November negotiations began on SALT II to reduce the number of intermediate range missiles and tactical weapons with nuclear warheads.

While SALT negotiations continued, in February 1972, Nixon made an unprecedented visit to Beijing in order to have direct talks with communist party chairman Mao Zedong. The purpose of his visit was to end Chinese political and commercial isolation that had been U.S. policy after Chinese intervention in the Korean war. Ending isolation would allow China to reduce its military spending to support the North Vietnamese army.

After Nixon's visit to China, Soviet leaders eagerly seized the opportunity to expand the dialogue. Nixon was invited to Moscow and arrived in May 1972. The result of the Moscow trip was conceding the obvious: the nuclear parity of the Soviet Union and the United States in all weapons. This was the first step in conducting realistic negotiations for a SALT II treaty that would reduce the number and variety of nuclear weapons. The immediate result was Soviet cooperation in helping ease the United States out of Vietnam by reducing its support for North Vietnamese armies.

Although the signing of the SALT treaty was an important event to Soviet leaders, the most important event in 1972 was the withdrawal of U.S. troops from Vietnam. U.S. leaders assumed that Soviet leaders would use détente to increase participation in the global market. The United States and Common Market nations would help Soviet commodities enter the rapidly growing global market if Soviet leaders accepted the rules of global commerce. Henry A. Kissinger, Nixon's secretary of state, believed that "the problem of our age is to manage the emergence of the Soviet Union as a superpower." [9]

This was not the vision of Soviet leaders. Détente, coupled with American defeat in Vietnam was interpreted as a permanent decline in U.S. power and an opportunity for Soviet leaders to expand the Soviet sphere of influence into peripheral regions of global commerce. This was very bad strategy. It was equally expensive and equally futile because Marxist-Leninist revolutionary ideology had small and diminishing popular support. The best example was Castro in Cuba and his counterparts in other client nations of the Soviets. They were dictators that were little different from the ones they replaced. The Russian aid supplied to Marxist governing elites in politically unstable nations had little revolutionary content.

There were four Soviet adventures in politically unstable nations during the 1970s: 1) Chile (1970-1973) when Salvador Allende became president on the basis of 36 percent of the vote, the largest part from peasants and displaced peasants; 2) Angola that became independent in 1975 (after the collapse of the Portuguese empire), and where Marxists were one of the contending factions in a civil war; 3) Ethiopia in 1977, where a huge airlift of military supplies supported a Marxist dictator who refused to be a Soviet client; 4) intervention in Afghanistan in December 1979 to install a friendly president.

In Chile, Allende accepted Cuban political advisors to speed the nationalization of major industries. Peremptory nationalization created economic chaos. The army ended his experiment and restored political and economic stability. The Cubans were expelled. In Angola and Ethiopia Soviet leadership used Cuban troops (17,000 in Angola and 12,000 in Ethiopia) as proxies to support friendly regimes. In Afghanistan, the friendly regime installed by the Soviets could not suppress regional/tribal rivalries and it disintegrated. An invasion failed to restore order and the Soviets became enmeshed in a guerrilla war it could not win, like the United States in Vietnam.

Détente had a precarious existence during the 1970s but retained its viability because Soviet leaders wanted to maintain the political and military statusquo in Europe and U.S. political leaders never lost sight of the long range goal that stable political relations with the Soviet Union had to be based on some degree of mutual nuclear disarmament. Soviet armies were no longer an immediate threat to the security of NATO nations because a European war would mean mutual nuclear destruction. The recession of a Soviet threat to Europe allowed negotiations to continue without reference to political and military events in other parts of the world. The result was the SALT II agreement signed in November 1978. It was met with skepticism in the U.S. senate when it was submitted for ratification because of the Soviet invasion of Afghanistan. President Jimmy Carter was forced to withdraw the treaty from ratification.

After the death of general secretary Leonid Brezshnev in 1982, arms reduction negotiations with the Soviets continued. A large part of the problem was that he died without an apparent successor. The two general secretaries who followed him were his elder peers who were seriously ill when they gained power. Both died after about one year in office. The choice of Mikhail Gorbachev as general secretary in 1985 indicated that there was a real possibility for large scale mutual disarmament because he was more familiar with how Common Market nations had achieved prosperity and he wanted to devote more Soviet resources to producing consumer products and less to armaments.

Gorbachev's initiatives were a huge surprise to U.S. negotiators, but once they were recognized as genuine, both Secretary of State George Schultz and Soviet Foreign Minister Eduard Shevardnaze moved with great speed to put as much arms reductions as possible in treaty form. In 1987 a treaty was signed to remove all intermediate range nuclear missiles from Europe, and the treaty included on-site inspection. At the same time Gorbachev clearly stated that armed force would not be used to prevent changes in the governments in the Soviet sphere of influence in central and southern Europe. In particular, the Soviet Union would not intervene to preserve the government of East Germany. Furthermore, the Soviet Union would completely withdraw its armed forces from Afghanistan. In 1989 the client nations of central Europe resumed full independence.

IMPLEMENTING GLOBAL COMMERCIAL POLICIES

The Bretton Woods Agreement in 1944 looked forward to a general lowering of trade barriers brokered by a General Agreement on Tariffs and Trade (GATT). It also looked forward to establishing the International Monetary Fund (IMF) and World Bank. The World Bank became operational in June 1946, the IMF in March 1947, and GATT on January 1, 1948. GATT would broker multilateral reductions of tariffs among participating nations, but especially among the principal industrial nations. The IMF would supervise the operation of an international exchange rate mechanism, and the World Bank would make loans to help reindustrialize Europe, revive international commerce, and make loans to peasant nations to build infrastructure projects. From their inception GATT, IMF, and World Bank were intended to be global institutions with their policies managed by the group of seven (G7) of the principal noncommunist industrial nations (exclusive of Japan).

Japan's industrial recovery had a different origin than Marshall Plan aid. After 1950, reindustrialization was put on a sustaining basis by the privileged entry of manufactured products into the U.S. market. Japanese businessmen were very energetic and resourceful in establishing new industries (consumer electronics) to take advantage of this opportunity. They were also highly innovative in developing new management techniques that enormously improved the reliability of manufactured products, as well as reducing the costs of producing older products (automobiles, merchant ships).

In 1950, with its own recovery in process, western Europe would not have tolerated Japanese access to its markets. Nor would western European nations have accepted Japanese membership in GATT and the IMF. Japan's entry into these institutions would have been indefinitely delayed until western European nations were fully reindustrialized so that they could absorb Japanese competition. The astounding success of the Common Market and the equally astounding success of Japanese industrial recovery made it possible for the United States to sponsor Japanese membership in GATT, the IMF,

World Bank, and the other institutions that were evolving to manage the emerging global market.

GENERAL AGREEMENT ON TARIFFS AND TRADE

GATT was an agreement among participating nations to negotiate multilateral reductions of trade barriers on the basis of reciprocity, and provide rules for settling trade disputes. Trade barriers would be reduced by lowering tariffs on manufactured products and ultimately eliminating import licensing (quotas) on all products. The initial protocols were drafted in the U.S. state department in 1945 and were amended and consolidated at the Geneva conference of October 1947. Twenty-three nations signed the agreement. "The United States had made elimination of all preferences a major principle of its policy for the postwar organization of world trade" [10] in order to extinguish the commercial empires of western European nations.

GATT had no formal institutional structure, and had to operate without independent powers of enforcement. Disputes were settled by a mixture of negotiation and mediation using panels of expert consultants to decide the merits of complaints. It had no jurisdiction in monetary policies, financial aid, or in less visible commercial services like shipping, insurance, and financial transfers. The general rules of GATT allowed managers to relax rules for nations with persistent balance of payment problems but otherwise healthy economies.

The two rationales for reducing barriers to international trade were political and economic. The most important was political. United States strategy, strongly supported by many European political leaders, was to make international commerce as politically neutral as possible, based on the ability of corporations to compete in the global market. Corporate competition rather than imperial rivalry would help allay large amounts of national distrust that persisted after the end of WWII.

The economic rationale was increasing the efficiency of production and distribution of manufactured products. This would be done by more efficient management that could take advantage of economies of scale, favorable terms of trade, and increased efficiency in moving products long distances using container ships (and supertankers), roll-on-roll-off ferries, unit trains, and large trucks moving on high speed highways. Reciprocal tariff reduction was a bargain by which all industrial nations would profit.

The reduction of a tariff is a benefit to the country making the reduction. Tariff reduction raises the standard of living by lowering prices to consumers, contributes to the competitiveness of local industry by lowering the cost of inputs, and improves the allocation of resources by shifting production from relatively inefficient import-competing industries to relatively efficient export industries. If one concentrates on these aspects of tariff reduction, tariff negotiations become a joint, cooperative effort. [11]

GATT evolved to service the interests of the industrial nations that had the most efficient work forces performing commercial labor norms. These nations produced large volumes and varieties of manufactured products for export. The increased global commerce impelled by multilateral tariff reductions was highly concentrated in high value manufactured products. The proof of this generalization is statistics, not theory. Since 1950 the total volume of global commerce has increased at over twice the rate of the total production of all nations. For example, if the value of an industrial nation's total production doubled during a decade, its international commerce more than quadrupled.

Peasant nations with only commodities for export tried to compensate for their commercial weakness by organizing producer cartels. High prices would be sustained by withholding part of the annual production from the global market. During the 1970s cartels were organized for copper, tin, bauxite, bananas, coffee, sugar, and other commodities. They soon collapsed and prices plummeted because there was no discipline among participating nations to limit production to optimum levels of consumption in industrial nations. Only the oil cartel, Organization of Petroleum Exporting Countries (OPEC), has been able to maintain high global prices by controlling production.

From the inception of GATT, bargaining conferences have been held at periodic intervals to reduce trade barriers. Delegates to these conferences gain a global picture of how the elimination of trade barriers helps create new wealth. During negotiations the delegates from participating nations usually have little direct communication with senior managers of business corporations; however, they make their interests known to senior officials who are in constant communication with delegates. Between 1948 and 1961 there were five conferences. The results were highly effective. On average, tariffs declined 73 percent.

After most tariffs among industrial nations were reduced, there was a need for an organization to harmonize nontariff commercial policies. The Organization for Economic Cooperation and Development (OECD) was organized in 1960 for this purpose. Its principal members were Britain, France, Germany, Japan, and the United States. Its direct predecessor was the Organization of European Economic Cooperation (OEEC) that had managed the distribution of Marshall Plan aid among western European nations. OECD's mission was to negotiate bilateral reciprocity agreements and settle bilateral trade disputes among participating nations. OECD also sets the agenda for future bargaining conferences conducted by GATT (now the World Trade Organization).

Bargaining conferences after 1960 were the Kennedy sessions (1963-1967); the Tokyo sessions (1973-1979); and the Uruguay sessions (1986-1994). Seventy-four nations participated in the Kennedy sessions and remaining tariffs were reduced an additional 35 percent. The Tokyo sessions continued the process of reducing trade barriers so that after 1979 tariffs on manufactured products traded among industrial nations averaged 6.3 percent; and after the Uruguay sessions the average was reduced to about 3.9 percent. This tariff rate is equivalent to a sales tax collected at ports of entry rather than a barrier to trade.

The Uruguay sessions transformed GATT into the World Trade Organization (WTO) and gave it a permanent institutional existence. At its inception in August 1995, it had 128 member nations. A high priority for WTO was encouraging the harmonization of procedures for transferring investment capital, liquid funds, financial services, data processing, and telecommunication technologies among nations in order to increase the availability of commercial information and minimize the impact of speculation. After 1990, financial services across international boundaries were especially important to industrial nations because of the accelerating number of mergers that created global and multinational corporations. These corporations needed accurate financial information and there had to be generally accepted rules to maintain global competition. This was especially true for banks because the funds they control and the credit they allocate are extremely fluid. "The largest part of bank credits is now the product of syndicates of mixed nationality. The ease and intimacy with which financiers from different countries work together today would have seemed unthinkable, if not treasonous, three-quarters of a century ago." [1 2]

Currently (2003), the two principal concerns of the principal industrial nations are: 1) Removal of hidden protections that discourage imports or discriminate against them within domestic markets. Several of the most common hidden protections are production and export subsidies, opaque bureaucratic rules that require excessive time and expenses for entry, and regulations that purport to protect human and environmental health. 2) Protection of intellectual property (copyrights, patents, software, trade-marks) from infringement by non-industrial nations. The WTO is exerting continual pressure on non-industrial member nations to end the practices of making pirate copies of music, movies, books, and computer pro-grams; and using patented technologies without paying royalties or license fees.

The most concealed form of protection, however, is political. All governments participating in the process of tariff reduction and the elimination of opaque bureaucratic rules must deal with the reality that it is politically dangerous to reduce the welfare of any group that enjoys protection in order to improve the efficiency of the whole economy. One way or another, these groups must be safeguarded against precipitous declines in their incomes; therefore, removal of many barriers to global commerce must be done with caution.

The unwieldy size of the WTO has created a serious problem in dealing with the commercial problems that continually arise between the principal industrial nations. Annual meetings of delegates from these nations increasingly resolve these problems. The most impor-tant meeting is between the representatives of the United States, Canada, the European Union, and Japan. As regional trade organizations increase their effectiveness in reducing trade barriers among themselves, there is an increasing tendency to settle trade problems with similar annual meetings. The accomplishments of these associations will then be harmonized at periodic global conferences sponsored by the WTO. The apparent direction of evolution of the WTO is an umbrella organization for regional trade associations.

Since the end of the cold war (1991), the principal industrial nations have assigned the WTO the function of harmonizing the economic policies of Russia and China with WTO rules so they can increase their participation in the global market. Harmonization will not be easy or quick because both the Chinese and Russian governments continue to use credit subsidies to preserve the bloated number of employees in state owned industries. These subsidies must be substantially reduced; otherwise, trade in these products will not be fair. China's entry into the WTO in 2001 began an active process of harmonization. Russia cannot be far behind because its current government wants entry and its economy has the potential for producing large amounts of manufactured products for sale in the global market. It is now a question of when it is admitted and on what terms.

In the process of harmonization, Russia and China must: 1) lower tariffs and quotas that protect inefficient state owned industries from competition from more efficient producers in free market economies; 2) have clear bureaucratic rules for entry of imports; 3) have predictable schedules for payments for imports; 4) restructure their legal systems to define and enforce contracts on an equitable basis. Fair rules of trade and the number of years required to implement them will be a matter of negotiation, as it was when GATT assumed the function of reducing tariffs worldwide in the years immediately after WWII.

What are the results of the rules made for global commerce by GATT and WTO during the past 50 years? At one end of the spectrum are the populations of industrial nations that enjoy consumer cultures. At the other end are peasant nations with no industrial sectors and small commercial sectors where subsistence privation is a recurring event in poor crop years. In between are nations with various sized commercial and industrial sectors where the standard of living has variously increased depending on how successful the policies of central governments have been in increasing per capita agricultural production and promoting industrial growth. Improvements in living standards in these nations has usually been linked to increasing the production of manufactured products for export. In other words, employed persons in nations with small industrial sectors have increased their living standards in direct proportion to increased exports.

INTERNATIONAL MONETARY FUND

The intended purpose of the IMF was to operate a revolving fund to make loans to western European nations that had chronic imbalances of trade or temporary imbalances in current transactions during reindustrialization after WWII. Capital contributions came from member nations, and the amounts they contributed were the measure of how much they could borrow. The IMF did not fulfill its anticipated function because it had inadequate liquidity. Before 1952 it had minimal business because the Marshall Plan supplied the raw materials and machine tools that would otherwise have had to be purchased on credit.

After the currencies of western European nations were fully convertible (1960), IMF lending to European governments declined. It ceased after 1977 because its resources were inadequate to provide the liquidity required for the rapidly growing volume of products entering the global market. The necessary liquidity was supplied by eurodollars held by the central banks of Common Market nations and the international commercial banks with headquarters in Europe. These funds were sufficient to service the temporary trade imbalances of western European nations. During these years the IMF reinvented its mission. Its lending was increasingly focused on the financial and trade problems of peasant nations, especially post-colonial peasant nations.

The Yom Kippur war (October 1973—Israel against Egypt and Syria), and the oil embargo that followed, permanently increased the price of oil on the global market. By the end of 1973 the price of oil was five times what it had been in 1970, and this price was maintained during the following decade. Higher oil prices had a large impact on the industrial nations of western Europe, but it had a devastating impact on the commercial sectors of peasant nations. They needed credit for their commercial sectors to survive. The IMF became the arbiter for extending credit to the governments of peasant nations in order to ensure the survival of their commercial sectors; otherwise, many of these nations would have disintegrated.

Oil exporting nations were able to maintain higher prices after the Yom Kippur war because Common Market nations and Japan had become dependent on oil to fuel reindustrialization. At the end of WWII both western Europe and Japan were dependent on coal for most of their energy needs. In western European nations, communists were the principal leaders of miners unions and many strikes were politically motivated. It was strongly in the interests of the political leaders of western European nations to diminish the power of these unions by changing the principal sources of energy from coal to oil and nuclear power.

American companies that produced oil in the Persian Gulf supplied western Europe and Japan with the requisite oil. After WWII, the magnitude of Arab oil resources at tidewater locations made it possible to produce oil for 25 cents a barrel and deliver it to Europe for two dollars, and it was instantly available. By 1970, 60 percent of the energy used by western European nations and 73 percent of Japan's energy were supplied by oil. The availability of cheap oil from the Persian Gulf was one of the principal propellants for the rapid reindustrialization of western European nations and Japan. After the Yom Kippur war, the dependency of the principal industrial nations on Persian Gulf oil had two results. The immediate result was the nationalization of oil producing facilities, but not marketing. The long term result was higher oil prices that industrial nations could pay and peasant nations could not.

Higher oil prices also had a major impact on the economies of Arab exporting nations. They could not immediately absorb the huge amounts of money that flowed into their treasuries. In 1974 Arab oil producers had a current account surplus of 68 billion dollars and one year later it was 92 billion. The huge surge of petrodollars could not be converted into imported goods and services until Arab nations built adequate physical and educational infrastructures. Petrodollars were deposited in the largest international commercial banks in western Europe and the United States, which greatly increased their liquidity. How would these funds be used? One obvious use was loaning them to the governments of nations that wanted to initiate industrialization or accelerate it.

During the 1970s high prices for export commodities produced by these nations sustained their ability to incur new debts and pay the interest on existing debts. After petrodollars became available, nations with small manufacturing sectors increased their sovereign debts at the rate of 20 percent per year. Among the largest borrowers were Mexico, Brazil, Venezuela, and Chile.

In 1981, international commercial banks made 80 percent of the loans that were made to the governments of Latin American nations. In addition, 63 percent of the loans made by the IMF and World Bank were to the governments of Latin American nations. All loans were denominated in petrodollars. A high percentage of loans were invested in infrastructure improvements that would not yield immediate returns. Nonetheless, these loans required annual interest payments in dollars from the foreign exchange earnings of these nations. Payments were bearable if sufficient foreign exchange was earned from the export of commodities or manufactured products. The other principal use for petrodollar loans was subsidizing manufacturing corporations to supply domestic markets with products that were formerly imported (import substitution). The capital to start these businesses was often allocated to political favorites, not competent businessmen.

The excessive (profligate) lending of petrodollars by commercial banks, the mismanagement of the process of economic development by governing elites, and the general decline in commodity prices at the same time that petroleum prices increased, converged in 1982 to create a global financial crisis. In 1982 the sovereign debts of all Latin American nations was 330 billion dollars, and interest payments required 41 percent of the dollar denominated foreign exchange earnings of these nations. These debts stopped most policies of economic development. What occurred in Latin American nations between 1975 and 1982 occurred in other non-industrialized nations (Turkey, Indonesia). In 1982 they had equally large sovereign debts denominated in dollars. The total indebtedness of all non-industrial nations was 738 billion dollars. Many nations with small industrial sectors, particularly those in Latin America, had insufficient foreign exchange earnings to pay the annual interest on their sovereign debts. They were bankrupt.

Between 1981 and 1984, 84 nations rescheduled all or parts of their sovereign debts because servicing petrodollar debts threatened political stability. Alternatively, servicing petrodollars debts seriously retarded economic growth. The simultaneous bankruptcy of Mexico and Brazil in 1983 would have bankrupted nine of the largest international commercial banks in the United States that had made petrodollars loans to them. The bankruptcy of these banks would have undermined the increasingly integrated global banking system that sustained global commerce, as well as impacting the balance of power in the cold war. It was politically necessary to rescue both excessively indebted nations and technically bankrupt international banks that had loaned petrodollars to them.

The IMF treated the virtual defaults of sovereign debts as temporary suspensions of interest payments until new terms of repayment could be negotiated. The principal purpose of rescheduling debts was to prevent overt default. The IMF became the institution that negotiated rescheduling agreements to provide debt relief. This was done by: 1) reducing interest rates; 2) adding more years to repayment schedules of principals; 3) allowing smaller annual payments; 4) requiring no repayments of the principal, only the annual interest; 5) canceling some debts.

As part of the package, the IMF pressured international commercial banks to continue lending petrodollars on a pro-rata basis. The reward for rolling over loans of dubious quality was continued payments of annual interest but no repayments of principals. Renewing the loans was linked to reforms in political economy that bought time for these nations to increase the acquisition of foreign exchange to service their debts.

The experience of the 1970s clearly indicates that sovereign debts contracted by nations with small industrial sectors, in order to accelerate economic development, can have opposite results. Sovereign debts became counter-productive when prices of export commodities declined. Low commodity prices produced a crisis because these nations had few manufactured products to export. Manufactured products better retain their value in export markets than commodities. The experience of the 1980s indicates that direct foreign investments by global corporations is the safer way for nations with small industrial sectors to increase the size and scope of their industrial sectors because corporations assume the risks of their investments. Even more important, investments by global corporations transfers technical skills, and the efficient use of these skills increases tax bases instead of becoming drains on national revenue.

The United States, the IMF, and World Bank cooperated to reschedule the sovereign debts of these nations, provided they adopted remedial policies of political economy defined by the IMF. The IMF became the honest broker between the governments of excessively indebted nations and the international commercial banks that were forced to rollover petrodollars loans. This brokerage function defined the new mission of the IMF.

Nations that paid interest to international commercial banks on rescheduled loans did it because they had to have future access to external credit; and because the prices of export products had sufficiently increased so that interest costs were a bearable portion of national budgets. The reforms in political economy urged on nations with high sovereign debts were: 1) acceptance of much more direct investments by global corporations in order to produce manufactured products for sale on the global market. Unlike bank deposits, corporate investments cannot flee the country during financial crises, nor do their investments have to be serviced with national revenues; 2) privatization of state owned industries to make them more competitive; 3) ending high tariffs and other subsidies to inefficient manufacturing corporations; 4) in order to force import substitution industries to be competitive.

Reforms in political economy required by the IMF were strongly in the direction of creating export driven economies as the most efficient means of inducing continuous economic growth. Similar policies had been highly successful in South Korea, Taiwan, Hong Kong, and Singapore (Asian tigers) during the years following the 1973 oil crisis, as well as during the debt crisis of the 1980s, compared to nations with high sovereign debts. In addition, the IMF and other international lending agencies urged the privatization of many utilities, especially telecommunications. Global or multinational corporations were preferred buyers because they could make the capital investments in the newest technologies needed to increase the scope and efficiency of operations.

How effective was the brokerage function of the IMF? It was most effective for nations that had small industrial sectors (Mexico, Venezuela, Brazil, Turkey). After reforms in political economy were negotiated, the IMF certified a nation's credit worthiness. Thereafter, the IMF, World Bank, and international commercial banks made loans to cover the transition period until reforms took effect or prices of export commodities increased.

During the 1990s the IMF expanded its brokerage function to the governments of central European nations that were formerly in the Soviet sphere of influence. The conditions required for loans from the IMF and international commercial banks (especially banks in the European Union) were designed to prepare these nations for entry into the EU in the immediate future. The conditionality of loans was designed to speed the transition to free market economies by financing the privatization of state enterprises and, at the same time, help establish political institutions that could sustain democratic governments. The conditionality of these loans had a much higher rate of success than rescheduling agreements with excessively indebted Latin American nations because both lenders and borrowers had a common political goal—entry into the EU.

In contrast, the IMF has had almost no leverage with post-colonial peasant nations with fragile central governments that are ruled by presidents for life. These nations have no manufacturing sectors and their commercial sectors are small and mismanaged. These nations had little credit worthiness before the increase in oil prices in 1973, and none afterwards. These nations faced catastrophe. They could not pay higher oil prices because both the volume and market value of their export commodities stagnated or declined. These nations had permanent foreign exchange deficits and were in a continual state of bankruptcy. They survived because they received gift loans from the IMF and World Bank to purchase petroleum products; otherwise, their commercial sectors would have collapsed.

Before approving loans the IMF brokered reforms in political economy but the conditions were seldom implemented because economic development was not the goal of presidents for life. Their first priority was retaining power and this depended on patronage. Governing elites of these nations knew they could ignore the reforms required by the IMF and World Bank because there were no alternative governments. It was either them or anarchy. Slippage is the usual euphemism used by IMF and World Bank apologists to describe the wastage of funds on patronage rather than investments in infrastructure projects.

Two other euphemisms describe wastage. They are domestic stabilization policies and structural adjustment measures. From the moment of their approval, these were not loans. They were ongoing gifts concealed by involuted verbiage: "a series of standby arrangements, often interspersed with drawings under the compensatory financing facility and sometimes followed in later years by an extended arrangement." [13] In other words, the IMF expected structural adjustment loans to most post-colonial peasant nations to be serially defaulted. For similar purposes and with similar results, the United States allocated funds to the peasant nations of Central America as part of military and economic assistance programs. There was, however, no provision for repayment.

In 1981 the IMF established a special fund to purchase food grains in order to prevent famines in the post-colonial nations of sub-Saharan Africa. This fund complemented the International Development Association (IDA) established by the World Bank in 1960 for similar purposes. IMF loans to purchase food were similar to the ongoing loans used to purchase petroleum products. Food imports were necessary because during the previous ten years these nations had failed to increase per capita food production because governing elites failed to initiate reforms in political economy mandated by the IMF. Nonetheless, funds were forthcoming because the senior managers of the IMF and World Bank refused to admit that the agricultural policies devised by the theoretical economists of the World Bank, and approved by the IMF, had failed to end endemic hunger (alleviate absolute poverty).

All the loans made by the IMF and World Bank in the 1970s and 1980s failed to reduce high birth rates (where populations doubled in 25 years) or reduce the frequency of famine conditions. The opposite occurred. Per capita food production declined because increasing numbers of peasants migrated to shantytowns surrounding the largest cities where they were fed with imported food purchased with IMF and World Bank gifts (loans).

IMF and World Bank cooperation in making structural adjustment gifts has kept the governing elites of these nations in power. The inadvertent result is protecting the statusquo of subsistence labor norms and perpetuating the endemic privation that is inherent in subsistence agriculture. Ernest Stern uses slippery language to apologize for this policy and, at the same time, blame the global market for the permanency of subsistence privation in peasant nations. "Since the early 1970s the developing countries have faced a difficult and volatile international economic environment in which major developments seem neither transitory nor cyclical."[14] The venality, incompetence, and greed of the governing elites of these nations are ignored.

IMF and World Bank managers accept the indifference of the governing elites of most peasant nations to the poor performance of their commercial and agricultural sectors. They continue to prescribe the same failed economic policies, and continually accept non-compliance with the conditions for making gifts. Although IMF and World Bank managers vehemently deny it, the purpose of structural adjustment gifts is to maintain the statusquo in peasant nations. The "slow growth and an inherently weak balance of payments position which prevents pursuit of an active development policy"[15] is not blamed on venal governing elites or failed economic policies prescribed by the managers of the IMF and World Bank. In other words, economic development is not a priority policy of senior managers of the IMF and World Bank.

WORLD BANK

The delegates who drafted the Bretton Woods Agreement envisioned a World Bank that would provide long term loans to European nations to reconstruct their industrial sectors. Its legal name was the International Bank of Reconstruction and Development. The bank obtained its capital by selling long term bonds to governments and commercial banks in the principal industrial nations. The bank, however, did not have sufficient capital to finance the reconstruction of the industrial sectors of western European nations. Its loans were supplemented by Marshall Plan gifts that supplied most of the machine tools and raw material needed to sustain reindustrialization.

During the mid-1950s the bank began shifting its lending to nations that had small industrial sectors and to post-colonial peasant nations without industrial sectors. These nations required large amounts of capital to build infrastructure projects that required large upfront investments before they became productive. The most prominent were electric generation facilities, enlarged port facilities, trunkline roads, and mining projects. A second policy was to create or enlarge manufacturing sectors to produce products that were consumed in large quantities by the populations of these nations (import substitution). In effect, the bank assumed the financial risk of loaning money to nations where the risk of economic mismanagement and political turmoil were high. Lending to these nations after they had exhausted whatever credit worthiness they possessed (least credit-worthy nations), was an extension of the late colonial policy of expanding infrastructure facilities to increase commercial penetration into peasant villages where most people lived.

In 1960, a subsidiary fund, the International Development Association (IDA), was created to "combine economic growth with greater social justice." [16] It preferentially funded programs designed to increase agricultural production and improve education facilities. IDA

loans were interest free (soft loans, concessionary loans) and had a repayment period of 50 years, but no payments were required for the first
ten years. Unofficially these loans were called credits but they were really
gifts. Most IDA funds came from the budgets of the United States, Britain, Germany, France, Canada, and Japan. Between 1960 and 1990
IDA funds were replenished nine times, and during these years the United
States contributed 14.7 billion dollars, which was 27 percent of the total
funds disbursed.

Why did the United States and the other principal industrial nations contribute huge amounts of money to peasant nations that had
governing elites that were unable or unwilling to use it to expand
their commercial sectors? The broad answer is that the United States
considered the bank and IDA to be instruments of foreign policy.
During the cold war, U.S. policy makers believed that the bank's lending policies should complement the long term political interests (and
short term economic interests) of the United States, western Europe,
and Japan. Other contributing nations usually agreed, but not always.
When they disagreed, they were usually able to secure World Bank or
IDA funding for projects in nations where they wanted to maintain a
special or historical relationship.

Between 1961 and 1971 the World Bank allocated 1.1 billion dollars to agricultural development. This was 10 percent of all loans. Transportation, mainly building or repairing trunkline roads, accounted for 32
percent of the bank's loans; electric power generation accounted for
another 32 percent; and education accounted for 2 percent. Until 1965
IDA gifts were concentrated in India and Pakistan, but after 1965 increasing amounts were allocated to sub-Saharan African nations. Between 1961 and 1971, 25 percent of IDA disbursements were for agricultural projects or programs; 27 percent for transportation, mainly to
build trunkline roads that could take food and export commodities to
market; and 6 percent of disbursements were for education programs.
Only 8 percent of disbursements were allocated to the generation and
transmission of electric power. Allocations to agriculture were made on
the assumption they would help increase per capita food production.
Based on the experience of industrial nations these investments, if properly managed, would have accelerated economic development.

Robert S. McNamara, who was president of the World Bank from 1968 to 1981, personally selected economic advisors who believed that social justice required all international agencies to use their resources to reduce the incidence of absolute poverty in peasant nations, particularly the nations of sub-Saharan Africa. The great flaw in McNamara's good intentions was that he did not understand the difference between subsistence and commercial labor norms, nor did any of his economic advisors.

Economists interpret seasonal hunger and recurrent privation as absolute poverty. It is not absolute poverty. It is subsistence, and it is embodied in the subsistence compromise. The subsistence compromise is most visible in Muslim peasant societies that are male dominated and polygamous. On a west African rice irrigation project that was capable of growing two crops of rice per year, the second crop was seldom planted because an acceptable level of subsistence was obtained from one crop:

By controlling land use and the money acquired from the sale of rice, male strategy was to: 1) transfer as much of the labor of rice cultivation as possible to women in their households; 2) hire migrant laborers to do the rest of the labor of cultivation and harvesting; 3) use government credit to hire tractors to plow; 4) use the money acquired from the sale of rice to make marriage payments for a second wife who would contribute her labor to rice cultivation; 5) reject cultivating a rice crop in the dry season if the labor of cultivation could not be transferred to women or migrant laborers. [17]

In normal crop years enough rice was harvested during the rainy season to provide households with adequate nutrition plus a small surplus. Money acquired from the sale of this surplus (their exchange commodity) was enough for male heads of households to hire a tractor to plow (turning the soil was male labor if done by hoes or draft animals); and purchase textiles and steel tools for household use. In poor crop years households experienced seasonal hunger and made few purchases of manufactured items. Privation was endured.

In 1972, McNamara restructured the bank's management because he wanted to use theoretical quantification techniques to measure the feasibility of projects and programs that were designed to alleviate absolute poverty. His principal advisors claimed that their econometric models could predict the results of poverty alleviation loans made by the bank. Their model, however, was a pyramid of assumptions based on the false assumption that peasants were eager to adopt Green Revolution technologies and expend the additional labor to make them productive.

The assumption behind the attempt to alleviate absolute poverty was that per capita and gross agricultural production (particularly food grains) would automatically increase after international agencies funded Green Revolution technologies and programs to teach literacy. Peasants would escape privation, nations would become self-sufficient in food production, balance of payment problems would be mitigated by increased production of export commodities, and consumers worldwide would benefit from competitively priced commodities from nations that took advantages of favorable terms of trade.

None of this happened. Instead of increasing money acquisition by using Green Revolution technical inputs to grow a second crop for market sale, adult male peasants selectively used Green Revolution inputs to reduce their agricultural labor. Selective use of Green Revolution inputs allowed them to perform less agricultural labor. Males were unwilling to expend the necessary labor to grow a second crop because their subsistence needs had been satisfied.

Because post-colonial peasant nations lacked personnel capable of envisioning and planning the technical inputs into poverty alleviation programs, this had to be done by World Bank experts. "Increasingly, the new ideas implemented by the organization came from the top down, from the economists and planners in Washington, D.C." This strategy of economic development and poverty alleviation "reflected the new role that the economists and policy planners had acquired." The reorganized management structure of the World Bank/IDA "became less of a lending agency and more of a development-directing organization." In the process, "development theory and its spokespersons became more important in guiding change" than the observations and experiences of persons (in other disciplines) who actually observed subsistence labor norms in peasant villages. [18]

A wonderful example of the futility of econometric analysis applied to peasant nations is an article by Gary S. Becker, Kevin M. Murphy, and Robert Tamura: "Human Capital, Fertility, and Economic Growth."[19] In 25 pages, the word assume is used 25 times, there are 13 implies, 2 suggestions, and 1 suppose; and 17 of these pages have algebraic equations or graphs on them. This method of analysis was especially appealing to McNamara because it strengthened his "mission ideology . . . to rid the world of absolute poverty."[20]

In September 1973, in Nairobi, Kenya, McNamara announced that the lending policies of the World Bank/IDA would be directed to peasant nations in order to increase agricultural production by 40 percent within five years. It was a policy that had:

strong support from Governors of developing and developed countries alike to launch a sustained attack on the problems of what I have called absolute poverty. I sense wide agreement with my judgment that the heart of a strategy for this attack must be the development of policy and project techniques that will raise the productivity of small-scale, subsistence farms.[21]

He believed it was possible "to increase production on small farms so that by 1985 their output will be growing at the rate of five percent per year." He then identified the policies that could alleviate the subsistence privation (absolute poverty) of peasants. They would be embedded in new commercial institutions closely linked to teaching how to use the Green Revolution technologies that had increased agricultural production by (commercially motivated) farmers in North America and western Europe.[22]

The policy of poverty alleviation was based on three false assumptions shared by McNamara and his economist advisors: 1) all persons are motivated to increase their money incomes when opportunities are available; 2) peasants desire access to Green Revolution technologies and are eager to learn how to use them; 3) poverty alleviation is equated with social justice. McNamara and his economic advisors were profoundly ignorant of the social values that govern peasant behavior. There is a revolutionary difference between subsistence and poverty. Poverty is measured by money incomes and, although all contemporary peasant societies are monetized, monetization is not the same as income. Poverty does not exist in peasant societies. Subsistence exists in peasant societies because, as long as peasants control land use, they are not motivated to labor in sufficient amounts to acquire enough money to constitute incomes. They labor to acquire target sums of money and when that is acquired they cease laboring. Subsistence privation is not absolute poverty. It is famine conditions—mostly of the peasantry's own making.

Poverty exists in commercial cultures where money incomes are the source of social security. Subsistence in peasant societies and poverty in commercial cultures have radically different social origins. Therefore, ending subsistence in peasant societies and alleviating poverty in commercial cultures requires two radically different sets of policies. Increasing per capita agricultural production in peasant nations is primarily a political process. Commercializing food and commodity production requires coercion as well as inducements to sustain the process. The necessity of using coercion to induce increased per capita production was invisible to the visiting economists and senior bank managers who were momentary observers of African subsistence agriculture.

Neither economists nor bank managers questioned the assumption that the principal means for inducing increased per capita agricultural production was the introduction of technical inputs and economic incentives. Based on theoretical models they considered themselves uniquely qualified to prescribe policies and inputs. They believed that if the market incentives and technical inputs that increased per capita agricultural production in North America and western Europe were applied to peasant nations, peasants would automatically produce assured food surpluses. The core policies that were successful in western Europe and North America were: 1) adequate funding to promote the use of Green Revolution technologies; 2) institutional credit for cultivators; 3) free market prices paid to cultivators; 4) roads to carry commodities to market.

The simplistic analysis of the development economists who advised bank managers was further aggravated by the lack of a generally accepted definition of what constitutes social justice. In practice, social justice is a term that means whatever its users want it to mean. The managing directors of the World Bank and IDA wanted to do good; therefore, they closed their eyes to the indifference of the governing elites of sub-Saharan African nations to increasing food and commodity production. Then they retreated into their Washington, D.C. offices, looked into their computer screens and refused to believe that per capita food and commodity production actually declined during the years the bank and IDA increased its funding of agricultural programs and projects. During McNamara's tenure and during the tenure of his chosen successor, IDA funds had to be used to pay for imported food in order to avert famines.

Most of the imported food was used to feed peasants who moved to cities where parastatal marketing boards subsidized low prices. Displaced peasants acquired money to purchase food by performing monetized subsistence tasks. Peasants who remained on the land continued to practice the subsistence compromise without any pressure being imposed on them to perform commercial labor norms.

Apologists for the lending policies of the World Bank/IDA disagree. They claim that "Africa presents a special problem with food imports rising rapidly in recent years."[23] Alternatively, they claim that the strategy to alleviate absolute poverty "is a complex and controversial topic" because "it is difficult to formulate criteria for evaluating the Bank's work, particularly its work under McNamara on behalf of poverty alleviation."[24] The reason why Africa is a special problem is never explained because it does not fit econometric models.

Passive acceptance of the subsistence compromise by the managers of the World Bank/IDA and the governing elites of sub-Saharan African nations is why per capita food production stagnated from 1968 to 1979, and declined from 1980 to 1985. The decline actually accelerated after the World Bank/IDA began disbursing funds to cure absolute poverty. In 1985 the average per capita welfare in sub-Saharan African nations was less than in 1960.

How much money did it cost industrial nations to try to cure absolute poverty? Between 1960 and mid-1992 the IDA disbursed 71 billion dollars. Fifty billion of this came after 1972. The U.S. share was 18 billion (25 percent). A charitable appraisal of the impact of U.S. contributions computes a "net negative effect of support for IDA of some $9,564,500,000."[25] A more accurate assessment substitutes the word waste for effect. Waste is the accurate term because most nations where IDA funds were disbursed failed to increase per capita food and commodity production. The dual policies of economic development and poverty alleviation implemented by the World Bank/IDA during the years of McNamara's presidency were abject failures.

Structural adjustment gifts have made most post-colonial peasant nations into neocolonial dependents of the IMF and World Bank/IDA. These nations will remain neocolonial dependents for the foreseeable future because neither the IMF nor World Bank have policies to induce the governing elites of these nations to enforce commercializing policies.

REGIONAL TRADE AGREEMENTS

Parallel to the formation of the Common Market in 1957 and the European Free Trade Association in 1960 were agreements that focused on the possibilities for increasing trade in geographic regions. Regional trade agreements would be similar to the Common Market, but without commitments to political integration.

The more important regional agreements are: 1) LAFTA, 1960: Latin American Free Trade Association that evolved into LAIA, Latin American Integration Association in 1980; 2) ASEAN, 1967: a free trade association of southeast Asian nations to reduce tariffs; 3) CARICOM, 1973: a customs union among 14 small former British colonies in the Caribbean sea; 4) CER, 1983 and ANZERTA, 1989: trade agreements between New Zealand and Australia; 5) CUSTA, 1988: Canada-United States Free Trade Agreement that evolved from the 1965 agreement for free trade in autos and auto parts; 6) MERCOSUR (Mercado Comun del Sur), 1991: agreement between Argentina, Brazil, Paraguay, and Uruguay to form a common market by 1996; 7) NAFTA, 1994: North American Free Trade Agreement between Canada, Mexico, and the United States; 8) CIS, 1995: the Commonwealth of Independent States, an attempt by Russia to maintain the economic unity of the former Soviet Union. [26]

Except for the EU, most regional trade agreements had minimal success before the debt crisis of 1983. From the mid-1980s to the mid-1990s, the number of regional trade agreements accelerated in response to the end of the cold war and the continuing prosperity of the European Union. Between 1990 and 1994 33 regional trading agreements were negotiated. Political leaders of nations with small industrial sectors (and high sovereign debts) faced the reality that import substitution policies contributed to industrial stagnation and inflation. Import substitution policies that operated behind protective tariffs hindered the transfer of the newest technologies possessed by global and multinational corporations without necessarily increasing the tax base, as well as forcing consumers to pay higher prices for manufactured products.

Direct investments by global or multinational corporations increased employment opportunities for both skilled labor trained to use the newest technologies, as well as unskilled labor employed in labor intensive manufacturing. Products made for export by global corporations also increased the acquisition of foreign exchange. Without optimal amounts of foreign exchange obsolescent machinery used by many protected manufacturing corporations could not be replaced, nor were there any incentives for managers in protected industries to make more efficient use of labor and machines.

I will now examine the political reasons for the formation of the North American Free Trade Agreement (NAFTA) between Canada, Mexico, and the United States that became operational on January 1, 1994. The broader questions involved in this analysis are whether regional trading agreements are impediments to the further integration of global commerce, or are useful intermediaries that help produce additional new wealth in neighboring nations.

NAFTA was partly a response to the increased economic integration of western Europe after the EU became operational in 1993, and partly a response to the perception of Carlos Salinas, president of Mexico, that direct investments by global and multinational corporations could rapidly increase employment. Between 1986 and 1989, Mexico began to actively reconstruct its economy by joining GATT, ending its import substitution policy by unilaterally lowering tariffs on many manufactured products, allowing foreign corporations to

own 100 percent of Mexican subsidiaries, and agreeing not to expropri-
ate corporations owned by NAFTA investors except for public purposes.

Salinas was afraid that the end of the cold war, that followed the breach
of the Berlin wall in 1989, would divert investments from Mexico to central Europe. A free trade agreement, if properly implemented, would
keep investments by U.S. and Canadian corporations on the American
side of the Atlantic, as well as attracting investments from other nations
that desired easier entry into the U.S. market. It was essential for Mexico
to receive substantial direct foreign investments because Mexico's domestic savings were insufficient to supply the investment capital needed to
utilize the available labor. Mexico's availability of lower cost labor relative to the United States and Canada meant that imported capital and
technology supplied by global and multinational corporations could make
Mexican products competitive in the global market. Based on this competitiveness, foreign direct investments could rapidly increase the size of
Mexico's industrial sector.

Canadian business leaders were receptive to freer trade with the United
States because continuing prosperity depended on enlarged markets. This
meant increased entry into the U.S. market where Canadian corporations
were successfully competing under terms of the Canadian-United States
Free Trade Agreement (CUSTA) of 1989. Like Mexico, Canada wanted
free trade with the United States to increase exports because jobs in export industries paid higher wages than other job categories; and higher
wages meant increased tax revenues. Canada and Mexico initiated negotiations for NAFTA.

United States president George W. Bush was receptive for a number of reasons. By far the most important was that most business
leaders and policy makers in Washington were convinced that lowering or removing trade barriers wherever possible would improve the
welfare of participating nations; and the end of the cold war was an
opportunity that should not be missed. Including Mexico in free trade
negotiations was a gamble because the closely integrated industrial
sectors of the United States and Canada had a gross national product
20 times that of Mexico. Furthermore, Mexico's legal system was

different, and its protected banking system was backward in recognizing commercial opportunities. Finally, peasants in Mexico's large subsistence sector continued to have high birthrates and experience frequent seasons of hunger, a situation that triggered the peasant rebellion in Chiapas in January 1994.

Two subsidiary considerations for the United States were frustration with the slow progress of the Uruguay session of GATT in negotiating multilateral agreements, and the desire to increase employment opportunities in Mexico in order to reduce the entry of illegal immigrants into the United States. The final agreement provided for free trade of manufactured products between the three nations by 2009. Neither agricultural commodities nor labor mobility were part of the agreement. [27]

What has been the effect of NAFTA on the participating nations? NAFTA conferred considerable benefits on Mexico in the crisis that followed the devaluation of the peso in December 1994. This crisis required 47 billion dollars of short term loans in order to avert the financial collapse of the Mexican economy. In the crisis year of 1995, and in the two following years, exports to the United States increased at annual rates of 13 percent, 23 percent, and 20 percent. The investments that made these exports possible helped Mexico reestablished financial stability. Thereafter, investments in factories by global and multinational corporations continued to increase. NAFTA was also highly positive for Canada. Employment has increased and much of the additional employment is in high wage industries.

It is more problematic with the United States. Exports to Mexico and Canada from the U.S. increased but imports increased at a greater rate. Much of the imports from Mexico came from factories concentrated along the border (maquiladora factories). It is probable that imports from Mexico and Canada put downward pressure on the wages of U.S. industrial workers—with the highly positive effect of helping to reduce inflationary pressures.

A final consideration is the effect of NAFTA on the other trading partners of the United States and Canada. An undetermined amount of trade was diverted to Mexico from South Korea and other Pacific rim nations. Diversion was most visible in clothing, but also in other products that are labor intensive. The amount of diversion, however, is difficult to measure. Most economists, using what statistics are available, believe that NAFTA has done what was intended—increased commercial wealth in the three nations. On this basis, in December 2002, NAFTA was made quadrilateral by the inclusion of Chile. This was done by the U.S. signing a bilateral free trade agreement that duplicated bilateral free trade agreements that Chile had with Canada and Mexico.

In 2003, the positive effect of reducing global trade barriers was readily visible. Since the end of WWII, wealth has increased at a faster rate in the industrial nations that have fully participated in the global market than in those nations that pursued policies of self-sufficiency. In 1946, the United States produced half of the world's commercial wealth. In 1993 the United States produced 26 percent of the gross world product; the European Union 30 percent, and Japan 15 percent, but the world's commercial wealth was enormously larger in 1993 than in 1946. Although the United States produces a smaller share of global wealth in 2003 than in 1946, there are many more people in the world enjoying consumer cultures comparable with the United States.

AGRICULTURE

Immediately after WWII, most nations in western Europe and Japan subsidized their agricultural sectors in order to feed displaced populations. Increased food production was necessary to reduce expenditures for imported food because food imports created balance of payment problems. Retaining cultivators on the land slowed migration to cities where there were neither jobs nor housing for them. Although pre-WWII agriculture in western Europe was commercialized and cultivators could feed national populations, as they did during the war, the food they produced was expensive compared to food produced in the United States, Canada, Australia, and Argentina. In 1950, about 20 percent of the populations of the six nations that formed the Common Market (1957) were cultivators. As reindustrialization accelerated after 1950, and especially after 1952, the labor came from a steady rationalization of agricultural production. Small cultivation units were consolidated into larger farms, tractors replaced horses, and Green Revolution inputs were applied. Although farms became larger and were increasingly mechanized, the average per capita production of food and feed grains did not match average per capita production in the United States, Canada, Australia, and Argentina.

Between 1950 and 1970 agricultural employment in Common Market nations declined to about 10 percent of the population, and these cultivators supplied about 90 percent of the Common Market's food needs. After Common Market cultivators sold their harvests, imports were admitted to supply remaining needs. The success of the Common Market created powerful agricultural interests in all nations that wanted to preserve the statusquo of the remaining cultivators by guaranteeing them a reasonable standard of living. They achieved their goal in 1968 with the adoption of a common agricultural policy (CAP).

CAP created a single market for agricultural commodities produced and consumed in the Common Market, and a single price (less transport costs). CAP is maintained by a common tariff and a common fund that guarantees minimal prices for producers of non-perishable commodities. Grain cultivators, dairy farmers who produce milk for butter and cheese, wine makers, and olive oil producers receive guaranteed prices that preserves excessive numbers of inefficient yeomen cultivators on small land units. The same policy generously rewards efficient large scale farmers.

Blocs of agrarian voters have successfully preserved subsidies for marginal cultivators with three results: 1) attempts to further consolidate land in order to lower the costs of production have failed; 2) too many yeomen households continue to cultivate small land units; 3) large landowners in southern Spain and Portugal have taken advantage of subsidies to cultivate their land much more intensively than during the Franco and Salazar dictatorships when they were more interested in political office than earning incomes from the efficient cultivation of their land. In 2003, western European cultivators produce an agricultural surplus but agricultural subsidies continue because rural areas have disproportionately large representation in national legislatures, and urban consumers do not object.

Agriculture has been a chronic problem in the Common Market because Greece, Ireland, Portugal, Finland, and Spain have very inefficient agricultural sectors. These nations share a desire to prevent rural depopulation or deal with the political instability that results when there is insufficient urban employment to absorb aging men who have been forced off of the land, and who have minimal skills that are transferable to urban employment. For example, after Spain and Portugal entered the Common Market in 1986, the fruit, vegetables, and oil seeds they produced were not granted free entry into the Common Market for ten years. The ten year delay was essential to make their agricultural sectors more efficient. More efficient meant reducing the number of households cultivating small land units that qualified for subsidy payments under the rules of CAP. The ten year delay was not long enough. Agriculture in these nations is still the most inefficient within the EU and CAP subsidies annually threaten to bankrupt the EU treasury.

Subsidies averaged 92 billion dollars per year between 1986 and 1990, and in 1999, half of the annual budget of the EU was used to subsidize agriculture. A similar situation exists in Japan where subsidies force Japanese consumers to pay over four times the global market price for rice, compared to the price they would pay if Japan imported most of its rice needs from the United States or Australia. The political necessity of preserving inefficient cultivators within western Europe and Japan has meant that negotiations to reduce trade barriers for agricultural commodities have been largely outside of GATT; and they continue to be largely outside of the WTO. The political necessity of protecting cultivators means that a high percentage of agricultural commodities sold on the global market are by direct negotiations between the governments of producing and consuming nations. These bilateral contracts are for fixed prices and for fixed quantities; and the prices received are often concessionary, with sales dependent on export subsidies. Free trade in agricultural commodities does not operate in the current global market and is not likely to operate in the foreseeable future.

In the World Bank section of this chapter and in the previous chapter, I have strenuously emphasized that the governing elites of most post-colonial nations, particularly those in sub-Saharan Africa and India, are indifferent to enforcing policies of political economy that are necessary to commercialize agriculture. The opposite problem confronts the political leaders of the EU. Their major problem is how to reduce production in order to reduce subsidies to inefficient commercial (yeomen) cultivators.

Four hundred years ago most nations in western Europe had frequent seasons of hunger and occasional famines when the population was less than one-third of what it is today and 70 percent or more of the population was engaged in agriculture. Why was the requisite food not produced? What were the revolutionary policies that induced European cultivators to produce the assured food surpluses of the nineteenth and twentieth centuries without using Green Revolution inputs? This is not the place to go into the details. Explanations are available in my books *Famine in Peasant Societies* (1986) and *Subsistence and Economic Development* (2000). What is relevant to this chapter is that abundant food is produced in all commercial cultures where cultivation is a business. Arable land is a capital asset. It has a specific owner (freehold tenure), a market value, and it pays taxes like other businesses. Farmers are rural businessmen who measure their social security by money incomes like all city residents. Compared to the past, the size of current harvests in western European nations is clear evidence that commercial labor norms in agriculture, combined with scale of operations, can increase per capita production of food crops comparable to the economies of scale in manufacturing.

DEMISE OF THE LAST COMMERCIAL EMPIRE

The collapse of the Soviet sphere of influence in central Europe in 1989, followed by the reunification of Germany in October 1990, had a huge spillover effect in the Soviet Union. Gorbachev's policy of opening political discussion (glasnost) was the opportunity for suppressed nationalities that had been forcibly incorporated into the Soviet Union to assert a desire for autonomy or independence.

A power struggle in the Kremlin made it possible for these nationalities to peaceably achieve independence and, in the process, escape the centralized economic planning that sustained the existence of the Soviet Union. Boris Yeltsin, the elected president of Russia, challenged Gorbachev who wanted to preserve the Soviet Union. Yeltsin accepted the right of the republics that constituted the Soviet Union to become independent nations because this was the best way to legitimatize his tenure as president of Russia. In 15 elections the 15 constituent republics of the Soviet Union voted to become independent, including Russia. In December 1991, the Soviet Union dissolved and Gorbachev had no political base. He became a pensioner.

The collapse of the Soviet Union, the dissolution of the Soviet sphere of influence in central and southern Europe, and the end of the cold war created huge problems and equally huge opportunities for the political leaders of the European Union and the United States. It was immediately evident that a high percentage of the populations of central European nations wanted to join the EU as soon as possible. They wanted to participate in its economic prosperity and the freedom to travel within Europe and the world. The political leaders of EU nations clearly recognized that the inclusion of central European nations in the EU was desirable for both the EU and these nations.

The end of the cold war created two imperatives: 1) maintaining political order in nations peripheral to the EU where ethnic violence were events waiting to happen; 2) integrating central European nations and Russia into the EU. EU leaders knew that eastward expansion would require enormous political and economic changes in the governments of nations that had centrally planned economies. Neither the post-Soviet political leaders nor the citizens of these nations fully understood how great the changes had to be; nor did they fully understand the social dislocations that had to be navigated during the transition period.

The abrupt end of central planning in the Soviet Union and the nations of central and southern Europe coincided with the end of communist party governance. Russia and all of the successor nations of the Soviet Union, as well as the nations in its former sphere of influence required: 1) some variety of governance by consent to replace the communist party; 2) some variety of market economy to replace central planning. In 2003 these two institutions were operational in central European nations, but they are fragile. In southern European nations these institutions are still experimental.

The failure of Russia to achieve prosperity is due to the reluctance of political leaders to adopt policies that speed the replacement of political managers of manufacturing corporations with managers who are commercially motivated. New men are required to efficiently manage the available manpower and material resources to build more and better housing and produce more consumer products for domestic consumption. A consumer culture is clearly possible in Russia if privatized corporations are more efficiently managed. Lack of efficient managers in manufacturing corporations means that the economic stability of Russia in 2003 depends on exporting raw materials.

An equal impediment to efficient production is the bureaucracy that extorts a share from existing production rather than encouraging business corporations to efficiently use labor and raw materials to increase per capita production. In 2003 the tentative acceptance of market institutions in Russia, and the successor nations of the Soviet Union, and in the nations of southern Europe, has prolonged the transitional distress of the economies of these nations.

In comparison, the governments of the Baltic nations and central European nations have been much more aggressive in restructuring their economies. In spite of restructuring, however, most privatized industrial corporations in these nations are inefficient producers compared to similar corporations in the EU. A principal cause of their inefficiency is an acute shortage of managers who can reduce bloated labor forces and reorganize those who remain into efficient workers. Nonetheless, the governments of the Baltic and central European nations have made the institutional changes required to establish governance by consent and sustain market economies. This made them candidates for rapid inclusion in the EU.

In December 2002 the EU invited Poland, Estonia, Latvia, Lithuania, Czech Republic, Slovakia, Hungary, and Slovenia, plus the

Greek part of Cyprus and Malta to join in May 2004. Referendums will endorse or reject the invitations. Membership is a two way street. The EU will provide large amounts of money to help increase average incomes, but new members will have to restructure their agricultural sectors. This will be politically difficult. In fact, agriculture is the biggest gamble on the eastward expansion of the European Union. The Baltic and central European nations have three times the percentage of cultivators in their populations as the EU (about 20 percent versus about 6 percent), and their productivity is one-third. The new members will have ten years to restructure their agricultural sectors before they qualify for full CAP subsidies. Before that subsidy level is reached the EU will probably be forced to restructure CAP payments or face bankruptcy.

After the collapse of the Soviet Union in 1991, NATO has had to redefine its mission. Its original mission was guaranteeing peace among the principal industrial nations of Europe, including the Soviet Union, by preventing the Soviet Union from forcibly expanding its sphere of influence into western Europe. This mission ended with the end of the cold war. Where does NATO fit into the new political order of Europe, and what mission will it perform? In 2003 this is an unanswered question, although, on an emergency basis, it has participated in ending ethnic and communal violence in southern Europe.

NATO may find a new mission in helping to create a stable political order in southern Europe that will eventuate in Serbia, Croatia, Romania, Bulgaria, Albania, Bosnia, Montenegro, Macedonia, the Ukraine, and Moldavia joining the EU. Maintaining civil order in some of these nations may be extremely difficult. Much of the difficulties are due to the abrupt dissolutions of communist governments. The political uncertainties following this change have created conditions for demagogues to mobilize suppressed ethnic and religious identities (and animosities) in order to force the redrawing of political boundaries on the basis of religious or language dominance. In some way the coercive glue of communist governments must be replaced with institutions that establish governance by consent. As of 2003, the governments of all of these nations are in transition. If some variety of governance by consent does not evolve, the southern boundary of the EU may remain perpetually unstable and the full integration of these nations into the global economy will be indefinitely postponed.

Finally, the key measure for sustaining global peace is the inclusion of Russia within the global economy. The best available institution to manage its inclusion is the EU. Hopefully, during the next ten years as the EU consolidates its presence in central Europe, Russia will be integrated into the EU and be militarily neutralized in the same way that German militarism was neutralized when it was integrated into the Common Market, NATO, and the European Union.

Hopefully, Russia will be able to manage the Commonwealth of Independent States so that these post-colonial nations can qualify for associate membership in the EU. A second hope is that association agreements will be an incentive for nations in the Commonwealth of Independent States to become more productive participants in the global economy than most of the post-colonial nations of the British, French, Dutch, and Portuguese empires.

SUMMARY

Maintaining peace was the vision that motivated the political leaders who created the six principal institutions of the post-WWII global economy. These institutions are GATT/WTO, IMF, World Bank, Common Market/EU, OECD, and NATO. All six are cooperative and five of the six were designed to reduce barriers to international commerce as the best way of: 1) reducing tensions among the principal industrial nations that were capable of waging global war; 2) encouraging the production of new wealth. The reciprocal of policies designed to create new wealth was discouraging policies that were designed to share existing wealth. In industrial nations, full employment and the acquisition of new skills and the capital to make them productive are the best ways to produce new wealth; and if increased per capita production is coupled with favorable terms or trade, or an ability to create favorable terms of trade, the material welfare of workers can improve dramatically.

The sixth institution was NATO. Its mission was to protect the nations of western Europe so that governance by consent could become institutionalized in democratic governments. With the end of the cold war, NATO must redefine its mission. As of 2003, this has not happened. Nonetheless, there must be some multi-national organization to deal with the political instabilities of southern European nations, or counter the Islamic terrorists groups that reject the secular foundation the global market. NATO is a candidate to perform these functions. The September 11, 2001 terrorist attack on the World Trade Center in New York City was a clear signal to all industrial nations that: 1) there are huge numbers of people who reject secular governments; 2) reject governance by consent; 3) reject consumer cultures; 4) and that tolerance for terrorist activities are highly concentrated in Islamic cultures.

The United States, Canada, the nations of the EU, and Japan cooperated to create the global market and they are the current managers of its operation. It is, however, an open ended management team. The rules governing the global market are based on bilateral and multilateral negotiations among the principal industrial nations. The purpose of its rules are to accelerate global commerce as the most efficient way to produce new taxable wealth and increase per capita material welfare. The primary beneficiaries of the global market are industrial nations; however, participation is open to all nations that industrialize, provided they to conform to WTO rules.

Most post-colonial nations are minimal participants in the global market and will retain this status for the foreseeable future. With the possible exception of oil, export commodities produced by post-colonial nations are not essential to industrial nations. If the exports of post-colonial nations declined or ceased, competitively priced substitutes are available from elsewhere. Peasant nations will remain passive onlookers to the accelerating production of new wealth in industrial nations because few persons in them have commercial skills or are willing to perform full-time commercial labor norms that are essential for producing commodities or manufactured products for sale on anonymous markets (urban markets or export markets).

Forty years after decolonization the volume and value of commodities produced for export by post-colonial nations are a minor part of global commerce. Decolonization was a dramatic event that continually made front page news, but in economic terms the commodities produced by post-colonial nations are marginal to the prosperity of industrial nations Because of their commercial weakness, the post-colonial peasant nations of sub-Saharan Africa, plus the peasant nations of Latin America and Asia, are, to a greater or lesser extent, neocolonial dependents of the principal industrial nations. They are dependents because the governing elites of these nations failed to adopt policies to induce increased per capita production of all commodities, whether for export or domestic consumption.

The survival of many of these nations depends on continuous neocolonial interventions. The principal ones are gifts of food to mitigate recurring famine conditions, and funds to build and maintain essential infrastructure projects. Without these interventions, the commercial sectors of many of these nations would collapse. The World Bank, IMF, and various agencies of the United Nations supply the funds. These organizations are the new imperial protectors of post-colonial peasant nations because the principal industrial nations have assigned them the task of ensuring their survival.

NOTES

1. A. George Kenwood, Alan L. Lougheed, *The Growth of the International Economy*, chapters 4, 5.
2. Cheryl Payer, *The World Bank*, 20.
3. Cheryl Payer, *The World Bank*, 11.
4. Raymond Vernon, Louis T. Wells, *Economic Environment of International Business*, 212.
5. William David McIntyre, *British Decolonization*, Table of Independence dates.
6. David Reynolds, *One World Divisible*, 162.
7. Lawrence S. Kaplan, *NATO and the United States*, 18.
8. Lawrence S. Kaplan, *NATO and the United States*, 18.
9. David Reynolds, *One World Divisible*, 352.
10. Kenneth W. Dam, *GATT*, 42.
11. Kenneth W. Dam, *GATT*, 65.
12. Benjamin J. Cohen, *Crossing Frontiers*, 66-67.
13. Richard Goode, *Economic Assistance to Developing Countries Through the IMF*, 20.
14. Ernest Stern, "World Bank Financing of Structural Adjustment," in John Williamson, ed. *IMF Conditionality*, 87.
15. Richard Goode, *Economic Assistance to Developing Countries Through the IMF*, 25.
16. Escott Reid, *Strengthening the World Bank*, 19.
17. Ronald E. Seavoy, *Subsistence and Economic Development*, 131.
18. Louis Galambos, David Milobsky, "Organizing and Reorganizing the World Bank, 1946-1972," *Business History Review*, Vol. 69, 1995, 178.
19. Gary S. Becker, Kevin M. Murphy, Robert Tamura, "Human Capital, Fertility, and Economic Growth," Journal of Political Economy, Vol. 98, 1990, 12-37.

20. David Milobsky, Louis Galambos, "The McNamara Bank and Its Legacy, 1968-1987," Business and Economic History, Vol. 24, 1995, 184, 187, 189. Ronald E. Seavoy, Famine in Peasant Societies, chapter 1.
21. Aart J. M. van de Laar, The World Bank and the Poor, 109 (quote), 143.
22. Deborah Shapley, Promise and Power, 510-512.
23. Barend A. de Vries, Remaking the World Bank, 20-21.
24. Robert L. Ayres, Banking on the Poor, 11.
25. Catherine Gwin, U.S. Relations with the World Bank, 48-55, 87 (quote).
26. Jeffrey A. Frankel, Regional Trading Blocs in the World Economic System, chapters 1, 3, Appendix A. Kym Anderson, Richard Blackhurst, eds.Regional Integration and the Global Trading System, xviii-xxi. Miles Kahler, International Institutions and the Political Economy of Integration, chapter 3.
27. Jeffrey A. Frankel, Regional Trading Blocs, 37. Norris C. Clement, et al. North American Trade Integration, 19-20, 256-264.

REFERENCES

Anderson, Kym, Richard Blackhurst, eds. *Regional Integration and the Global Trading System*, New York, St Martins Press, 1993

Ayittey, George B. N. "Aid for Black Elephants: How Foreign Assistance Has Failed Africa," in Doug Bandow, Ian Vasquez, eds. *Perpetuating Poverty: The World Bank, the IMF, and the Developing World*, Washington, Cato Institute, 1994

Ayres, Robert L. *Banking on the Poor: The World Bank and World Poverty*, Cambridge, MIT Press, 1983 (chapters 1, 4, 6)

Becker, Gary S., Kevin M. Muphy, Robert Tamura. "Human Capital, Fertility, and Economic Growth," *Journal of Political Economy*, Vol. 98, 1990

Bird, Graham. *IMF Lending to Developing Countries: Issues and Evidence*, London, Routledge, 1995 (chapter 1)

Bordo, Michael D. "The Bretton Woods International Monetary System: A Historical Overview," in Michael D. Bordo, Barry Eichengreen, eds. *A Retrospective on the Bretton Woods System: Lessons for International Monetary Reform*, Chicago, University of Chicago Press, 1993

Clement, Norris C., et al. *North American Economic Integration: Theory and Practice*, Cheltenham, Edward Elgar, 1999

Cline, William R. *International Debt: Systematic Risk and Policy Response*, Washington, Institute for International Economics, 1984 (chapter 4)

Cohen, Benjamin J. *Crossing Frontiers: Explorations in International Political Economy*, Boulder, Westview Press, 1991 (chapters 4, 6, 10, 11)

Cohen, Stephen D. *The Making of United States International Economic Policy: Principles, Problems, and Proposals for Reform*, Westport, Praeger, 1994 (chapters 1, 2)

Dam, Kenneth W. *GATT: Law and International Economic Organization*, Chicago, University of Chicago Press, 1970 (chapters 2, 3, 4, 5)

Easterly, William R. *The Elusive Quest for Growth: Economists Adventures and Misadventures in the Tropics*, Cambridge, MIT Press, 2001

Eichengreen, Barry. "Hegemonic Stability Theories in the International Monetary System," in Richard N. Cooper, et al. *Can Nations Agree? Issues in International Economic Cooperation*, Washington, Brookings Institution, 1989

Ellwood, David W. *Rebuilding Europe: Western Europe, America and Postwar Reconstruction*, London, Longman, 1992 (chapters 5, 6, 7, 8)

Frankel, Jeffrey A. *Regional Trading Blocs in the World Economic System*, Washington, Institute for International Economics, 1997 (chapters 1, 3, 10, appendix A)

Fratianni Michele, John Pattison. "International Organizations in a World of Regional Trade Agreements: Lessons from Club Theory," *The World Economy*, Vol. 24, 2001

Galambos, Louis, David Milobsky. "Organizing and Reorganizing the World Bank, 1946-1972," *Business History Review*, Vol. 69, 1995

Garrett, Geoffrey. "The Politics of Maastricht," in Barry Eichengreen, Jeffrey A. Frieden, eds. *The Political Economy of European Monetary Unification*, Boulder, Westview Press, 2001

Garthoff, Raymond L. *Détente and Confrontation: American-Soviet Relations from Nixon to Reagan*, Washington, Brookings Institution, 1994 (chapter 2)

Gilpin, Robert. *The Political Economy of International Relations*, Princeton, Princeton University Press, 1987 (chapter 8)

Goldberg, Ellen S., Dan Haendel. *On Edge: International Banking and Country Risk*, New York, Praeger, 1987 (chapters 2, 3)

Goode, Richard. *Economic Assistance to Developing Countries Through the IMF*, Washington, Brookings Institution, 1985

Grabbe Heather, Kirsty Hughes, *Enlarging the EU Eastwards*, London, Royal Institute of International Affairs, 1998 (chapter 7)

Gwin, Catherine. *U.S. Relations with the World Bank, 1945-1992*, Washington, Brookings Institution, 1994 (pp 48-55, 87)

Hathaway, Dale E. "Agricultural Trade Policy for the 1980s," in William R. Cline, ed. *Trade Policy in the 1980s*, Washington, Institute for International Economics 1983

Hoekman, Bernard M., Michel M. Kostecki. *The Political Economy of the World Trading System: From GATT to WTO*, Oxford, Oxford University Press, 1995 (chapters 1, 8, 9)

Jackson, John H. *The World Trading System: Law and Policy of International Economic Relations*, Cambridge, MIT Press, 1999 (chapter 2)

Kahler, Miles. *International Institutions and the Political Economy of Integration*, Washington, Brookings Institution, 1995

Kaplan, Lawrence S. *NATO and the United States: The Enduring Alliance*, Boston, Twayne Publishers, 1988

Kenwood, A. George, Alan L. Lougheed. *The Growth of the International Economy, 1820-2000*, London, Routledge, 1999 (chapters 4, 5)

van de Laar, Aart J. M. *The World Bank and the Poor*, Boston, Martinus Nijhoff Publishing, 1980 (chapters 4, 5, 6)

Lawrence Robert Z. *Regionalism, Multilateralism, and Deeper Integration*, Washington, Brookings Institution, 1996 (chapters 2, 3, 8)

McIntyre, William David. *British Decolonization, 1946-1997: When, Why and How Did the British Empire Fall?* New York, St Martins Press, 1998 (table of independence dates)

Mason, Edward S., Robert E. Asher. *The World Bank Since Bretton Woods*, Washington, Brookings Institution, 1973 (chapters 12, 20; tables E-4, E-5)

Milobsky, David, Louis Galambos. "The McNamara Bank and Its Legacy, 1968-1987," *Business and Economic History*, Vol. 24, 1995

Nafziger, E. Wayne. *The Debt Crisis in Africa*, Baltimore, Johns Hopkins University Press, 1993 (introduction, chapters 1, 2)

Payer, Cheryl. *The World Bank: A Critical Analysis*, New York, Monthly Review Press 1982 (chapters 1, 8)

Reid, Escott. *Strengthening the World Bank*, Chicago, Adlai Stevenson Institute, 1973 (chapter 3)

Reynolds, David. *One World Divisible: A Global History Since 1945*, New York, Norton, 2000

Rostow, Walt W. *The United States and the Regional Organization of Asia and the Pacific, 1965-1985*, Austin, University of Texas Press, 1986

Sachs, Jeffrey D. "Introduction," in Jeffrey D. Sachs, ed. *Developing Country Debt and Economic Performance: The International Financial System*, Chicago, University of Chicago Press, 1989

Sachs, Jeffrey D. "Conditionality, Debt Relief, and the Developing Country Debt Crisis," in Jeffrey D. Sachs, ed. *Developing Country Debt and Economic Performance: The Financial System*, Chicago, University of Chicago Press, 1989

Seavoy, Ronald E. *Famine in Peasant Societies*, Westport, Greenwood Press, 1986 (chapter 1)

Seavoy, Ronald E. *Subsistence and Economic Development*, Westport, Praeger, 2000

Shapley, Deborah. *Promise and Power: The Life of Robert McNamara*, Boston, Little, Brown, 1993 (chapter 22)

Stern Ernest. "World Bank Financing of Structural Adjustment," in John Williamson, ed. *IMF Conditionality*, Washington, Institute for International Economics, 1983

Urwin, Derek W. *The Community of Europe: A History of European Integration Since 1945*, London, Longman, 1955

Vernon, Raymond, Louis T. Wells. *Economic Environment of International Business*, Englewood Cliffs, N.J., Prentice-Hall, 1976 (chapter 12)

de Vries, Barend A. *Remaking the World Bank*, Washington, Seven Locks Press, 1987 (chapters 2, 3, 5)

Williams, Allan M., ed. *Southern Europe Transformed: Political and Economic Change in Greece, Italy, Portugal and Spain*, London, Harper and Row, 1984 (chapters 2, 4, 5, 9)

Winters, L. Alan. "Expanding EC Membership and Association Accords: Recent Experience and Future Prospects," in Kym Anderson, Richard Blackhurst, eds. *Regional Integration and the Global Trading System*, New York, St Martins Press, 1993

Wise, Mark. "The European Community," in Richard Gibb, Wieslaw Michalak, eds. *Continental Trading Blocs: The Growth of Regionalism in the World Economy*, Chichester, Wiley, 1994

GLOBAL CORPORATIONS IN THE TWENTY-FIRST CENTURY

PURPOSE OF GLOBALIZATION

Global corporations evolved to service the needs of the global market. Their purpose is to efficiently integrate global industrial production and related services. In the twenty-first century the most visible result of their activity will be raising the level of material welfare for the citizens of nations that increase their participation in the global commerce. Put another way, global and multinational corporations are the most efficient institutions for creating consumer cultures in nations where they are encouraged to invest. The three most important attributes of global and multinational corporations are: **1**) they reduce national commercial rivalries to manageable proportions; **2**) the employment they create helps reduce economic and social inequalities in industrial nations; **3**) they create new taxable wealth in nations with small industrial sectors.

1. Reducing National Commercial Rivalries: Competition in the global market is between corporations, not between rival empires. Corporations compete using rules that the governments of participating nations have assigned to the IMF, WTO, and regional trade organizations to manage and adjudicate. Corporate competition in the global market is as close to a level playing field as is politically possible.

In the day-to-day operation of the global market, global and multinational corporations have the ability to increase the volume and value of exports in all nations with industrial sectors because they are: 1) efficient at accumulating and investing capital; 2) efficient at distributing products in the global market; 3) much more flexible in operational strategies than centrally planned economies.

2. Creating Employment: Full employment in industrial nations is the best way to create new wealth that can sustain consumer cultures. In nations that have achieved consumer cultures, political differences focus on which political party can better manage prosperity. Confrontational politics based on competing ideologies are reduced or eliminated, which is the best possible way to institutionalize governance by consent.

3. Creating New Taxable Wealth: In nations with small industrial sectors lack of investment capital, deficient technology, inefficient management, and tax evasion are the principal causes of retarded development. Investments by global and multinational corporations usually carry with them modern technology and efficient management skills that local persons are trained to use. In addition, these investments are highly visible and more easily taxed.

BIG CORPORATIONS BECOME GLOBAL CORPORATIONS

Big business corporations with large international sales came into existence at an early date. The two most obvious were the English and Dutch East India companies, but big business corporations did not become common until the industrial revolution. Railroads were the earliest big corporations of the industrial revolution. Bigness was directly linked to the ability of railroads to mobilize large amounts of capital for constructing rights-of-way and purchasing rolling stock. After operations began, railroads had to earn large amounts of money in order to maintain rights-of-way, replace obsolescent equipment, and service bonded indebtedness. The complexity of managing railroad operations required paid professional managers who were promoted on merit. The advent of large, highly capitalized corporations performing complex operations, like railroads, is inseparably linked to the institutionalization of managerial capitalism. Paid professional managers replaced management by descendents of founding entrepreneurs because direct descendents usually lacked essential technical and financial skills.

Experience gained in financing, building, and managing railroad corporations made a major contribution to developing the management and financial skills that were essential for building new high technical industries. Among the first of these industries was the generation and distribution of electricity to factories (to power electric motors), to residences (indoor lighting), and for urban transportation (streetcars). Like trunkline railroads, corporations that provided these products and services had to be big from the beginning of operations. These corporations appeared suddenly in the last quarter of the nineteenth century in the three principal industrial nations (United States, Britain, Germany).

What type of big corporation was likely to become global, and how was global growth achieved? Railroad corporations could not become global because their charters of incorporation usually had a geographic limitation; neither could most utility corporations or large banks become global because of political or geographic limitations. On the other hand, manufacturing corporations that had products or processes protected by patents did build factories in several nations. They became multinational. Oil and mining corporations, by the nature of their business of exploring the world for exploitable deposits, were likely to be multinational corporations from their inception; and if they distributed their products worldwide they became global corporations.

Most contemporary global and multinational corporations are engaged in manufacturing. They became global or multinational by using managerial strategies that were similar to the strategies they used to become big in their domestic markets: 1) mastery of a technology; 2) mastery of a process; 3) mergers; 4) access to large amounts of capital and credit; 5) substantial foreign sales conducted by agents. Alfred D. Chandler summarizes:

Manufacturing enterprises became multifunctional, multiregional and multiproduct because the addition of new units permitted them to maintain a long-term rate of return on investment by reducing overall costs of production and distribution, by providing products that satisfied existing demands, and by transferring facilities and skills to more profitable markets when returns were reduced by competition, changing technology, or altered market demand.

Whatever the initial motivation for its investments in new operating units, the modern industrial enterprise has rarely continued to grow or maintain its competitive position over an extended period of time unless the addition of new units (and to a lesser extent the elimination of old ones) has actually permitted its managerial hierarchy to reduce costs, to improve functional efficiency in marketing and purchasing as well as production, to improve existing products and processes and to develop new ones, and to allocate resources to meet the challenges and opportunities of ever-changing technologies and markets.

It was the development of new technologies and the opening of new markets, which resulted in economies of scale and of scope and in reduced transaction costs, that made the large multiunit industrial enterprise come when it did, where it did, and in the way it did. [1]

The application of new technologies to large national markets in the United States, Britain, and Germany required management teams that could manage complex operations by delegating authority to persons who possessed technical and financial skills. In other words, the creation of big corporations that could manufacture industrial products (electricity or electrical generators) or consumer items (soft drinks, cooking pots) required managers who could optimize the use of labor and machinery, plan the arrival of raw materials or component parts when required, control inventories, efficiently distribute finished products, improve product design, speed production (by developing new machinery), create new products by research, and know how to efficiently use credit.

Almost as fast as big corporations appeared, serial mergers created oligopolies in order to economize high capital costs and accumulate capital to finance technical evolution. Oligopolistic competition made it much easier for managers to allocate capital investments, make annual budgets, and gain access to large amounts of capital and credit because market shares were more predictable. Corporations most likely to transform themselves into global or multinational corporations are oligopolistic manufacturing corporations servicing large national markets.

A substantial number of multinational and global corporations existed in the interwar years (1918-1938) because it was a necessary strategy to protect foreign markets from tariffs that threatened to restrict imports of products they manufactured. In this sense, becoming global or multinational in the first half of the twentieth century was a defensive strategy designed to avoid threatened or actual restrictions on the movement of manufactured products into foreign markets.

Most global corporations, however, evolved after 1960 when the reindustrialization in western Europe and Japan was complete. Thereafter, the operation of the Common Market and GATT continually lowered political barriers to global commerce and the advantages of global operations became more apparent and more easily attainable. The increase in the number and size of global corporations was a response to opportunities to earn profits by taking advantages of economies of scale, significantly lower costs of long distance transportation, and the ability of efficient management teams to expand operations to additional nations when political conditions became favorable.

Global and multinational manufacturing corporations usually have factories or preferred suppliers of component parts in more than one nation. Component parts can be manufactured or assembled anywhere in the world and final products marketed anywhere in the world. Efficient management of production for global distribution is possible because senior managers have near instant communication with managers of subsidiary corporations and they are seldom more than one day distant from any operation. As the number and size of global manufacturing corporations increased after 1980, the related services of banking, communication, information, and insurance services also underwent globalization.

After 1960, political leaders in the Common Market and the United States clearly recognized that the political and economic benefits of global commerce were infinite and that all participating nations would benefit. Benefits, however, would especially accrue to industrial nations because their governments actively sought to attract direct investments from any source. The governments of industrial nations have minimal political concern over how global corporations acquire ownership of factories (purchase, merger, new buildings), or the nationality of the banks that make loans to resident corporations, or the nationality of corporations that supply the supporting services they need.

Nor are the governments of industrial nations particularly concerned where global corporations transfer profits.

Full employment is the principal concern of industrial nations because this maximizes tax revenues that pay the costs of social services. Global corporations have an advantage in creating stable employment because they sell products in several nations and this smoothes fluctuations in demand. Democratic governments of industrial nations strongly desire stable employment because it minimizes political discontent.

These policies do not usually operate in nations with small industrial sectors; therefore, their participation in global commerce is limited. If, however, the governments of these nations adopt policies of political economy designed to maximize participation in the global market, direct investments by global corporations can supply the capital, technology, and management personnel. Global corporations are especially efficient creators of new wealth in nations seeking to expand their industrial sectors.

NATIONAL MARKETS BECOME GLOBAL MARKETS

By the mid-1890s the United States was the leading industrial nation, and by the beginning of WWI (August 1914), it was producing 36 percent of the world's industrial output compared to 16 percent for Germany and 14 percent for Britain. The United States had proportionally more big industrial corporations than either Britain or Germany, and many of these corporations had international operations prior to 1900; and many more had them after 1920. For this reason, big corporations with headquarters in the United States were, from the beginning of industrialization, major participants in the global market, even when managers concentrated their efforts on the rapidly expanding domestic market.

Political conditions became favorable for the expansion of the global market after 1960 when reindustrialization of western Europe was complete and the Common Market was an obvious success. In the 1960s a large majority of global corporations had headquarters in the

United States and Canada. Jean-Jacques Servan-Schreiber, an accurate observer of what was evolving, wrote a widely read book, *The American Challenge*. He predicted that U.S. corporations would dominate the global economy. It did not happen.

During the 1970s and 1980s big corporations operating in the Common Market and Japan transformed themselves into global corporations by copying and improving on the way U.S. global corporations did business. "The key to the internationalization of business during the post-World War II period was not the traditional export or import of goods, but foreign direct investment." [2] The growth of global corporations and the prospects for increased profits are best realized by direct investments because managers control production, distribution, and pricing. A global management team makes production and distribution decisions based on global demand for their products, not on the basis of seeing only the domestic market and its limitations. In the evolution of the global market that has occurred since the end of WWII, "the concept of individual national markets is obsolete." [3]

The success of European and Japanese catch-up strategies was impressive. Sometime after 1975 direct foreign investments by Common Market and Japanese global corporations surpassed investment by U.S. global corporations. Among the principal industrial nations, the process of technical convergence was complete by about 1980. Global and multinational corporations in the Common Market, United States, and Japan were competitive equals in global commerce. During the process of convergence, the services that accompanied global commerce (banking, accounting, advertisement, management consultants) increased at an even faster rate than direct foreign investments by global corporations. "The rate and extent of globalization of business during the second half of the 1980s, as measured by flows of foreign direct investment, was spectacular." [4]

By the best estimates, between 1985 and 1990, world income increased at a rate of about 6 percent per year and exports increased at a rate of about 9 percent per year. During this five year period, direct foreign investment increased somewhere between 23 and 29 percent per year. Concomitant with increases in direct foreign investments by all global corporations were increasing numbers of mergers across national boundaries that rapidly increased the number of global and multinational corporations. After the end of the cold war (1991) the number of these mergers surged.

Why did the surge of direct investment and mergers occur? In large part it was due to the perception of senior managers of many big corporations in large national markets that they could be squeezed into niche markets unless they produced a wider range of products or services at competitive prices for sale on the rapidly evolving global market. Transnational mergers and resourcing through intra-corporate networks of trade became compelling strategies because continued profits were increasingly dependent on growth as more nations reduced trade barriers. Deregulation of businesses that were national monopolies (telecommunications, banks, electric utilities) was a major propellant of growth after it became politically possible for global corporations to purchase them.

In small part, the surge in direct investments was the aftermath of the debt crisis after 1982 that affected most nations with small, highly protected industrial sectors and minimal participation in global commerce. These nations needed greater participation in the global market in order to acquire foreign exchange; and this participation could be accomplished relatively quickly by direct investments made by global corporations. During the late 1980s, many of these nations reduced tariffs and other barriers to trade in order to attract investments by global corporations. After reduction, protected manufacturing corporations were forced to become more efficient producers and distributors in order to survive competition with imports. This is the same policy that was applied to Spain, Portugal, and Greece when they entered the Common Market, and the same policy that will be applied to central European nations when they enter the European Union.

The efficiency of direct foreign investments is related to the efficiency of management. If management remained in the hands of the descendents of founding entrepreneurs, the tendency of second and third generation managers was to protect profit margins by forming cartels. Cartels retarded the adoption of new technologies and expansion into competitive foreign markets because profits were secure in domestic markets. Up until about 1870 Britain was the leading industrial nation. After 1870, Britain began losing its industrial leadership to U.S. and German industrial corporations.

Historians and economists generally agree that the principal reason for Britain's decline was failure of second and third generations of owner/managers to take full advantage of opportunities to produce for larger but more competitive markets. Instead of merging to increase economies of scale they formed cartels. Instead of making direct investments in foreign markets, and supplying experienced managers, they made portfolio investments. The principal portfolio investments were bonds or preferred shares of foreign railroad and utility corporations that appeared to have predictable profit margins. Most purchases were made in nations and in industries where there was less competition. The preferred places for portfolio investments were Canada, Australia, India, the United States, and South American nations.

Other causes for the decline in Britain's competitiveness in international commerce were: 1) slowness in introducing new mass production techniques to stay competitive; 2) a reluctance of hereditary owners to train and promote paid professional managers; 3) reduced incentives to invest in research and development; 4) reduced need to standardize product designs; 5) reduced need to develop brand loyalty for consumer items.

Managers of U.S. and German corporations understood that portfolio investments produced insufficient profits. The most efficient way to earn adequate profits was sending experienced management teams to manage direct investments. Only after about 1960, when Britain applied for membership in the Common Market, did the managers of many British corporations fully realize that participation in the global market required paid professional managers who were highly educated and promoted on merit. Family management and portfolio investments were failed business strategies because they did not contribute to creating oligopoly corporations that could effectively compete in the post-WWII global market.

The end of the cold war (1991) created political conditions that were overwhelmingly favorable for direct foreign investments by global corporations in central European nations, especially by corporations with headquarters in the EU. Frequently, the means of attracting direct investments is selling (privatizing) state owned corporations to global corporations. Privatization is the means of escaping the technological isolation and rigidities of planned economies and linking newly acquired subsidiary corporations to the competitive pressures of larger markets.

Most privatized corporations in central European nations require new management teams, updated technologies, and very large capital investments to become efficient. Global corporations can supply them. Especially, global corporations can supply capital where the domestic supply is small or nonexistent. Management teams supplied by global corporations are much more efficient at accumulating capital from retained earnings and paying taxes compared to socialist management. New management teams rapidly increase worker productivity if national laws allow flexible labor markets. Flexible labor markets allow managers to use fewer workers who are better trained, better paid, and better motivated to produce more products of higher quality than politically managed, undercapitalized, and overstaffed corporations that were typical of planned economies. The ability of global corporations to manage participation in larger markets makes them efficient agents for helping to manage the transition to free market economies.

The highly visible prosperity of nations where direct foreign investments are concentrated is clear evidence that there is a close linkage between reduced barriers to global commerce (negotiated by WTO, EU, NAFTA) and the ability of global corporations to produce products at competitive prices, compared to prices charged by protected corporations in small national markets. The *World Investment Report 1993,* published by the United Nations, estimated that there were 37,000 multinational corporations with 200,000 subsidiaries that had 73 million full time employees. Not all of these corporations operated globally but whether multinational or global, they were highly concentrated in the United States, Canada, European Union, and Japan. In the mid-1990s, the 600 largest global corporations produced more than 25 percent of the world's domestic product. About 80 percent of the production and sales of these corporations was within or between North America, EU, and Japan.

In 1991, products made in the U.S. for export to the foreign subsidiaries of U.S. based global and multinational corporations accounted for 26 percent of total U.S. exports; and products made in the U.S. by the subsidiaries of global corporations with headquarters outside the United States accounted for an additional 23 percent of U.S. exports. In one form or another, products produced by global corporations accounted for about 50 percent of total U.S. exports, and this trend continued through the 1990s when these corporations built networks of intra-corporate trade in order to take advantage of economies of scale and terms of trade. What occurred in the United States also occurred in the EU, but less so in Japan.

The complexity and scale of global commerce indicates that in the twenty-first century: The nature of international competition will be redefined by the globalization of economic activities of transnational corporations which can be increasingly viewed as networks of international production in which intra-firm flows of capital, goods, services, training, and technology play an important role and their major value adding function is the integration, organization, and management of those international flows. [5]

GLOBAL CORPORATIONS

Why have so many big corporations in national markets become global? There are three principal reasons. The most important is that it is politically possible. The second is that peace has been maintained among the principal industrial nations, and the prospect for maintaining peace dramatically increased after the end of the cold war. The third reason is competition.

The end of the cold war was a clear signal to managers of global and multinational corporations that peace (instead of a tense military standoff) was sustainable for the foreseeable future. In response, senior managers accelerated mergers in order to optimize operations in an expanding global market. Participation in domestic and global markets became a competitive race between domestic corporations and global corporations to increase profits by cost reductions that were increasingly possible with economies of scale and terms of trade achieved by intra-corporate trade across national borders. Empirical evidence has consistently indicated that when global corporations establish or acquire subsidiaries in foreign nations, the subsidiaries are more profitable (more efficiently managed) than domestic corporations until domestic corporations become better managed or bankrupt.

The largest and best managed global manufacturing corporations have muted their national identities in the sense that the majority of profits (and perhaps a high majority) are earned outside the nations where their headquarters are located. Senior managers are promoted on the basis of performance so that citizenship is usually a minor consideration in selecting executives. When these corporations introduce new products it is done globally, rather than treating international markets as an afterthought to domestic markets.

Global corporations preferentially invest in politically stable, industrial nations with predictable business polices, high disposable incomes, high rates of literacy, and the most technically advanced infrastructures. In practice this means that, in the 1990s, 80 percent of direct investments by global corporation were in North America, the EU, and Japan. Nations with small industrial sectors (Mexico, Brazil, Chile, South Korea, Taiwan) received most of the rest. Only one percent of direct foreign investments by U.S. corporations in 2000 were in peasant nations. Most of it was to produce oil and other raw materials.

Taken together, the exports of all the world's poor and middle-income countries (including comparative giants such as China, India, Brazil, and Mexico, big oil exporters such as Saudi Arabia, and large-scale manufacturers such as South Korea, Taiwan, and Malaysia) represent only about 5 percent of global output. This is an amount roughly equivalent to the gross domestic product of Britain. [6]

Only belatedly have the governing elites of nations with small industrial sectors recognized the advantages of direct investments by global corporations. The debt crisis of the mid-1980s forced them to see the positive results of maximizing participation in global commerce because the export driven economies of Singapore, Malaysia, Taiwan, and South Korea, as well as the prime example of Japan, were minimally affected. The majority of exports of these nations (usually a vast majority) are manufactured products, not commodities.

An alternative strategy to direct investments by global corporations is strong encouragement by central governments in nations with small industrial sectors for entrepreneurs to use abundant unskilled labor to manufacture labor intensive products like textiles and clothing for export markets. A second alternative is to encourage the creation of a limited number of big industrial corporations that can compete in the global market. In both of these strategies the usual encouragement is preferential access to credit. After markets are established the big corporations may attempt to transform themselves into multinational corporations. As long as WTO and OECD can maintain rules in global commerce, the global market is an opportunity for big corporations in less industrialized nations to become global.

Joint ventures are an alternative strategy to expand markets and increase profits of global corporations. Joint ventures have many variations. The most common is a partnership between global corporations and domestic corporations. The global corporation contributes capital, technology, and management skills and the domestic corporation contributes a factory and a domestic distribution network. It may also contribute political influence. Alternatively, a global corporation may sign a management contract to apply proprietary knowledge in order to increase the operating efficiencies of a domestic corporation, or for that corporation to produce one or more new products for export.

In joint ventures and management contracts, global corporations do not fully control management or growth strategies because domestic partners retain more or less control of business operations. This is especially true if the partner's principal contribution is political influence. Frequently, this leads to conflict because politically motivated middle managers may be more interested in increasing employment without a commitment to increasing profits. When conflicts occur global corporations have two options: buyout domestic partners or withdrawal from the venture. If buyouts are impossible because national laws forbids global corporations from majority or total ownership of businesses, then the only option is withdrawal by selling its share if a buyer is available. Because of the risk of management conflicts, global manufacturing corporations are very reluctant to enter into joint ventures in nations with small industrial sectors composed of highly protected industries.

PEASANT NATIONS

Global corporations ignore peasants because subsistence labor norms do not earn money incomes. For peasants, money acquisition has a low social priority because they choose to minimize production of commodities for market sale. Neither are yeomen cultivators attractive consumers of the products and services produced by global corporations. Although they perform commercial labor norms, their labor is inefficient because they produce middling amounts of agricultural surpluses for market sale. Their low incomes make them peripheral consumers of manufactured products.

After independence, the governing elites of many post-colonial nations rejected direct investments by global corporations because they claimed that global corporations were a new and more exploitive form of colonialism. These nations attracted almost no investment by manufacturing corporations because the Marxist ideology of governing elites claimed that socialist policies of political economy could initiate and sustain industrialization. They could not. It has taken 40 years for the governing elites of some of these nations to realize that the requisite human and capital resources are nonexistent in the subsistence cultures they govern.

Except for investments in mining and oil production, that only have export markets, most of the industrial facilities in peasant nations are gifts (foreign aid). For example, the government of Tanzania accepted gifts of factories to make textiles, footwear, and cement to supply the domestic market. These factories are not in continuous production due to irregular supplies of raw materials, and when they are in production they operate at less than 30 percent, to a maximum of 50 percent of capacity. Likewise, the paved roads built with foreign aid carry little commercial traffic and they have seriously deteriorated because they receive little maintenance.

If mines were operating in colonies they were usually nationalized after independence. In Zambia and Congo Republic the results have been disastrous. Investments that were essential to sustain copper production and keep it competitive in the global market were continually deferred. Production continually declined because a high percentage of revenues were used for patronage in order to retain governing elites in power. Currently (2003), the mines, mills, and smelters of the African copperbelt are piles of junk.

NOTES

1. Alfred D. Chandler, *Scale and Scope*, 14, 17, 18.
2. Lewis D. Solomon, *Multinational Corporations and the Emerging World Order*, 9.
3. Stephen D. Cohen, *The Making of United States International Economic Policy*, 26.
4. Edward M. Graham, *Global Corporations and National Governments*, 9.
5. Karl P. Sauvant, "Transnational Corporations as Engines of Growth," in Phillip D. Grub, Dara Khambata, eds. *The Multinational Enterprise in Transition*, 506.
6. *The Economist*, "Globalization and its Critics," September 29, 2001, 11.

REFERENCES

Blomstrom, Magnus, Ari Kokko, Mario Zejan. *Foreign Direct Investment: Firm and Host Country Strategies*, London, Macmillan, 2000 (chapters 7, 8, 9)

Chandler, Alfred D., ed. *The Railroads: The Nation's First Big Business*, New York, Harcourt, Brace, and World, 1965 (parts 1, 2, 3)

Chandler, Alfred D. *The Visible Hand: The Managerial Revolution in American Business*, Cambridge, Belknap Press, 1977 (chapters 12, 13, 14)

Chandler, Alfred D. "The Growth of the Transnational Industrial Firm in the United States and the United Kingdom: A Comparative Analysis," *Economic History Review*, Vol. 33, 1980

Chandler, Alfred D. "The Emergence of Managerial Capitalism," *Business History Review*, Vol. 58, 1984

Chandler, Alfred D. *Scale and Scope: The Dynamics of Industrial Capitalism*, Cambridge, Belknap Press, 1990 (chapters 1, 2, 3, 4)

Cohen, Stephen D. *The Making of United States International Economic Policy: Principles,Problems, and Proposals for Reform*, Westport, Praeger, 1994 (chapters 1, 2)

Dunning, John H. *Multinationals, Technology and Competiveness*, London, Unwin Hyman, 1988 (chapter 3)

Dunning, John H., Rajneesh Narula, eds. *Foreign Direct Investments and Governments: Catalysts for Economic Restructuring*, London, Routledge, 1996 (chapters 8, 9, 12, Mexico, Taiwan, China)

Dunning, John H. "Does Ownership Really Matter in a Globalizing Economy?" in Douglas Woodward, Douglas Nigh, eds. *Foreign Ownership and the Consequences of Direct Investment in the United States: Beyond Us and Them*, Westport, Quorum Books, 1998 *The Economist*, "Globalization and Its Critics," September 29, 2001, 11

Eden, Lorraine. "Bringing the Firm Back In: Multinationals in the International Political Economy," in Lorraine Eden, Evan H. Potter, eds. *Multinationals in the Global Political Economy*, New York, St Martins Press, 1993

Franko, Lawrence G. "The Origins of Multinational Manufacturing by Continental European Firms," *Business History Review*, Vol. 48, 1974

Graham, Edward M., Paul R. Krugman. "The Surge in Foreign Direct Investment in the 1980s," in Kenneth A. Froot, ed. *Foreign Direct Investment*, Chicago, University of Chicago Press, 1993

Graham, Edward M. *Global Corporations and National Governments*, Washington, Institute for International Economics, 1996

Holstein, William J. "The Stateless Corporation," in Phillip D. Grub, Dara Khambata, eds. *The Multinational Enterprise in Transition: Strategies for Global Competitiveness*, Princeton, Darwin Press, 1993

Molz, Rick. "Privatization of Government Enterprise: The Challenge of Management," in Phillip D. Grub, Dara Khambata, eds. *The Multinational Enterprise in Transition: Strategies for Global Competitiveness*, Princeton, Darwin Press, 1993

Robock, Stefan H. "U.S. Policies Toward Transnationals," in Weizao Teng, N. T. Wang, eds. *Transnational Corporations and China's Open Door Policy*, Lexington, Lexington Books, 1988

Sauvant, Karl P. "Transnational Corporations as Engines of Growth," in Phillip D. Grub, Dara Khambata, eds. *The Multinational Enterprise in Transition: Strategies for Global Competitiveness*, Princeton, Darwin Press, 1993

Solomon, Lewis D. *Multinational Corporations and the Emerging World Order*, Port Washington, Kennikat Press, 1978 (chapters 1, 2, 3, 9)

Stopford, John M. "The Origins of British-Based Multinational Manufacturing Enterprises," *Business History Review*, Vol. 48, 1974

Stopford, John M., Susan Strange. *Rival States, Rival Firms: Competition for World Market Shares*, Cambridge, Cambridge University Press, 1991 (chapters 2, 3)

Yoshino, M. Y. "The Multinational Spread of Japanese Manufacturing Investment Since World War II," *Business History Review*, Vol. 48, 1974

CONCLUSION

The global economy of the twenty-first century is the lineal descendent of European commercial imperialism that began in the fifteenth century with the voyages of discovery financed (in part) by the governments of Portugal and Spain. European commercial imperialism was the forcible intrusion of global commerce into subsistence cultures whether the cultures were primitive tribal societies, as they were in the Philippines and much of sub-Saharan Africa, or were highly sophisticated feudal kingdoms and principalities, as in much of India, China, and Japan. The evidence for the success of European commercial intrusion is the large number of coastal and riverine cities that grew at peripheral locations to existing subsistence societies, where previously there had been only fishing villages or vacant beaches. Some of these cities are Accra, Bombay, Calcutta, Cape Town, Dakar, Durban, Hong Kong, Irkutsk, Jakarta, Karachi, Kuala Lumpur, Lagos, Lima, Madras, Manila, Medan, Nagasaki, Rangoon, Shanghai, Singapore, Surabaya, and Vladivostok.

During the sixteenth and following centuries the search for global profits evolved into the rival commercial empires of Portugal, Spain, England, the Netherlands, and France and, at a later date, Russia, Germany, United States, and Japan. The unimaginable amount of wealth that has been produced by global commerce in the twentieth century could not have been foreseen in the sixteenth century. Nonetheless, much of this wealth is the direct result of commercial policies initiated by the central governments of European nations and implemented by merchant adventurers. The success of merchant adventurers was due to central governments supplying the naval and military forces that were essential for intruding imperial commerce into subsistence cultures.

From the first arrival of European merchants, a high percentage of indigenous merchants assisted the intrusion of imperial commerce and imperial governance into their societies. Indigenous merchants were coopted into imperial commerce because: 1) the rules of imperial governance were constrained by laws that made official conduct more predictable than that of indigenous feudal and tribal rulers; 2) imperial governance offered more protection for merchants and their wealth than provided by indigenous rulers; 3) participation in imperial commerce raised the status of indigenous merchants as well as increasing their fortunes; 4) and lowered the status of indigenous warriors. Under imperial governance warriors became the servants of merchants, not the reverse, and bureaucratic rules replaced unpredictable decisions by feudal and tribal rulers.

The greatest social benefit of imperial governance was the imposition of peace on warring feudalities and ending endemic tribal warfare because maximizing commerce requires peace. Tax revenues were no longer the personal property of feudal rulers to be used to wage war on neighbors or indulge in opulent luxury. They were used to enforce internal peace and build technically modern infrastructure facilities that were paid for by regularized taxation. Peace and infrastructure investments promoted a vast increase in domestic and export commerce; and the most visible result of this commerce was the creation of new wealth concentrated in new cities.

The European foundation for increasing the commercial wealth of European nations was applying commercial labor norms to agriculture, artisan manufacturing, and seamanship. Both the English and Dutch had commercialized agriculture by 1650 and the assured food surpluses produced by English and Dutch cultivators fed artisan manufacturers, city workers, and seamen. This was a principal reason why

England and the Netherlands emerged as imperial nations (and major European powers) in the seventeenth century. The failure of Spanish rulers to induce the commercialization of agriculture or encourage artisan manufactories were principal reasons why Spain failed to maintain itself as a major European power after precious metal imports from the Americas declined.

The last region to be incorporated into imperial commerce was sub-Saharan Africa. Imperial penetration did not begin until the second half of the nineteenth century, and imperial governance was not securely established until about 1910. Because of the paucity of human skills, the short duration of imperial governance, and the retarding effects of two world wars and the Great Depression, political unity and the commercial sectors created by imperial governance were small and weak at the time of independence in the 1960s. Decolonization was premature but inevitable because of the weakness of imperial rule and the skill of indigenous political leaders in uniting diverse ethnicities for the single purpose of ending imperial governance. Premature independence meant that the central governments and commercial sectors of most post-colonial nations have remained fragile because governing elites have opted to maintain the subsistence statusquo rather than continue the process of economic development begun by imperial governors.

After the end of WWII (1945) political leaders in the United States and western Europe were determined to end the imperial commercial rivalries of the nineteenth and early twentieth centuries that had contributed to WWI and WWII. Their overwhelming concerns were: 1) creating institutions that could sustain a lasting peace (absence of nuclear war) among the principal industrial nations; 2) integrating the economies of the principal industrial nations so tightly that it would be impossible for any one of them to wage global war. This integration would not take place unless there was protection from the potential aggression of the last commercial empire builder (Soviet Union). NATO provided the protection.

Imperial rivalries would be replaced by cooperative commercial policies among the principal industrial nations (except the Soviet Union). Behind the shield of NATO the rules governing global commerce changed. Rivalry was replaced by cooperation. Cooperation required the dissolution of rival European commercial empires. Concurrently, new institutions had to be created that could manage global commerce so that all industrial nations had equalized opportunities to share in the creation of new wealth. Restructuring required cooperation on a continuing basis in order to sustain prosperity. The best measure of prosperity is a consumer culture. Full employment was the means of achieving prosperity and full employment could best be sustained by maximizing participation in global commerce.

The key policy in restructuring global commerce was devolving competition to global and multinational corporations. Decentralizing competition made it manageable. But there had to be rules for competition and only cooperation could make rules acceptable to the principal industrial nations. The rules were embedded in bilateral and multilateral trade agreements brokered by GATT/WTO, IMF, Common Market/European Union, and NAFTA. These agreements defined fair competition and adjudicated commercial disputes between nations in which global and multinational corporations had a strong interest. These organizations put competition on as level a playing field as was politically possible.

From their inception, these organizations were designed to operate for the benefit of the principal industrial nations; and their continued operation is primarily for their benefit. Five assumptions guide the policy decisions of the managers of these organizations. 1) There is no limit to the amount of new wealth that can be produced. 2) There is an infinite amount of new technologies that can be discovered by research and transferred across national borders. 3) Persons and corporations ought to be encouraged to apply new technologies to produce new wealth. 4) There is an infinite supply of raw materials in politically stable nations that can be produced using requisite technologies. 5) Nations that want to maximize the production of new wealth must institutionalize social change in order to apply technologies that are essential for producing new wealth.

These organization, however, are not exclusive clubs. The benefits they confer on participating nations are freely available to all nations that adopt policies that actively expand their commercial sectors and adhere to the rules of global commerce that have evolved since 1945. The industrialization of South Korea and Taiwan (from a near zero base) and their competitiveness in the global market conclusively demonstrates that political leadership can transform peasant nations into industrial nations—if governing elites are united for this purpose.

Put in other terms, the industrial wealth produced in North America, the European Union, and Japan after WWII was not at the expense of any industrial nation, nor was it at the expense of nations with small or no industrial sectors. The new wealth in industrial nations resulted from political, economic, and education policies that were implemented by central governments that wanted to maximize the prosperity of their citizens. These policies encouraged global and multinational corporations to develop and apply new technologies, build new infrastructure facilities, invest in new factories, and train persons to maximize per capita production of products and services. In sum, these policies institutionalized the social changes that accompany the application of new technologies and the expansion of markets.

Managers of global and multinational corporations are very sensitive to political policies that favor or discourage direct foreign investments. Before investments are made they must be sure that profits are recognized as legitimate rewards for efficient economic and social performance. They must also be assured that profits will be reasonably taxed. If reasonable taxation is a national policy most managers of global and multinational corporations favor increased public expenditures for health care, education, and transportation, as long as these services are preferentially allocated to persons who perform the commercial labor norms that produce new taxable wealth. It cannot be otherwise if prosperity is to be sustained. Only after commercial labor norms have been fully institutionalized (full-time paid labor becomes the social norm) can social services be more broadly shared.

Stimulating the production of all varieties of manufactured products that can be sold on the global market was one of the principal purposes for reducing trade barriers between the principal industrial nations. In the process, nations that fully participate in the global market become less self-sufficient in the production of manufactured products and raw materials. This economic integration has three beneficial effects: 1) the economies of the principal industrial nations are so tightly integrated that war between them is impossible; 2) consumer cultures are created in nations where none existed; 3) increased varieties of products and services are available for purchase in nations where consumer cultures already exist. The global market is a bargain in which all participating nations profit.

To summarize: **1.** The global economy and the prosperity it confers on participating nations has evolved during the more than 50 years of peace following WWII. The global economy could not have evolved without peace. The cooperation that was essential for its evolution could not have been sustained unless all industrial nations gained advantages from the increased volume of global commerce. Nor could global commerce have increased in scope and efficiency unless rules of fair competition were defined and organizations created to adjudicate disputes. Nor could these organizations have performed their functions unless the principal industrial nations agreed that they were essential for continuing prosperity. Looked at from a different perspective, the principal industrial nations have prospered because they have institutionalized social change that is inherent in commercial cultures.

2. Prosperity is simply measured in industrial nations. It is full employment and the enjoyment of consumer cultures. Consumer cultures include not only an abundance of possession but a large variety of public and social services that are paid for with tax revenues. There is only one source of tax revenue that is sufficiently large to pay for these services. It is income taxes paid by corporations and by persons who are full-time employees. The only way to sustain these sources of revenue is reasonable tax rates so that corporations can accumulate capital for reinvestment. In a world where there are fewer barriers to trade and financial transactions, industrial nations must be competitive in their taxation policies because competition for investments and transfers of technology confers sustaining social benefits on electorates.

Four final observations: **1. Why has low per capita industrial productivity persisted in some nations that have substantial in-**

dustrial sectors? There are two principal causes. 1) Centrally planned economies were designed to be largely self-sufficient in many manufactured products. 2) Minimal participation in global commerce greatly reduced access to new technologies and the accompanying pressure to be efficient producers of products and services. Both causes are due to failures in political leadership.

2. What has been the impact of global commerce on peasant nations? In all cases it is highly disruptive of customary social norms because enlarging commercial sectors accelerates social change. As long as commercial sectors continue to expand, the direction of change is always toward opportunities to improve the material welfare of people who perform commercial labor norms to produce products that are sold on anonymous markets. These markets could be in the nearest city or a continent away. Production of commodities for sale on anonymous markets always contributes to dissolving the subsistence social values that govern peasant conduct.

There have been two forms of resistance to social changes induced by global commerce. The first is blind fury. Blind fury is most likely to originate in Muslim nations awash in petrodollars where governing elites have been indifferent or hostile to creating institutions that induce social change. Large numbers of Muslim males are profoundly alienated by the impact of technology on their cultures because they perceive that their non-technical cultures have lost control of the future. They are politically impotent in the global economy. Global commerce requires secularization and secularization has a strong dissolving effect on customary social values, especially male dominance that pervades Muslim cultures. Terrorists portray themselves as god appointed protectors of the past. In Muslim cultures a principal response to the commercialization and secularization of culture is reinvigorating religious laws that sanction male dominance, coupled with terrorist attacks against the most visible institutions that propagates secular social change.

The September 11, 2001 terrorist attack on the World Trade Towers in New York City was a dramatic act their fury. All of the political leaders of industrial nations immediately recognized that the destruction of the World Trade Towers was really an attack on the secular basis of all commercial cultures; and similar attacks could happen at any time within the borders of all industrial nations.

The second form of resistance is using central governments to maintain a subsistence statusquo. The governing elites of most post-colonial peasant nations are indifferent to economic development that requires inducing more persons to perform commercial labor norms (continuous paid labor). Their commitment to maintaining the statusquo is indicated when a high percentage of national revenue is used for patronage instead of making improvements in infrastructure facilities. This use of revenue converts the central governments of these nations into modern versions of feudal principalities. Instead of being ruled by kings, rajahs, or emirs, they are ruled by presidents for life.

3. Tenuous participation of peasant nations in global commerce. In spite of debilitating weaknesses, they must participate in the global market to survive. Survival requires a neocolonial relationship with the principal industrial nations; otherwise, they are likely to dissolve into anarchy. The principal industrial nations have assigned neocolonial responsibilities to the IMF and World Bank, supplemented by assistance (gifts) from the United Nations and various western European nations, Japan, the United States, and Canada. Neocolonial dependency will persist for the foreseeable future because there is no alternative.

4. Confusion of development economists: Economists are seriously handicapped trying to refute critics of the global economy who assert that investments in peasant nations (to take advantage of lower labor costs) enforces poverty. They have difficulty refuting this assertion because both economists (who favor the expansion of the global market) and critics (who oppose expansion) accept the same definition of poverty. Both parties fail to understand the revolutionary difference between subsistence labor norms and commercial labor norms. For both economists and critics, subsistence does not exist. This word is not part of their vocabularies. What exists is absolute poverty, a favorite term of both parties.

Neither economists nor critics of the global economy understand that illiterate peasants who are paid low wages accept them because the alternative (subsistence privation) is worse. Subsistence privation and poverty have totally different origins and totally different policies must be used to mitigate their effects. Economists do not understand the distinction between subsistence and poverty because they have little understanding of the causes of the social stresses that were experienced by the populations of western European nations, Japan, and Russia during the process of commercialization. They have less understanding of agriculture and the enormous amount of coercion that was exercised by central governments to overcome peasant resistance to performing commercial labor norms in food production.

The real issue is how to manage the commercialization process; and this requires political leaders and economic advisors who understand the revolutionary difference between subsistence social values (and their supporting institutions) and commercial social values (that can operate only when social change has been institutionalized). Until economists understand these distinctions, and equally understand that economic development is primarily a political process, they can only apologize for the failure of the policies they have prescribed (for the past 50 years) to cure subsistence privation.

BIBLIOGRAPHY

Abernethy, David B. "Nigeria," in David G. Scanlon, ed. *Church, State, and Education in Africa*, New York, Teachers College Press of Columbia University, 1966

Afigbo, Adiele E., Emanuel A., Ayandele, R. J. Gavin, John D. Omer-Cooper, Robin Palmer. *The Making of Modern Africa: The Nineteenth Century*, London, Longman, 1986

Afigbo, Adiele E., Emanuel A. Ayandele, R. J. Gavin, John D. Omer-Cooper, Robin Palmer.*The Making of Modern Africa: The Twentieth Century*, London, Longman, 1986

Anderson, Kym, Richard Blackhurst, eds. *Regional Integration and the Global Trading System*, New York, St Martins Press, 1993

Armytage, W.H.G. *Four Hundred Years of English Education*, Cambridge, Cambridge University Press, 1970

Arnold, David, ed. *Imperial Medicine and Indigenous Societies*, Manchester, Manchester University Press, 1988

Ashby, Eric. *African Universities and Western Tradition*, Cambridge, Harvard University Press, 1964

Axelson, Eric. *Congo to Cape: Early Portuguese Explorers*, New York, Barnes and Noble, 1973

Ayittey, George B. N. "Aid for Black Elephants: How Foreign Assistance Has Failed Africa," in Doug Bandow, Ian Vasquez, eds. *Perpetuating Poverty: The World Bank, the IMF, and the Developing World*, Washington, Cato Institute, 1994

Ayres, Robert L. *Banking on the Poor: The World Bank and World Poverty*, Cambridge, MIT Press, 1983

Bairoch, Paul. "European Trade Policy, 1815-1914," in Peter Mathias, Sidney Pollard, eds. *Cambridge Economic History of Europe: The Industrial Economies: The Development of Economic and Social Policies*, Vol. 8, Cambridge, Cambridge University Press, 1989

Ball, J. N. *Merchants and Merchandise: The Expansion of Trade in Europe, 1500-1630*, New York, St Martins Press, 1977

Barnes, Donald G. *A History of the English Corn Laws from 1660-1846*, New York, Crofts, 1930

Basye, Arthur H. *The Lords Commissioners of Trade and Plantations: Commonly Known as the Board of Trade, 1748-1782*, New Haven, Yale University Press, 1925

Becker, Gary S., Kevin M. Murphy, Robert Tamura. "Human Capital, Fertility, and Economic Growth," *Journal of Political Economy*, Vol. 98, 1990

Beer, George L. *The Origins of the British Colonial System, 1578-1660*, Gloucester, Peter Smith, 1959 (reprint of 1908 edition)

Berg, Elliott J. "The Development of a Labour Force in Sub-Saharan Africa," *Economic Development and Cultural Change*, Vol. 13, 1965

Bird, Graham. *IMF Lending to Developing Countries: Issue and Evidence*, London, Routledge, 1995

Blakemore, Priscilla. "Assimilation and Association in French Educational Policy and Practice: Senegal, 1903-1939," in Vincent M. Battle, Charles H. Lyons, eds. *Essays in the History of African Education*, New York, Teachers College Press of Columbia University, 1970

Blau, Peter M. *Bureaucracy in Modern Society,* New York, Random House, 1956

Blomquist, Thomas W. "Commercial Associations in Thirteenth-Century Lucca," *Business History Review*, Vol. 45, 1971

Blomstrom, Magnus, Ari Kokko, Mario Zejan. *Foreign Direct Investment: Firm and Host Country Strategies*, London, Macmillan, 2000

Bordo, Michael D. "The Bretton Woods International Monetary System: A Historical Overview," in Michael D. Bordo, Barry Eichengreen, eds. *A Retrospective on the Bretton Woods System: Lessons for International Monetary Reform*, Chicago, University of Chicago Press, 1993

Boxer, Charles R. *The Dutch Seaborne Empire, 1600-1800*, New York, Knopf, 1965

Boxer, Charles R. *Francisco Vieira de Figueiredo: A Portuguese Merchant-Adventurer in South East Asia, 1624-1667*, Gravenhage, Martinus Nijhoff, 1967

Boxer, Charles R. *The Portuguese Seaborne Empire, 1415-1825*, New York, Knopf, 1969

Boxer Charles R. *Jan Compagnie in War and Peace, 1602-1799: A Short History of the Dutch East-India Company*, Hong Kong, Heinemann Asia, 1979

Braudel, Fernand. *Civilization and Capitalism 15th-18th Century*, New York, Harper Row, 1984

Brewer, John. *The Sinews of Power: War, Money and the English State, 1688-1783*, New York, Knopf, 1989

Bridenbaugh, Carl. *Vexed and Troubled Englishmen, 1590-1642*, New York, Oxford University Press, 1968

Carlos, Ann W., Stephen Nicholas. "Giants of an Earlier Capitalism: The Chartered Trading Companies as Modern Multinationals," *Business History Review*, Vol. 62, 1988

Cell, John W. "Colonial Rule," in Judith M. Brown, William R. Louis, eds. *Oxford History of the British Empire: The Twentieth Century*, Vol. 4, Oxford, Oxford University Press, 1999

Chandler, Alfred D., ed. *The Railroads: The Nation's First Big Business*, New York, Harcourt, Brace, and World, 1965

Chandler, Alfred D. *The Visible Hand: The Managerial Revolution in American Business*, Cambridge, Belknap Press, 1977

Chandler, Alfred D. "The Growth of the Transnational Industrial Firm in the United States and the United Kingdom: A Comparative Analysis," *Economic History Review*, Vol. 33, 1980

Chandler, Alfred D. "The Emergence of Managerial Capitalism," *Business History Review*, Vol. 58, 1984

Chandler, Alfred D. *Scale and Scope: The Dynamics of Industrial Capitalism*, Cambridge, Belknap Press, 1990

Charlton, Kenneth. *Education in Renaissance England*, London, Routledge and Kegan Paul, 1965

Chartres, John, David Hey, eds. *English Rural Society, 1500-1800*, Cambridge, Cambridge University Press, 1990

Cheong, Weng E. *The Hong Merchants of Canton: Chinese Merchants in Sino-Western Trade*, Richmond, Curzon, 1997

Cipolla, Carlo M. *Guns, Sails, and Empires: Technological Innovation and the Early Phases of European Expansion, 1400-1700*, Manhattan, Sunflower University Press, 1985 (reprint of 1965 edition)

Cipolla, Carlo M. *Literacy and Development in the West*, Baltimore, Penguin Books, 1969

Cipolla, Carlo M., ed. *The Emergence of Industrial Societies,* Part 1, Glasgow, Fontana/Collins, 1973

Cipolla, Carlo M., ed. *The Industrial Revolution, 1700-1914*, London, Harvester Press/Barnes and Noble, 1976

Clement, Norris C., et al. *North American Economic Integration: Theory and Practice*, Cheltenham, Edward Elgar, 1999

Cline, William R. *International Debt: Systematic Risk and Policy Response*, Washington, Institute for International Economics, 1984

Clough, Shepard B., Charles W. Cole. *Economic History of Europe*, Boston, Heath, 1952

Cohen, Benjamin J. *Crossing Frontiers: Explorations in International Political Economy*, Boulder, Westview Press, 1991

Cohen, Patricia C. *A Calculating People: The Spread of Numeracy in Early America*, Chicago, University of Chicago Press, 1985

Cohen, Stephen D. *The Making of United States International Economic Policy: Principles, Problems, and Proposals for Reform*, Westport, Praeger, 1994

Coquery-Vidrovitch, Catherine. "Western Equatorial Africa," in Roland A. Oliver, G. N. Sanderson, eds. *Cambridge History of Africa: From 1870 to 1905*, Vol. 6, Cambridge, Cambridge University Press, 1985

Cressy, David. *Education in Tudor and Stuart England*, New York, St Martins Press, 1976

Cressy, David. *Literacy and the Social Order: Reading and Writing in Tudor and Stuart England*, Cambridge, Cambridge University Press, 1980

Crowder, Michael. *West Africa Under Colonial Rule*, London, Hutchinson, 1968

Crowder, Michael. "The White Chiefs of Tropical Africa," in Lewis H. Gann, Peter Duignan, eds. *Colonialism in Africa, 1870-1960: The History and Politics of Colonialism, 1914-1960*, Vol. 2, Cambridge, Cambridge University Press, 1970

Curtin, Philip D. *Death by Migration: Europe's Encounter with the Tropical World in the Nineteenth Century*, Cambridge, Cambridge University Press, 1989

Dam, Kenneth W. *GATT: Law and International Economic Organization*, Chicago, University of Chicago Press, 1970

Davies, Kenneth G. *The Royal African Company*, New York, Atheneum, 1970 (reprint of 1957 edition)

Davis, Clarence B., Kenneth E. Wilburn, eds. *Railway Imperialism*, Westport, Greenwood Press, 1991

Davis, Ralph. "English Foreign Trade, 1700-1814," in Walter E. Minchinton, ed. *The Growth of English Overseas Trade in the Seventeenth and Eighteenth Centuries*, London, Methuen, 1969

Deane, Phyllis. "The Industrial Revolution in Great Britain," in Carlo M. Cipolla, ed. *Fontana Economic History of Europe: The Emergence of Industrial Societies*, Vol. 4, Glasgow, Fontana/Collins, 1973

Dickson, Peter G. M. *The Financial Revolution in England: A Study in the Development of Public Credit, 1688-1756*, London, Macmillan, 1967

Diffie, Bailey W., George D. Winius. *Foundations of the Portuguese Empire, 1415-1580*, Minneapolis, University of Minnesota Press, 1977

Disney, Anthony R. *Twilight of the Pepper Empire: Portuguese Trade in Southwest India in the Early Seventeenth Century*, Cambridge, Harvard University Press, 1978

Douglas, Roy. *Taxation in Britain Since 1660*, London, Macmillan, 1999

Dowell, Stephen. *A History of Taxation and Taxes in England from the Earliest Times to the Year 1885* (2 volumes), London, Longmans Green, 1888

Dunning, John H. *Multinationals, Technology and Competitiveness*, London, Unwin Hyman, 1988

Dunning, John H., Rajneesh Narula, eds. *Foreign Direct Investments and Governments: Catalysts for Economic Restructuring*, London, Routledge, 1996

Dunning, John H. "Does Ownership Really Matter in a Globalizing Economy?" in Douglas Woodward, Douglas Nigh, eds. *Foreign Ownership and the Consequences of Direct Investment in the United States: Beyond Us and Them*, Westport, Quorum Books, 1998

Easterly, William R. *The Elusive Quest for Growth: Economists Adventures and Misadventures in the Tropics*, Cambridge, MIT Press, 2001

Eden, Lorraine. "Bringing the Firm Back In: Multinationals in the International Political Economy," in Lorraine Eden, Evan H. Potter, eds. *Multinationals in the Global Political Economy*, New York, St Martins Press, 1993

Edwardes, Michael. *British India, 1772-1947: A Survey of the Nature and Effects of Alien Rule*, London, Sidgwick and Jackson, 1967

Edwardes, Michael. *Plassey: The Founding of an Empire*, London, Hamilton, 1969

Eichengreen, Barry. "Hegemonic Stability Theories in the International Monetary System," in Richard N. Cooper, et al. *Can Nations Agree? Issues in International Economic Cooperation*, Washington, Brookings Institution, 1989

Ellwood, David W. *Rebuilding Europe: Western Europe, America and Postwar Reconstruction*, London, Longman, 1992

Falola, Toyin A., A. D. Roberts. "West Africa," in Judith M. Brown, William R. Louis, eds. *Oxford History of the British Empire: The Twentieth Century*, Vol. 4, Oxford, Oxford University Press, 1999

Farley, John. "Bilharzia: A Problem of Native Health, 1900-1950," in David Arnold, ed. *Imperial Medicine and Indigenous Societies*, Manchester, Manchester University Press, 1988

Farley, John. *Bilharzia: A History of Imperial Tropical Medicine*, Cambridge, Cambridge University Press, 1991

Fieldhouse, David K. *The Colonial Empires: A Comparative Survey from the Eighteenth Century*, New York, Delacorte Press, 1967

Fieldhouse, David K. "The Economic Exploitation of Africa: Some British and French Comparisons," in Prosser Gifford, William R. Louis, eds. *France and Britain in Africa: Imperial Rivalry and Colonial Rule*, New Haven, Yale University Press, 1971

Fieldhouse, David K. *Economics and Empire, 1830-1914*, Ithaca, Cornell University Press, 1973

Fieldhouse, David K. *Colonialism, 1870-1945: An Introduction*, New York, St Martins Press, 1981

Fisher, Michael H. *Indirect Rule in India: Residents and the Residency System, 1764-1858*, Delhi, Oxford University Press, 1991

Fohlen, Claude. "The Industrial Revolution in France, 1700-1914," in Carlo M. Cipolla, ed. *Fontana Economic History of Europe: The Emergence of Industrial Societies*, Vol. 4, Glasgow, Fontana/Collins, 1973

Foster, William, ed. *The Embassy of Sir Thomas Roe to the Court of the Great Mogul 1615-1619: As Narrated in His Journal and Correspondence*, Nendeln/Liechenstein, Kraus Reprint, 1967 (reprint of 1899 edition)

Foster, William, ed. *The Journal of John Jourdain, 1608-1617: De-scribing His Experiences in Arabia, India, and the Malay Ar-chipelago*, Nendeln/Liechtenstein, Kraus Reprint, 1967 (reprint of 1905 edition)

Foster, William, ed. *The Voyage of Sir Henry Middleton to the Moluccas, 1604-1606*, London, Kraus Reprint, 1990 (reprint of 1943 edition)

Frankel, Jeffrey A. *Regional Trading Blocs in the World Economic System*, Washington, Institute for International Economics, 1997

Frankel, Sally Herbert. *Capital Investment in Africa: Its Course and Effects*, London, Oxford University Press, 1938

Franko, Lawrence G. "The Origins of Multinational Manufacturing by Continental European Firms," *Business History Review*, Vol. 48, 1974

Fratianni Michele, John Pattison. "International Organizations in a World of Regional Trade Agreements: Lessons from Club Theory," *The World Economy*, Vol. 24, 2001

Furber, Holden. *Rival Empires of Trade in the Orient, 1600-1800*, Minneapolis, University of Minnesota Press, 1976

Galambos, Louis, David Milobsky. "Organizing and Reorganizing the World Bank, 1946-1972," *Business History Review*, Vol. 69, 1995

Galenson, David W. *White Servitude in Colonial America: An Economic Analysis*, Cambridge, Cambridge University Press, 1981

Garrett, Geoffrey. "The Politics of Maastricht," in Barry Eichengreen, Jeffrey A. Frieden, eds. *The Political Economy of European Monetary Unification*, Boulder, Westview Press, 2001

Garthoff, Raymond L. *Détente and Confrontation: American-Soviet Relations from Nixon to Reagan*, Washington, Brookings Institution, 1994

Gifford, Prosser, William R. Lewis, ed. *France and Britain in Africa: Imperial Rivalry and Colonial Rule*, New Haven, Yale University Press, 1971

Gifford, Prosser, Timothy C. Weiskel. "African Education in a Colonial Context: French and British Styles," in Prosser Gifford, William R. Louis, eds. *France and Britain in Africa: Imperial Rivalry and Colonial Rule*, New Haven, Yale University Press, 1971

Gilpin, Robert. *The Political Economy of International Relations*, Princeton, Princeton University Press, 1987

Glamann, Kristof. *Dutch-Asiatic Trade, 1620-1740*, Copenhagen, Danish Science Press, 1958

Goldberg, Ellen S., Dan Haendel. *On Edge: International Banking and Country Risk*, New York, Praeger, 1987

Gomes, Leonard. *Foreign Trade and the National Economy: Mercantilist and Classical Perspectives*, New York, St Martins Press, 1987

Goode, Richard. *Economic Assistance to Developing Countries Through the IMF*, Washington, Brookings Institution, 1985

Grabbe, Heather, Kirsty Hughes. *Enlarging the EU Eastwards*, London, Royal Institute of International Affairs, 1998

Graham, Edward M., Paul R. Krugman. "The Surge in Foreign Direct Investment in the 1980s," in Kenneth A. Froot, ed. *Foreign Direct Investment*, Chicago, University of Chicago Press, 1993

Graham, Edward M. *Global Corporations and National Governments*, Washington, Institute for International Economics, 1996

Gras, Norman S. B. *The Evolution of the English Corn Market: From the Twelfth to the Eighteenth Century*, Cambridge, Harvard University Press, 1915

Greene, Jack P., ed. *Great Britain and the American Colonies, 1606-1763*, New York, Harper and Row, 1970

Gruber, Lloyd. *Ruling the World: Power Politics and the Rise of Supranational Institutions*, Princeton, Princeton University Press, 2000

Gutteridge, William F. "Military and Police Forces in Colonial Africa," in Lewis H. Gann, Peter Duignan, eds. *Colonialism in Africa, 1870-1960: The History and Politics of Colonialism, 1914-1960*, Vol. 2, Cambridge, Cambridge University Press, 1970

Gwin, Catherine. *U.S. Relations with the World Bank, 1945-1992*, Washington, Brookings Institution, 1994

Hale, John R. *Renaissance Exploration*, New York, Norton, 1968

Hanna, Willard A. *Indonesian Banda: Colonialism and Its Aftermath in the Nutmeg Islands*, Philadelphia, Institute for the Study of Human Issues, 1978

Hargreaves, John D. "British and French Imperialism in West Africa, 1885-1898," in Prosser Gifford, William R. Louis, eds. *France and Britain in Africa: Imperial Rivalry and Colonial Rule*, New Haven, Yale University Press, 1971

Hargreaves, John D. "Western Africa, 1886-1905," in Roland A. Oliver, G. N. Sanderson, eds. *Cambridge History of Africa: From 1876 to 1905*, Vol. 6, Cambridge, Cambridge University Press, 1985

Haring, Clarence H. *Trade and Navigation Between Spain and the Indies in the Time of the Hapsburgs,* Cambridge, Harvard University Press, 1918

Harper, Lawrence A. *The English Navigation Laws: A Seventeenth-Century Experiment in Social Engineering*, New York, Columbia University Press, 1939

Hathaway, Dale E. "Agricultural Trade Policy for the 1980s" in William R. Cline, ed. *Trade Policy in the 1980s*, Washington, Institute for International Economics 1983

Headrick, Daniel R. *The Tools of Empire: Technology and European Imperialism in the Nineteenth Century*, New York, Oxford University Press, 1981

Hoekman, Bernard M., Michel M. Kostecki. *The Political Economy of the World Trading System: From GATT to WTO*, Oxford, Oxford University Press, 1995

Hogendorn, Jan S. "The Origins of the Groundnut Trade in Northern Nigeria," in Carl K. Eicher, Carl Liedholm, eds. *Growth and Development of the Nigerian Economy*, East Lansing, Michigan State University Press, 1970

Holstein, William J. "The Stateless Corporation," in Phillip D. Grub, Dara Khambata, eds. *The Multinational Enterprise in Transition: Strategies for Global Competitiveness*, Princeton, Darwin Press, 1993

Houston, Robert A. *Literacy in Early Modern Europe: Culture and Education, 1500-1800*, London, Longman, 1998

Jack, Sybil M. *Trade and Industry in Tudor and Stuart England*, London, Allen and Unwin, 1977

Jackson, John H. *The World Trading System: Law and Policy of International Economic Relations*, Cambridge, MIT Press, 1999

Jackson, Robert H. *Quasi-States: Sovereignty, International Relations, and the Third World*, Cambridge, Cambridge University Press, 1990

Jeffries, Charles J. *The Colonial Empire and Its Civil Service*, Cambridge, Cambridge University Press, 1938

John, Arthur H. "English Agricultural Improvement and Grain Exports, 1660-1675," in Donald C. Coleman, Arthur H. John, eds. *Trade, Government and Economy in Pre-Industrial England*, London, Weidenfeld and Nicholson, 1976

Jones, Eric L., ed. *Agriculture and Economic Growth in England, 1650-1815*, London, Methuen, 1967

Jones, Mary G. *The Charity School Movement: A Study of Eighteenth Century Puritanism in Action*, Hamden, Conn., Archon Books, 1964 (reprint of 1938 edition)

Kahler, Miles. *International Institutions and the Political Economy of Integration*, Washington, Brookings Institution, 1995

Kamarck, Andrew M. *The Economics of African Development*, New York, Praeger, 1967

Kaplan, Lawrence S. *NATO and the United States: The Enduring Alliance*, Boston, Twayne Publishers, 1988

Keay, John. *The Honourable Company: A History of the English East India Company*, New York, Macmillan, 1991

Kennedy, William C. *English Taxation, 1640-1799: An Essay on Policy and Opinion*, London, Bell, 1913

Kenwood, A. George, Alan L. Lougheed. *The Growth of the International Economy, 1820-2000*, London, Routledge, 1999

Kerridge, Eric. *Agrarian Problems in the Sixteenth Century and After*, London, Allen and Unwin, 1969

Kilson, Martin. "The Emergent Elites of Black Africa, 1900-1960." In Lewis H. Gann, Peter Duignan, eds. *Colonialism in Africa, 1870-1960: The History and Politics of Colonialism, 1914-1960*, Vol. 2, Cambridge, Cambridge University Press, 1970

Kingsley, J. Donald. "Bureaucracy and Political Development, with Particular Reference to Nigeria," in Joseph LaPalombara, ed. *Bureaucracy and Political Development*, Princeton, Princeton University Press, 1963

Kirk-Greene, Anthony. *On Crown Service: A History of HM Colonial and Overseas Civil Services, 1837-1997*, London, Tauris Publishers, 1999

Kitchen, Helen, ed. *The Educated African: A Country-by-Country Survey of Educational Development in Africa*, New York, Praeger, 1962

Klein, Martin A. "Slavery and Emancipation in French West Africa," in Martin A. Klein, ed. *Breaking the Chains: Bondage and Emancipation in Modern Africa and Asia*, Madison, University of Wisconsin Press, 1993

Kranzberg, Melvin, Carroll W. Pursell, eds. *Technology in Western Civilization: The Emergence of Modern Industrial Society, Earliest Times to 1900*, New York, Oxford University Press, 1967

van de Laar, Aart J. M. *The World Bank and the Poor*, Boston, Martinus Nijhoff Publishing, 1980

Landes, David S. *The Unbound Prometheus: Technical Change and Industrial Development in Western Europe from 1750 to the Present*, Cambridge, Cambridge University Press, 1969

Lawrence, Robert Z. *Regionalism, Multilateralism, and Deeper Integration*, Washington, Brookings Institution, 1996

Lawson, John. *Medieval Education and the Reformation*, London, Routledge and Kegan Paul, 1967

Lewis, Oscar. *Five Families: Mexican Case Studies in the Culture of Poverty*, New York, Wiley, 1962

Lilley, Samuel. "Technological Progress and the Industrial Revolution, 1700-1914," in Carlo M. Cipolla, ed. *Fontana Economic History of Europe: The Industrial Revolution, 1700-1914*, Vol. 3, London, Harvester Press/Barnes and Noble, 1976

Lofchie, Michael F. "Political and Economic Origins of African Hunger," *Journal of Modern African Studies*, Vol. 13, 1975

Lofchie, Michael F. "The Decline of African Agriculture: An Internalist Perspective," in Michael H. Glanz, ed. *Drought and Hunger in Africa*, Cambridge, Cambridge University Press, 1987

Louis, William R., Ronald Robinson. "The Imperialism of Decolonization," *Journal of Imperial and Commonwealth History*, Vol. 22, 1994

McIntyre, William David. *British Decolonization, 1946-1997: When, Why and How Did the British Empire Fall?* New York, St Martins Press, 1998

MacLeod, Roy, Milton Lewis, eds. *Disease, Medicine, and Empire: Perspectives on Western Medicine and the Experience of European Expansion*, London, Routledge, 1988

McPhee, Allan. *The Economic Revolution in British West Africa*, London, Frank Cass, 1971 (reprint of 1926 edition)

Marshall, Peter J. *Bengal: The British Bridgehead: Eastern India, 1740-1828*, Cambridge, Cambridge University Press, 1988

Marshall, Peter J. *Trade and Conquest: Studies on the Rise of British Dominance in India*, Aldershot, Variorum, 1993

Mason, Edward S., Robert E. Asher. *The World Bank Since Bretton Woods*, Washington, Brookings Institution, 1973

Miers, Suzanne, Igor Kopytoff, eds. *Slavery in Africa: Historical and Anthropological Perspectives*, Madison, University of Wisconsin Press, 1977

Miers, Suzanne, Martin Klein, eds. *Slavery and Colonial Rule in Africa*, London, Frank Cass, 1999

Milobsky, David, Louis Galambos. "The McNamara Bank and Its Legacy, 1968-1987," *Business and Economic History*, Vol. 24, 1995

Minchinton, Walter E., ed. *The Growth of English Overseas Trade in the Seventeenth and Eighteenth Centuries*, London, Methuen, 1969

Molz, Rick. "Privatization of Government Enterprise: The Challenge of Management," in Phillip D. Grub, Dara Khambata, eds. *The Multinational Enterprise in Transition: Strategies for Global Competitiveness*, Princeton, Darwin Press, 1993

More, Thomas. *Utopia*, Harmondsworth, Penguin Books, 1965

Morison, Samuel E. *The European Discovery of America: The Southern Voyages, 1492-1616*, New York, Oxford University Press, 1974

Nafziger, E. Wayne. *The Debt Crisis in Africa*, Baltimore, Johns Hopkins University Press, 1993

Newton, A. P. "The Establishment of the Great Farm of the English Customs," *Transactions of the Royal Historical Society, Fourth Series*, Vol. 1, 1918

Nixon, Charles R. "The Role of the Marketing Boards in the Political Evolution of Nigeria," in Carl K. Eicher, Carl Liedholm, eds. *Growth and Development of the Nigerian Economy*, East Lansing, Michigan State University Press, 1970

Nwauwa, Apollos O. *Imperialism, Academe and Nationalism: Britain and University Education for Africans, 1860-1960*, London, Frank Cass, 1997

Pakenham, Thomas. *The Scramble for Africa: White Man's Conquest of the Dark Continent from 1876 to 1912*, New York, Avon Books, 1992

Parker, Irene. *Dissenting Academies in England: Their Rise and Progress and Their Place Among the Educational Systems of the Country*, New York, Octagon Books, 1969 (reprint of 1914 edition)

Parry, John H. *The Establishment of the European Hegemony, 1415-1715: Trade and Exploration in the Age of the Renaissance*, New York, Harper Torchbooks, 1961 (reprint of 1949 edition)

Parry, John H. *The Age of Reconnaissance*, New York, Mentor Books, 1964

Payer, Cheryl. *The World Bank: A Critical Analysis*, New York, Monthly Review Press 1982

Penrose, Boies. *Travel and Discovery in the Renaissance, 1420-1620*, New York, Atheneum, 1971 (reprint of 1952 edition)

Phillips, Carla R., William D. Phillips. *Spain's Golden Fleece: Wool Production and the Wool Trade from the Middle Ages to the Nineteenth Century*, Baltimore, Johns Hopkins University Press, 1997

Pike, Ruth. *Enterprise and Adventure: The Genoese in Seville and the Opening of the New World*, Ithaca, Cornell University Press, 1966

Plumb, John H. *England in the Eighteenth Century*, Baltimore, Penguin Books, 1965 (reprint of 1950 edition)

Plumb, John H. *The Growth of Political Stability in England, 1675-1725*, Baltimore, Penguin Books, 1969

Prakash, Om. *The Dutch East India Company and the Economy of Bengal, 1630-1720*, Princeton, Princeton University Press, 1985

Price, Jacob M. "Transaction Costs: A Note on Merchant Credit and the Organization of Private Trade," in James D. Tracy, ed. *The Political Economy of Merchant Empires*, Cambridge, Cambridge University Press, 1991

Price, Jacob M. "The Imperial Economy, 1700-1776," in Peter J. Marshall, ed. *Oxford History of the British Empire: The Eighteenth Century*, Vol. 2, Oxford, Oxford University Press, 1998

Reid, Escott. *Strengthening the World Bank*, Chicago, Adlai Stevenson Institute, 1973

Reynolds, David. *One World Divisible: A Global History Since 1945*, New York, Norton, 2000

Ringrose, David R. *Transportation and Economic Stagnation in Spain, 1750-1850*, Durham, Duke University Press, 1970

Robock, Stefan H. "U.S. Policies Toward Transnationals," in Weizao Teng, N. T. Wang, eds. *Transnational Corporations and China's Open Door Policy*, Lexington, Lexington Books, 1988

Rosenberg, Nathan, L. E. Birdzell. "Science, Technology and the Western Miracle," *Scientific American*, Vol. 263, November, 1990

Rostow, Walt W. *The United States and the Regional Organization of Asia and the Pacific, 1965-1985*, Austin, University of Texas Press, 1986

Russell-Wood, A.J.R. *A World on the Move: The Portuguese in Africa, Asia, and America, 1415-1808*, Manchester, Carcanet Press, 1992

Sachs, Jeffrey D. "Introduction," in Jeffrey D. Sachs, ed. *Developing Country Debt and Economic Performance: The International Financial System*, Chicago, University of Chicago Press, 1989

Sachs, Jeffrey D. "Conditionality, Debt Relief, and the Developing Country Debt Crisis," in Jeffrey D. Sachs, ed. *Developing Country Debt and Economic Performance: The Financial System*, Chicago, University of Chicago Press, 1989

Sauvant, Karl P. "Transnational Corporations as Engines of Growth," in Phillip D. Grub, Dara Khambata, eds. *The Multinational Enterprise in Transition: Strategies for Global Competitiveness*, Princeton, Darwin Press, 1993

Schremmer, D. E. "Taxation and Public Finance: Britain, France, and Germany," in Peter Mathias, Sidney Pollard, eds. *Cambridge Economic History of Europe: The Industrial Economies: The Development of Economic and Social Policies*, Vol. 8, Cambridge, Cambridge University Press, 1989

Schurz, William L. *The Manila Galleon*, New York, Dutton, 1959 (reprint of 1939 edition)

Seavoy, Ronald E. "The Shading Cycle in Shifting Cultivation," *Annals of the Association of American Geographers*, Vol. 63, 1973

Seavoy, Ronald E. "The Origin of Tropical Grasslands in Kalimantan, Indonesia," *Journal of Tropical Geography*, Vol. 40, 1975

Seavoy, Ronald E. "Social Restraints on Food Production in Indonesia Subsistence Culture," *Journal of Southeast Asian Studies*, Vol. 8, 1977

Seavoy, Ronald E. *Famine in Peasant Societies*, Westport, Greenwood Press, 1986

Seavoy, Ronald E. "Hoe Shifting Cultivation in East African Subsistence Culture," *Singapore Journal of Tropical Geography*, Vol. 8, 1987

Seavoy, Ronald E. *Famine in East Africa: Food Production and Food Policies*, Westport, Greenwood Press, 1989

Seavoy, Ronald E. *The American Peasantry: Southern Agricultural Labor and Its Legacy, 1850-1995, A Study in Political Economy*, Westport, Greenwood Press, 1998

Seavoy, Ronald E. *Subsistence and Economic Development*, Westport, Praeger, 2000

Shapley, Deborah. *Promise and Power: The Life of Robert McNamara*, Boston, Little, Brown, 1993

Simon, Brian, ed. *Education in Leicestershire, 1540-1940: A Regional Study*, Leicester, Leicester University Press, 1968

Simon, Joan. *Education and Society in Tudor England*, Cambridge, Cambridge University Press, 1966

Simon, Joan. "Was There a Charity School Movement? The Leicestershire Evidence," in Brian Simon, ed. *Education in Leicestershire, 1540-1940: A Regional Study*, Leicester, Leicester University Press, 1968

Solomon, Lewis D. *Multinational Corporations and the Emerging World Order*, Port Washington, Kennikat Press, 1978

Spufford, Margaret. *Contrasting Communities: English Villagers in the Sixteenth and Seventeenth Centuries*, Cambridge, Cambridge University Press, 1974

Stern, Ernest. "World Bank Financing of Structural Adjustment," in John Williamson, ed. *IMF Conditionality*, Washington, Institute for International Economics, 1983

Stone, Lawrence. "The Educational Revolution in England, 1560-1640," *Past and Present*, No. 28, 1964

Stopford, John M. "The Origins of British-Based Multinational Manufacturing Enterprises," *Business History Review*, Vol. 48, 1974

Stopford, John M., Susan Strange. *Rival States, Rival Firms: Competition for World Market Shares*, Cambridge, Cambridge University Press, 1991

Thirsk, Joan. *The Rural Economy of England*, London, Hambledon Press, 1984

Urwin, Derek W. *The Community of Europe: A History of European Integration Since 1945*, London, Longman, 1955

Verlinden, Charles. *The Beginnings of Modern Colonization,* Ithaca, Cornell University Press, 1970

Vernon, Raymond, Louis T. Wells. *Economic Environment of International Business*, Englewood Cliffs, N.J., Prentice-Hall, 1976

de Vries, Barend A. *Remaking the World Bank*, Washington, Seven Locks Press, 1987

Watson, Foster. *The English Grammar Schools to 1660: Their Curriculum and Practice*, Cambridge, Cambridge University Press, 1908

Watson, Ian B. *Foundation for Empire: English Private Trade in India, 1659-1760*, New Delhi, Vikas Publishing, 1980

Watts, Michael J. *Silent Violence: Food, Famine and Peasantry in Northern Nigeria*, Berkeley, University of California Press, 1983

Williams, Allan M., ed. *Southern Europe Transformed: Political and Economic Change in Greece, Italy, Portugal and Spain*, London, Harper and Row, 1984

Wills, John E. *Pepper, Guns and Parleys: The Dutch East India Company and China, 1622-1681*, Cambridge, Harvard University Press, 1974

Wilson, Charles H. *England's Apprenticeship, 1603-1763*, New York, St Martins Press, 1965

Winius, George D., Marcus P. M. Vink. *The Merchant-Warrior Pacified: The VOC (The Dutch East India Company) and Its Changing Political Economy in India*, Delhi, Oxford University Press, 1991

Winters, L. Alan. "Expanding EC Membership and Association Accords: Recent Experience and Future Prospects," in Kym Anderson, Richard Blackhurst, eds. *Regional Integration and the Global Trading System*, New York, St Martins Press, 1993

Wise, Mark. "The European Community," in Richard Gibb, Wieslaw Michalak, eds. *Continental Trading Blocs: The Growth of Regionalism in the World Economy*, Chichester, Wiley, 1994

Yoshino, M. Y. "The Multinational Spread of Japanese Manufacturing Investments since World War II," *Business History Review*, Vol. 48, 1974

INDEX

About the Author

RONALD E. SEAVOY is professor emeritus of history at Bowling Green State University, Bowling Green, Ohio. Previous books by the author are *The Origins of the American Business Corporation, 1784–1855* (Greenwood, 1982); *Famine in Peasant Societies* (Greenwood, 1986); *Famine in East Africa* (Greenwood, 1989); *The American Peasantry: Southern Agriculture Labor and Its Legacy, 1850–1995* (Greenwood, 1998); *Subsistence and Economic Development* (Praeger, 2000); and *A New Exploration of the Canadian Arctic* (2002).